BY THE SAME AUTHOR:

Topography

PURBECK: THE INGRAINED ISLAND

Poetry

RIDDLES FOR JACK

DOMINGUS

POEMS OF Z

THE STUBBORN FOREST

WIGHT

BIOGRAPHY OF AN ISLAND

by

PAUL HYLAND

———

LONDON
VICTOR GOLLANCZ LTD
1984

Recommended by the Isle of Wight Tourist Board

British Library Cataloguing in Publication Data
Hyland, Paul
  Wight
  1. Isle of Wight—Description and travel
  —Guide-books
  I. Title
  914.22'804858   DA670.W6

ISBN 0-575-03319-3
ISBN 0-575-03426-2 paperback

Printed in Great Britain
at The Camelot Press Ltd, Southampton

ACKNOWLEDGEMENTS

I thankfully acknowledge the Isle of Wight Tourist Board and its Director, Ewen Brenchley, for generous help in accommodating me on the Island, and Sealink UK Limited, Isle of Wight Services, for freely transporting me across the Solent.

Many people have given me their time, hospitality and advice, as well as access to documents and photographs in their possession. I thank them all, especially: Revd and Mrs Robert Bowyer, Simon Dabell, Patience Daldy, Jean Daniels, James S. Dearden, Col. W.J. Eldridge, Mr and Mrs Robin Freeman, Norman Gaches, Mr and Mrs David Gascoyne, Mr and Mrs Anthony Goddard, Mr and Mrs M.J. Green, Michael Harris, Gladys Harrison, John Hart, Brian Hinton, Dom S.F. Hockey, Michael J. Howley, Dr Allan Insole, Dr Jack D. Jones, Mr and Mrs Charles Jones, Mr and Mrs Clifford Matthews, The Lord Mottistone DL, National Farmers' Union (Newport), George Newberry, Sir John Nicholson Bt., C.I.E., Mr and Mrs Arthur Peters, Malcolm Pinhorn, Dr and Mrs Robert Piper, Messrs Ratsey & Lapthorn Limited, Mr and Mrs Graham Redfern, Mr and Mrs Colin Riches, Gill Rook, Elizabeth Saunders, Count Slade de Pomeroy, Harry Spencer, Mr and Mrs Frank Sweasey, Bridget Trehair, Mr and Mrs Edward Upward, Mr and Mrs Jack Whitehead, Colin Wickham and Mr and Mrs Raymond Young.

The many literary sources on which I have drawn are named in the text. Acknowledgements for permission to quote from works in copyright are due to: Faber & Faber Ltd for lines from W.H. Auden's *Collected Poems*; A.D. Peters & Co Ltd for quotation from *The Cruise of the Nona* by Hilaire Belloc (Constable); Cassell Ltd for *A History of the English Speaking Peoples* by Winston Churchill; Chatto & Windus for *Forays* by Robert Conquest; Hodder & Stoughton Ltd for *Give Us This Day* by R.F. Delderfield and *Launch* by J.E.B. Seely (Lord Mottistone); Oxford University Press for *Collected Poems* of David

Gascoyne; Carcanet New Press Ltd for *Solent Shore* by Jeremy Hooker; Methuen & Co Ltd (London) for *Lions & Shadows* by Christopher Isherwood; Hugh Noyes for *No Other Man* by Alfred Noyes (Lippincott & Co); Granada Publishing Ltd for *Isle of Wight* by Aubrey de Selincourt (Paul Elek); William Heinemann Ltd for *The Railway Accident* and *The Spiral Ascent* by Edward Upward; The Hogarth Press for *Freshwater, A Comedy* by Virginia Woolf; and Michael Joseph Ltd for *The Day of the Triffids* by John Wyndham.

I am indebted to articles in newspapers, magazines and journals, especially *Isle of Wight County Press*, *Isle of Wight Weekly Post*, *Wight Life*, *Islander*, *Proceedings of the Hampshire Field Club* and *Proceedings of the Isle of Wight Natural History and Archaeological Society*, and to numerous guide-books to churches and other places of interest. I am grateful to the staffs of the Isle of Wight County Library and Record Office for their help.

I am most grateful to George Tucker for the verve and expertise he brought to the job of photographing the Wight. I thank my wife, Noëlle, for her help with research, for reading the manuscript and compiling the Index.

P.H.

"She thinks of nothing but the Isle of Wight, and she calls it *the Island*, as if there were no other island in the world."

Jane Austen, *Mansfield Park*

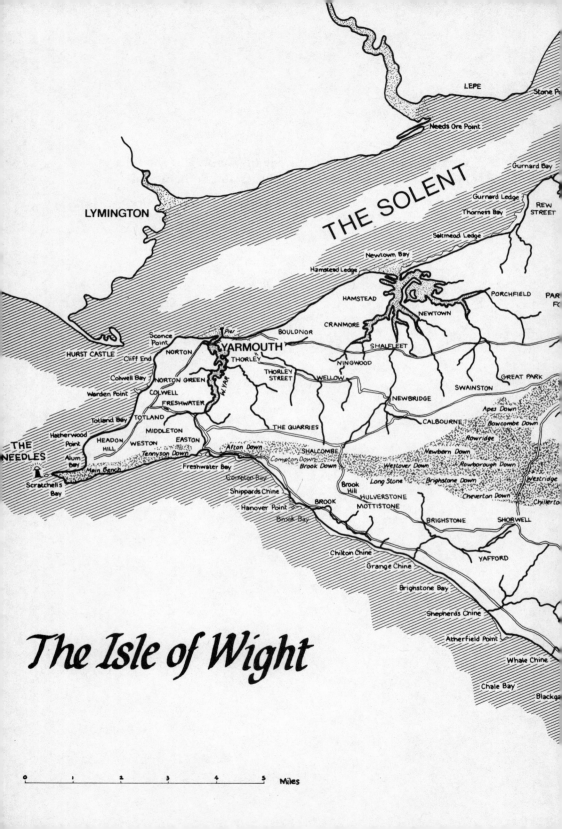

The Isle of Wight

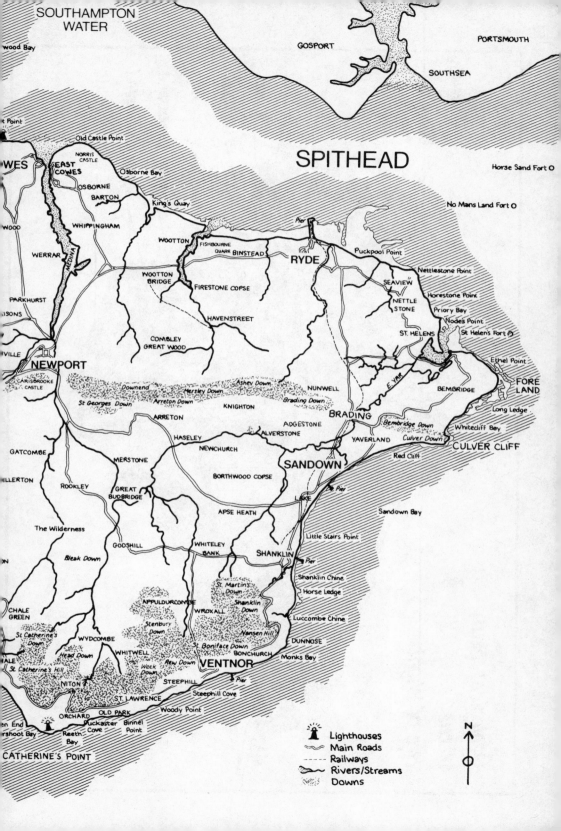

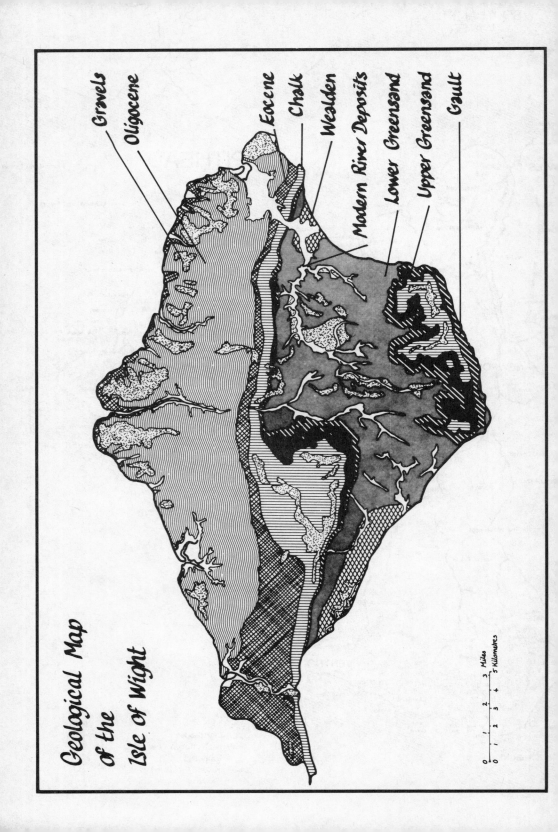

Geological Map
of the
Isle of Wight

Gravels
Oligocene
Eocene
Chalk
Wealden
Modern River Deposits
Lower Greensand
Upper Greensand
Gault

0 1 2 3 Miles
0 1 2 3 4 5 Kilometres

CONTENTS

LIST OF ILLUSTRATIONS

Photographs by George Tucker

Following page 68

The Needles and Scratchell's Bay
Highdown and Tennyson Down
Freshwater Bay
Alum Bay and Hatherwood Point
Colwell Bay and Fort Albert
St Michael the Archangel, Shalfleet
Yarmouth
Newtown Creek
All Saints', Calbourne
Ratsey's sail-loft, Cowes
The Royal Yacht Squadron, Cowes
Warrior figurehead, Spencer (Thetis) Yard
Quarr Abbey ruins
St Mildred's Church, Whippingham
Quarr Abbey Church
Brading Haven
Appley Tower, Ryde
Brading church tower and Wax Museum
Sweetshop, Brading
St Mary's Church, Brading
Princess Elizabeth's memorial, St Thomas's, Newport

Following page 196

Carisbrooke Castle
Quay Street, Newport

PART ONE

LANDFALLS

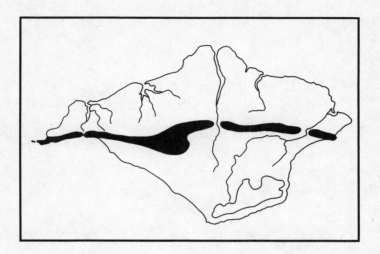

The Solent River plundered by the ebb
long since; a relic of its southern shore
still tethered to the mainland by a web
of wake, above an oozy, scoured sea-floor
wreck-thick between the Needles and the Nab.
The hovercraft and hydrofoils' roar
drowns muffled rowlocks at Wight's back: each tub
importing treason's taint and draught of war.

The Island bobs like cork in history's tide.
Accomplices and enemies in France,
Spaniards, Jutes, Germans planned to override
the swell of chalk; English Victorians,
possessed by dreams of little empire, tried.
Still Wight, stiff-necked and broken-backed, will dance.

I

A ROUGH DIAMOND

What weary imposture, what ghost-life, what Devil's Island in the heart have you allowed yourself to be cheated with until now?
Edward Upward *The Island*

"THIS ISLAND IS a little paradise", Karl Marx wrote to Friedrich Engels in mid-July 1874. The *Mercurius Anti-Pragmaticus* of November 1647 lamented Charles I's transfer to the safe custody of Wight with the words, "He forsook Paradice for this Isle". One man's heaven-on-earth is another man's purgatory.

Places mean something to us, but what they mean depends upon our experience of them, the length and intensity of our relationship with them, and our knowledge of elsewhere. "Caulkheads" are born on the Isle of Wight and some, even now, never leave it; they may treat the place with familiar contempt but will defend it against "overners" with a stubbornness born of tribal loyalty. Work brings a few mainlanders here to live, who grow either to revel in the freedom of the island they have been granted or to suffer the torments of insular claustrophobia. For thousands each summer it is the Garden Isle or Captain Sunshine's Treasure Island promoted by the Tourist Board, a kind of floating Pleasure Park, a honeymoon hide-away, where the real world stops at the ferry terminal and lets you get off—on to the Island. Eccentrics and outlaws have always found real or illusory escape here. Memories of childhood holiday bliss bring settlers in search of a retirement refuge. It is a retreat, an escapist's paradise or a prison. It is exile or Elysium.

If you set yourself a northerly course from Pointe de Barfleur towards St Catherine's Point, the southernmost tip of the Island, the prow of your craft cuts a fading swathe of foam through the slabby

21

grey-green waters of the Channel towards the barely perceptible curve of the horizon. Then what seems to surface, what erupts lazily into view, is the long low shoreline of an island land-mass: a vision of plunder, business and pleasure familiar to generations of invaders, traders and yachtsmen: the island of Britain. The whites, greys and ochres of the cliffs would seem continuous, if you could see as far, from Dartmouth to Dungeness. But just west of St Catherine's revolving white light is the occulting red, white and green of the Needles' lighthouse and the narrow channel, between Hurst Castle and Fort Albert, into the Solent; while east of the Bembridge Ledge and between Horse Sand and No Man's Land Forts is the doorway to the Solent's Spithead arm. Wight is a bulwark between Portsmouth and the Channel, a loosely-fitting stopper in the neck of Southampton Water.

The disuniting sea, *pelagus solvens* from which the Venerable Bede dubiously derived the *Solent Sea*, varies from one to six miles in width. Because Wight nestles where it does against the southern shore of Britain, the Solent benefits from a freak of nature: "in this sea, two tides of the ocean sea that spring from the boundless northern seas around Britain do daily meet and oppose one another off the mouth of the river Homelea . . . and when their striving together is ended they return and flow again into the ocean from whence they came." Bede's account of 731 is dramatized in Michael Drayton's *Polyolbion* of 1622:

> And to the Northe, betwixt the fore-land and the firme,
> She hath that narrow Sea, which we the *Solent* terme:
> Where those rough ireful Tides, as in her Straits they meet,
> With boysterous shocks and rores each other rudely greet.
> Which fierclie when they charge, and sadlie make retreat,
> Upon the bulwarkt Forts of *Hurst* and *Calsheot* beat,
> Then to *Southampton* run.

One tide comes the short way from the Atlantic, up-Channel from the west, and provides the first high water; then, after two hours, a second tide arrives, that originated in the Atlantic twelve hours or so before the first, but which has taken the scenic route around Scotland, the North Sea, through the Dover Straits and along the Channel from the east. It is as though high water holds for two hours during the neaps, while at the spring tides an hour's ebb may follow the first high water, only to flow back to give a second, higher high water followed by six-hours'-worth of ebb packed into four. Briefly, and crudely, this explains the tidal advantages of the Solent, countered only by the violence of the divided ebb which has contributed its share to the terrible tally of wrecks which stud the scoured sea-floor and pock the sediments that lie beneath the waters of the Wight.

The eccentric strip of water is responsible for a good deal. It gives what might otherwise be just one of the smallest counties in the United Kingdom a unique sense of itself. It distinguishes Islanders from mainlanders, Caulkheads from overners. Porters at Yarmouth, embarking passengers on the ferry for Lymington, used to cry, "This way to England!", and natives still talk of England, Scotland, Wales and the Isle of Wight. From the air it might be misconstrued as an aborted bit of Hampshire, a stray blot of cartographer's ink caught in the fold of the map and squeezed into rough diamond-shaped symmetry; but it is its own country, with its own air, its own climate and, with the tenacious remnants of its own dialect, its particular consciousness. The diamond's north-south axis, from Cowes to St Catherine's, measures thirteen miles and is marked by the aptly-named River Medina which rises in the southern downs, winds through the Wilderness and Newport, the Island's capital, then broadens during its tidal stretch through the northern half of Wight and issues into the Solent between East and West Cowes. The east-west axis, from Bembridge's Foreland to the Needles, is twenty-three miles long and is roughly, if sinuously, indicated by the massive chalk backbone of the Island, whose northern edge is the boundary between the Palaeogene, or Lower Tertiary, rocks to the north and the Cretaceous rocks to the south. The diamond's symmetry is reinforced by the rivers of its north-western and north-eastern facets, Newtown River and Wootton Creek, and by the two Rivers Yar which almost cut off the Island's extremities. Only efforts to prevent the sea running into the Western Yar at Freshwater Gate and into the Eastern Yar near Sandown have postponed the era of the *Isles* of Wight.

Until well after the last Ice Age, Wight was part of the mainland; the great Frome-Solent River drained the counties of Dorset and Hampshire with their now-eroded southern territories and emptied

into the sea somewhere south of Littlehampton. Stour and Lower
Avon, Nadder, Wily, Upper Avon, Test and Itchen fed the great
river from the north, while its southern tributaries included the
Corfe River in Purbeck and the Medina and the two Yars in Wight,
all of them larger than they are today and rising in what is now the
sea. The spine of Purbeck was continuous with Wight's backbone
until stream and sea together conspired to breach the hard chalk and
scoured out the clays and sands behind to create Poole Harbour,
Poole and Christchurch Bays, the Solent and Southampton Water,
and the harbours of Portsmouth, Langstone and Chichester. So
much flux, so much alchemy of rock and water to bring forth
Wight's rough symmetry, its uncouth diamond.

> The Island showed plainly
> what it was: the splintered foot
> of a bridge, and on a surface
> hacked into crests
> the chalk blue waves reflected it.

So the poet Jeremy Hooker sees it. I grew up with the Wight in the
corner of my eye. From my high window I looked south across
Poole Bay to the Isle of Purbeck's Foreland. There the glowing white
rock petered out in Old Harry's stacks ... and my eye moved
eastwards, skimming the sail-specked mirror of the sea for twenty
miles, when rain and mist allowed, to glimpse the rocks' mirror-
image where the geological tale is taken up once more ... the
Needles' bleached stacks stepping up out of the water, marked at
night by the distant glimmer of the Needles' light. That was chalk:
plinth for gulls and darkly glinting cormorants. Those were the
standing stones that marked the horizon of my childish imagination.
Hence my puzzlement, in the claustrophobia of the class-room, at
discovering that the sticks with which crow-gowned masters
scratched and squeaked their way across a drab blackboard claimed a
nobility which the transmission of all the education in the world
could never give, the name of *chalk*. In those days, knowledge and
imagination seemed quite distinct. How could a child obtain a grasp
on the world through books and blackboards? Books can be closed
and blackboards are wiped clean. It was things and places and their
creatures that I wished to get my hands on. I played in my territory;

and back at my window I stretched the evidence of my senses into imaginings about the paradise signalled on my horizon by ghostly rocks looming out of the dusk above the darkening water.

Perhaps I became a biologist because the first teachers to stir my imagination were scientists; they demonstrated a grasp on the world. Perhaps I became an obsessed magician in adolescence because I wanted to over-rule the facts by the force of the imagination. Later, perhaps I became a poet because I learned that the nearest we can get to the mastery of nature is, like Adam exercising his God-given voice in Eden, to name the creatures of the world and the creatures of imagination. Now I am writing a book naming Wight. But do not be misled; like the heart fed on illusions, the imagination not fed and disciplined by facts will always be disappointed. Wight is not paradise. It is a rough diamond.

2

THE APPROACHES

Vortigern invited the Angles hither ... they fought against the Picts
... Then they sent to Angel; ordered to send more aid and to be told
of the worthlessness of the Britons and of the excellence of the land
... These men came ... from the Old Saxons, from the Angles,
from the Jutes. From the Jutes came the people of Kent and the
people of the Isle of Wight.

The Anglo-Saxon Chronicle

What is cosier than the shore
  Of a lake turned inside out?
How do all these other people
  Dare to be about?

W.H. Auden *Islands*

THE ISLAND'S 94,000 acres are inhabited by 120,000 people and
were visited, in 1980, by nearly ten times that number of tourists
clutching £84 million in their collective hot hand. Since Wight
became a fashionable resort in the last century and a popular one in
this, a vital element of its attraction to overners is its islandness.
However, for holiday-makers and commuters, the gap is an
expensive one: ferry fares are high and add fifteen or twenty pounds
to the cost of every ton of imported or exported freight. For this
reason, and in order to forge a link that foul weather cannot break,
there have been a number of plots to tether the Island to the
mainland. The 1945 Solent Tunnel Scheme eventually was rejected,
but it seemed that anything was possible in the euphoric 'sixties,
when Buchananite planners, or schemers, envisioned a Solent City
comprising ten towns of London overspill benignly engulfing
Southampton and Portsmouth and much more; where the workforce
were to be the unsung heroes of a new industrial revolution focussed

26

on the growth areas of petro-chemicals, vehicles, hovercraft and new power projects. For them the Wight, the west Solent, the New Forest, and perhaps a new New Forest were to be utilized as on-the-doorstep amenities. How *nice* for Caulkheads, to be the denizens of a water-walled garden where suburbanites could breathe. In 1982 the Isle of Wight County Council voted narrowly against a new feasibility study for a bridge or tunnel link, and has also declared the Island a nuclear-free zone. An island linked to the mainland is no island, and Councillors have decided to live on one. I applaud their resolve.

"In due time we approached the Needles. The spectacle was grand," Mr Rush, a nineteenth-century American ambassador, noted in his journal. "The most exact steerage seemed necessary to save the ship from the sharp rocks that compress the waters into the narrow straits below. But she passed easily through. There is something imposing in entering England by this access." And sometimes more than imposing: intimidating, for while the Island now is desperate to seduce tourists and industry on to its shores, for much of its history it was not only content to live unto itself but was compelled to equip itself to repel invaders: with watches and beacons, forts and castles, garrisons and redoubts. In August 1914, Cowes Week was cancelled at short notice. The fleet, which a month earlier in Spithead had passed for six solid hours in review before the Royal Yacht *Victoria & Albert*, was now passing through the Straits of Dover. The Kaiser's yacht *Meteor* was being towed back home by its destroyer, and his contribution to the prizes—Dresden china and a silver cup—was carefully boxed up and stored for the duration. Krupp's schooner *Germania* was taken into safe custody at South-ampton. All ferries to the Island abruptly stopped. At Stone Point, Lepe, a watch stood by to open fire on any vessel that attempted the crossing.

The Isle of Wight is not only a sandbag for the defence of Portsmouth, it is also a potential stepping-stone on to the mainland. Camden wrote that it "is not so well fortified by its rocks and castles as by its inhabitants, who are naturally warlike and courageous"; and in the fourteenth century, when French invasion was always imminent, 29 beacons were primed to blaze their warning along skyline and shoreline, to mobilize the men of the Island's nine military districts. In Edward III's time, when the Wight was under unusually direct Crown control, the Warden of the Island was empowered to compel the return of absentees and to levy provisions and forces, including the men of Hampshire. The king supplied Carisbrooke Castle with ten tuns of wine, one hundred quarters of wheat, of malt and of oats, 50 quarters of pease and beans, as well as coals, wood, salt and munitions. Gentlemen held estates on condition that in time of war they should spring to the defence of Carisbrooke for 40 days at their own expense. None but licensed boats, excepting those of the Abbot of Quarr and two other gentlemen, were permitted to cross the Solent; and then only from three ports, each with its warden to prevent anyone absconding or exporting goods without a licence.

The three ports—La Riche (Ryde), Shamblord (East Cowes) and Yarmouth—are, with West Cowes and Fishbourne, still the main ports of entry. The ferries that hurry invaders across the moat have names that bow to more belligerent times: *Cenwulf, Cenred, Cuthred, Caedmon, Cowes Castle* and *St Catherine*. It takes about half an hour to steam, or diesel, sedately out of Lymington down Horn Reach past the yacht haven, jinking between the mud-flats through Short Reach and Long Reach and out past Jack-in-the-Basket to Yarmouth. There is a 50-minute passage from Southampton to Cowes, while the hydrofoil does the same trip, with more noise and effort, in twenty minutes. From Portsmouth you enter the mouth of Wootton Creek and roll off at Fishbourne, or disembark from the passenger ferry nearly half a mile offshore at Ryde, on to the Pier Head from which you can catch the Shanklin train. If you want to get a little closer, you must take the seven-minute hovercraft ride from Southsea, which beaches you asthmatically at a concrete terminal.

One of my most pleasurable approaches to the Island was on a brilliant June day with a fair wind. I was on board Charles Jones' gaff-rigged *Foam*, built "by the blow of the eye" in Ilfracombe about 120 years ago on the scaled-down lines of a Bristol Channel Cutter. With the weight of wind and tide on her tiller, her venerable planking and caulking under our buttocks and a formidable bowsprit asserting our bearing, we could look with a touch of enjoyable disdain at the fibre-glass hulls and bellying nylon around us. Unlike light modern boats strung taut as a metal tennis-racket, she tensed herself to windward, her leeward shrouds jangling slack and her whole organism responding to the elements. She rode us through rather than over the water, living up to her name. A full jib, foresail and mainsail—there was no need for the topsail we had hoisted in the earlier windless part of the day—heeled her over and drove her decisively towards Yarmouth Green.

Seen at a distance, the Island could be uninhabited. Bouldnor Cliff's wildly tumbled clays are topped by apparently impenetrable forest which meets the water westwards; but then at Sconce Point appears the shell of Fort Victoria, looking like a stretch of railway viaduct going nowhere; and beyond, at Cliff End, like a stranded steel-works, Fort Albert's inhabited hulk seems as though it might float off on the next tide to join its older ally Hurst Castle, that hard nose on the end of a shingle spit, the mainland's proboscis. Together they make a gateway for a vision of the Needles. In 1814 a large whale was grounded on the Shingles by the ebb-tide, and a 75-foot-long one was caught nearby during the winter of 1841. In the light of a January dawn the Island itself might be a great inert creature beached off the English coast, until on the humped back of the down the morning sun lights upon the Tennyson memorial cross, symbol of a grand past; or, recently, upon the crooked arm of a crane poised above a bright heap of raw chalk on Afton Down, where Freshwater's new reservoir was being bedded down in mundane provision for the future.

Then the town of Yarmouth comes into focus: its yacht club, castle, pier, ferry terminal, lifeboat station and, across Yar mouth, the villas of Norton on the hillside packed, like fragile ornaments, amongst a generous supply of greenery. That June afternoon, we brought *Foam* into harbour under power, put out the fenders and moored her on trots between piles so that she would ride with the tide's ebb and flow. We furled and coiled and stowed until she was ship-shape. That slowed down the process of arrival, slowed us down to Island pace while we breathed Island air, and by the time we had landed from the dinghy we were acclimatized to the sea-change which the Solent passage had wrought. You can see the sudden shock of it in visitors' faces as they debouch, dazed, from the hydrofoil. It is a change of air in the fullest sense, a shift of perspective, and it demands an imaginative response.

Look, stranger, on this island now

29

The leaping light for your delight discovers,
Stand stable here
And silent be,
That through the channels of the ear
May wander like a river
The swaying sound of the sea.

So wrote W.H. Auden; that he would ever express such sentiments must have seemed unlikely to Christopher Isherwood when Wystan, thinly disguised as Weston in *Lions and Shadows*, came to stay on the Wight in July 1926: "I see him striding towards me, along Yarmouth Pier, a tall figure with loose violent impatient movements, dressed in dirty grey flannels and a black evening bow-tie. On his straw-coloured head was planted a very broad-brimmed black felt hat." Isherwood disliked the hat from the start because it represented something self-conscious and sham, and caused "a considerable sensation" in Freshwater. It seems that Auden was out to make an impact on the Island, rather than *vice versa*; an impression reinforced by his loud Oxonian remarks in the bus from Yarmouth: "Of course, intellect's the only thing that matters at *all* . . . Man's got to assert himself against Nature, all the *time* . . . Poetry's got to be made up of images of form. I hate sunsets and flowers. And I loathe the *sea* . . ." Still, even if Tennyson would not have approved of every particular, it was one way of arriving in West Wight.

It was eighty years earlier, on a visit with Edward Moxon to James White of Bonchurch, that Tennyson had rowed around the Needles. He came back in 1849, and his third incursion of 1853 saw him on the look-out for a house. He heard of Farringford and summoned Emily, his wife, from Twickenham. Her journal records that "the railway did not go further than Brockenhurst then and the steamer, when there was one, from Lymington felt itself in no way bound to wait for the omnibus which brought as many of the passengers as it could from the train. We crossed in a rowing boat. It was a still November evening. One dark heron flew over the Solent backed by a Daffodil sky. We went to Lambert's, then Plumbly's Hotel & smaller than now. Next day we went to Farringford & looking from the drawing-room window I thought 'I must have that view', and I said so to him when alone." She got it. She and Alfred, in his broad-brimmed black hat, were to make the crossing many times in the succeeding years; more happily, though not always as comfortably, than in November 1888 when the poet, in his eightieth year, was conveyed to Lymington by special train, transferred into an invalid's chair for the boat trip, and towed in it down Yarmouth Pier. At Aldworth he had suffered bad attacks of arthritic gout and visions and delusions; he dreamed that he was the Pope with the weight of the world on his back; but by the time of the journey he was recovered enough to make a game of looking at the legs of the people he passed on the quay and guessing their characters from this novel perspective. The memory of that crossing must have been painfully vivid eleven months later when he and Emily and his nurse made the short voyage once more. Sixteen lines of poetry were born, almost whole, in his mind and he had jotted them on a scrap of paper by the time the boat docked. Later he boasted, "I began and finished it in twenty minutes, didn't I, Nurse?" It was *Crossing the Bar*:

> ... Twilight and evening bell,
>   And after that the dark!
> And may there be no sadness of farewell,
>   When I embark;
>
> For tho' from out our bourne of Time and Place
>   The flood may bear me far,
> I hope to see my Pilot face to face
>   When I have crost the bar.

Another twilight crossing, this time from near Titchfield to Cowes, was full enough of foreboding and the sadness of farewell: farewell to a kingdom and, effectively, to life. Three days after the event, John Oglander of Nunwell scratched the news into his notebook with an incredulous quill, "King Charles came into our Island Sunday the 14th November, to my great astonishment. For, as a great while I could not be brought to believe it, so, when I was certain of it I could do nothing but sigh and weep for two nights and a day. And the reason for my grief was that I verily believed he could not have come into a worse place for himself, or where he could be more securely kept. This being the chief yet I knew also it would be half an undoing to our poor Island, and I pray God I be no true prophet." The king and his party were smuggled into Cowes, like contraband, under cover of darkness by an escort led by the Island Governor, Colonel

Hammond. He was not taken directly to Carisbrooke and, as Henry VIII's castle was not sufficiently commodious, the royal visitor was provided with a bed at the Plume of Feathers. The king threw himself down upon it in fervent prayer beneath a carved and gilded admonition on the headboard that rubbed superfluous salt into his wounds. It read, "Remember thy end".

One hundred and ten years later, in the imagination of J. Meade Falkner, under a full moon and with a spring tide, the wind set the *Bonaventure* with John Trenchard and Elzevir Block on board up-Channel from the Isle of Purbeck and at daybreak put them ashore at Cowes. They too were *en route* for Carisbrooke Castle. They followed clues decoded from the Psalms, inscribed on a parchment that John had found in a locket taken from the neck of the corpse of Blackbeard in the Mohune vault at *Moonfleet*. Their quarry was the Mohune diamond, hidden in the castle well.

On the authority of Edward Upward and Christopher Isherwood we learn that, earlier this century, *The Javanese Sapphires* came into the hands of that grotesque native of Mortmere, Gunball, on the very threshold of the Island. "That they really had been given him on the jetty at Portsmouth by an elderly man who, scarcely an instant later, boarded the paddle-steamer for the Isle of Wight, I didn't for an instant doubt." Unfortunately, after alarming alarums and excruciating excursions, one Moxon stole the jewels from Gunball's house, employing his obedient black serpent to ascend the bathroom wastepipe and swallow them one by one.... The elderly man presumably disembarked from the paddle-steamer at Ryde unless, adopting the habit of the tall gentleman in black on the St Helen's ferry who never paid his fare, he evaporated into the ether half-way across.

Henry Fielding did get to Ryde, eventually. The author of *Tom Jones* had quit the King's Bench, suffering from, in his own words, "no fewer or less diseases than a jaundice, a dropsy, and an asthma, altogether uniting their forces in the destruction of a body so entirely emaciated that it had lost all its muscular flesh." He had laboured on to perfect a scheme for the eradication of robbery and murder on London's streets. He was gratified by its success in the winter of 1753 but was, "in the opinion of all men, dying of a complication of disorders." He was tapped at intervals and up to fourteen quarts of water were drawn from his belly. He resolved to sail for Portugal and, with his wife and eldest daughter, boarded a ship at Rotherhithe on 26 June 1754, in his forty-eighth year. Contrary weather delayed them and Fielding records, in *The Journal of a Voyage to Lisbon*, that it was not until Wednesday 10 July that a fresh gale brought them within sight of the Island. The next day, after all hands were set to recover a kitten that had accidentally abandoned ship, the wind prevailed and forced them to anchor "at a place called Ryde". On Friday, the ladies were regaled with afternoon tea and fresh cream at a Ryde ale-house. On Saturday his wife persuaded Fielding to go ashore. But there was no Ryde Pier then, nor Hovertravel, and "the living luggage is more difficult to be moved or removed than an equal or much superior weight of dead matter." Luckily a large hoy, "which in some places would pass for a ship, and many people would go some miles to see the sight", delivered the present of a buck to their vessel. Fielding was shifted into the hoy which took him as far as the mud. He comments, with the wisdom of a man who understands local government, that the magistrates had begun the construction of a small causeway to low-water mark, "but as this work was of a public kind, and would have cost a large sum of money, at least ten pounds, and the magistrates, that is to say, the churchwardens, the overseers, constable, and tithing-man, and the principal inhabitants, had every one of them some separate scheme of private interest to advance at the expense of the public", it was not finished. At last he was lowered into a small boat and rowed nearer the shore. Then he was carried by two sailors who waded through the mud, set their distinguished and distended visitor upon a chair and conducted him "to a house which seemed to bid the fairest for hospitality of any in Ryde". The fairest it may have been, but its shortcomings fill several hilarious pages of the *Journal*, and Fielding was obliged to endure them for ten days before embarking once more for Lisbon, where he died on 8 October.

When young Richard Middlemas boarded a brig in Newcastle with his false friend Captain Hillary of the Honourable East India Company, the wind favoured him more than it had Fielding. "The voyage was performed with safety and celerity; and having coasted the shore of that beautiful island, which he who once sees never forgets, through whatever part of the world his future path may lead him, the vessel was soon anchored off the little town of Ryde." So, in the course of *The Surgeon's Daughter*, a tale of dreadful corruption, Sir Walter Scott pays his tribute to the Wight. At anchor, the captain of the brig and Hillary entertained Middlemas with delicacies of a naval description, including quantities of excellent strong punch which stimulated hopes of an early commission and put him into a deep sleep. He awoke in the hellish surroundings of Ryde Military Hospital, run by the crimp and kidnapper Mr Seelencooper, an expert in the art of "recruiting" troops to protect the Eastern trade for which the Island was the principal depot. Drugged, robbed and abused by the Hospital Governor: such was Richard Middlemas's delirious arrival on Wight.

In others, the approaches induce a more delicious delirium: "Siegmund watched the bluish bulk of the island. Like the beautiful women in the myths, his love hid in its blue haze. . . . On either hand the grim and wicked battleships watched along their sharp noses. Beneath him the clear green water swung and puckered as if it was laughing. In front Sieglinde's island drew nearer and nearer, creeping towards him, bringing him Helena." But the battleships are a symbol of threat to the fragility of love; illicit love, for Siegmund is *The Trespasser* in D.H. Lawrence's second novel. His island idyll is doomed, at last, to disappointment and death.

The history of Wight is full of unfortunate landfalls and illicit landings, of wrecks and smuggling whose cold-blooded facts are all too often romanticized away to cosy folksiness; not, however, in the journal-entries of contemporaries or in the imaginations of good writers. In John Wyndham's drily matter-of-fact apocalyptic, *The Day of the Triffids*, the Island is a last hope. Ivan Simpson tells Bill and Josella Masen why it has been chosen in the battle-strategy against the aggressive plants. The merits of a number of islands had been discussed, but the climate decided them. "When we got there," Ivan said, "the triffids seemed even thicker than where we'd left. No sooner had we begun to settle ourselves into a big country house near Godshill than they started collecting along the walls in thousands. We let 'em come for a couple of weeks or so, then we went for them with flame-throwers." The battle was a long one, because Island nurseries had bred such high-quality plants, but eventually they won. Continuing vigilance consisted in "an intensive search every spring on account of seeds blowing over from the mainland." The Masens' party is invited to join the Wight community, and the last page of the book has them doing just that. If you want to read the rest of the story, as Bill Masen says, "you will find it in Elspeth Cary's excellent history of the colony".

Mark Adams escaped global catastrophe because he had spent three days and nights trapped at the bottom of the sea in an abandoned enemy submarine. When he regained consciousness, he gathered his strength and his escape apparatus for the ascent to the surface. "He found himself only a few hundred yards away from the coast that he knew best in the world, the Undercliff of the Isle of Wight." This strangest of all landfalls is described in *No Other Man* by Alfred Noyes, who lived in the Undercliff until his death in 1958. A strong tide brought Mark inshore and he waded into Steephill Cove. "Outwardly everything looked as he had known it and loved it for years: the fisherman's cottage under the cliff; the boats drawn up above the high-water line; the herring-gulls clustering over their reflection in the wet sand; the dark heap of rusty-red fishing-nets. It was all as lazily peaceful as a picture by Morland ..." But Mark notices that young women are still sunbathing when the sunlight has deserted the beach. A seagull almost alights upon the bare flesh of a girl in a pale gold bathing-suit. She and the others and, as he frantically discovers, all the inhabitants of the Island are dead. A notice pinned on the Royal Yacht Squadron's notice-board reveals that both Grumkow and the French President have threatened to use their secret weapons as a last resort. Mark's realization is an horrific one. "My God," he said, "I do believe they've really done it. I believe I'm the last man!"

The Island has seduced many imaginations, and these are some of the possible factual and fictional, past and future approaches to it. If you are not already here, or if you are in it but not of it, you have still to make your own. As J.B. Priestley wrote, "Any man from America or Australia might take one glance at the island as something on a map, and then decide to give it a couple of hours. But you can spend days and days exploring the Isle of Wight, which, if you are really interested, begins magically enlarging itself for you."

3

SPINE OF THE WIGHT

Through the midst thereof runs a long tract or chaine of hills, yeilding plentie of pasture, and forrage for sheepe. The wool of which, next unto that of Lemster and Cotswold, is esteemed best. . . .

Camden *Britannia*

To make a traveller an agreeable companion to a man of sense, it is necessary, not only that he should have seen much, but that he should have overlooked much of what he hath seen.

Henry Fielding *A Voyage to Lisbon*

THE GARDEN ISLE has been the scene of many ghastly landfalls and grisly "comings-ashore", but it has also witnessed heroic rescues and miraculous escapes. It is dusk on 25 January 1890; the three-masted *Irex*, 2,200 tons, has suffered three weeks' punishment in the Irish Sea and the Bay of Biscay *en route* from Glasgow to Rio; retreating into more homely waters, she has come to grief in Scratchell's Bay, not four hundred yards from the Needles' light. All night the sea scours her decks. By morning her sails begin to fly in tatters. Above the cross-trees the crew clings to mainmast and fore-mast and mizzen. The Totland lifeboat tries, but turns back. From 400-foot-high cliffs, the rocket-apparatus—that Island invention—fires a line across the angry gulf. Hawser and breeches buoy are rigged between wreck and cliff-top. Three men are washed away. The rest are hauled clear, but for a petrified lad, left bound to the mizzen-mast. A black crew member volunteers to go back for him, "Haul me off". With the help of a coastguard he drops away into peril, runs the seas' gauntlet on deck, plucks the boy from his perch and sends him to safety. Dark rumours of mutiny—of the disappearance of the captain and officers—are eclipsed by hurrahs for the black man as he collapses exhausted on the turf. The hawser parts. The boy revives. The heroic negro has melted away. Waves will soon fell the *Irex*'s masts and, in days to come, beachcombers will glean a rich harvest of flotsam.

The Wight's hills are the thickest Chalk-beds in Britain. They are weathered relics of mountainous waves raised in the earth's crust twenty million years ago, the reverberations of the Alps' genesis. The Island's spine trails the Needles in the sea, like the bleached vertebrae of a prehistoric monster's tail that still lashes the water to white fury. Long before the lighthouse tamed it, an outer stack called Goose Rock raised not white feathers but hackles. In April 1753 its stump did for the *Assurance*, a 44-gun man-o'-war with the Governor of Jamaica and a cargo of coin aboard. Eleven years later, the 120-foot needle of chalk called Lot's Wife fell on a calm day, with a report that affrighted the citizens of Portsmouth and Southampton, leaving a gap between her sturdier fellows. Goose Rock pierced the *Pommone*'s hull in 1811, when the 38-gun frigate came from the east bearing Persian princes. Spume spouted to a great height from her hatches and ran back out of her gun-ports, until a real storm dashed her to pieces and laid her relics, only now being retrieved by underwater archaeologists, upon those of the *Assurance*. Five years or so after that, the arch that linked the inner stack with the main cliff crashed down and, on New Year's Day 1859, a light shone from the hundred-foot lighthouse for the first time, completing today's familiar picture.

The gentle Garden Isle thrives behind grim walls of cliffs. Here in 1795, J.M.W. Turner glimpsed an early vision of the vortex, that premonition of entropy, which was to dominate his later canvases. "Turner's first oil picture of any size or consequence," wrote the contemporary engraver E. Bell, "was a view of flustered and scurrying fishing-boats in a gale of wind off the Needles"; almost certainly the *Cholmeley Sea Piece* exhibited at the Royal Academy in 1796, in which chill moonlight between clouds and upon the swell spins a web to threaten the warm lamp-light in a fishing-boat. That master of apocalyptic horror and Gothic grandeur, in paintings like *The Deluge* and *Belshazzar's Feast*, John Martin, chose Scratchell's Bay as subject for a small watercolour of 1839: lowering clouds lie heavily above a livid setting sun that throws the Needles into dark relief. And here, where the waters pile against the cliffs, John

Baldwin of Lymington willed that his corpse should be submerged, to spite a wife who had promised to dance upon his grave.

Around from Suncorner's noble water-worn arched recess, Main Bench rises from rugged footings and buttresses, scored obliquely with mysterious parallel lines of dark flints. As the pearl is to the oyster, so flint is to the chalk, and its grain lifts the eye upwards to a mist-shrouded summit through a kingdom of birds; of gulls, cormorants and shags, auks, guillemots and razorbills, puffins, kittiwakes and fulmars. Egg and feather collectors used to drive a crow-bar into the turf up there, lasso it and abseil down the precipice in pursuit of a trade dreadful as that of the samphire-gatherers. Beyond Oldpepper Rock are towering caverns hacked out of the face of the chalk together with all the ledges, pillars and arches the sea can carve. In caves called Lord Holmes' Kitchen, Cellar and Parlour, that Governor of the Island is said to have feasted his guests. A fugitive prisoner-of-war is supposed to have starved to death in Frenchman's Hole. After Bar Cave and Neptune's Caves comes Watcombe Bay with its secret tunnel, and then Freshwater Bay breaching the Chalk, where the sea has almost gnawed through to the source of the Western Yar. But more of that later. For now we come ashore, don seven-league boots and step up on to the spine of the Wight. It is a causeway through the Island's heart; a road, sometimes green, sometimes flinty or metalled with gravel, sometimes tarmacadamed, along the roof of this small world; a high place in the imagination from which to gain perspective, a long view of the territory under our feet. It will be a staccato progress eastwards, overseeing—and overlooking—much.

Above Freshwater Cliffs is a memorial to E.L.M., aged fifteen, who fell to her death on 28 August 1846. Higher, on Afton Down, golfers tee off from one of many Bronze Age circular burial mounds that punctuate the downs' horizon from end to end. Here, not far from a Late Bronze Age urn cemetery, the earlier barrows surround a Neolithic long barrow. Here Island forces arrayed themselves for the Grand Review by Major-General Don, their Commander-in-Chief; an engraving shows the carriages, gentlemen, and ladies with parasols who turned out on that June day in 1798 to enjoy both the spectacle and the sensation of being ready for the French. Mightier forces were assembled, 182 years later, when thousands upon thousands of fans alighted like locusts on East Afton Down for the Pop Festival that was Wight's requiem for the 'sixties. High on the downs they were, high on music, and above all, high; the gods descended in helicopters or debouched from limousines, with lights and sweat, and decibels that seemed to make the white membrane of the moon, risen above the sea, shiver like a drum. Then the götterdämmerung: the clogged ferries, the rubbish, the paths like open sewers, and a million ring-pulls from cans glittering like moon-dust over the grazing.

Cows crop the robbed barrows on Brook Down. From a Bronze Age plinth set on the Upper Chalk of the Upper Cretaceous, you can look north over Shalcombe Forest and forwards in geological time, across a rising, falling, rising landscape of palms, tortoises and crocodiles; across Reading Beds and London Clay to the rainbow of the Solent Group of rocks; across the Headon and Osborne Beds of the Oligocene to where the line of Bembridge limestone is betrayed by quarry wounds, and beyond the Bembridge Marls to where the tributaries of the Newtown River delve deep into the clays of the Hampstead Beds before emptying into the Solent. Turn to face south, and you look back over Upper Greensand and Gault Clay, down the declensions of the Lower Greensand to the oldest rocks of the Wight, once called Wealden but now split between the Wessex and Vectis Formations. When the tide is low in Brook Bay, Hanover Point reveals its Pine Raft, fossil trees embedded in sandstone below the cliff's purple marls. Down there, too, are skeletal remains and footprints of a dynasty of dinosaurs; a vision, if one could see it, of a great tropical delta, another age, another landscape and, it would seem, another latitude.

In recent, Stone Age times, after the Ice Ages and the Woolly Mammoths had retreated, the then Islanders slowly felled the forest that clothed the downs and began to graze beasts along their length. Generation upon generation of cropping teeth suppressed the climax vegetation and nurtured a priceless turf of grasses, milkwort, restharrow, dwarf thistle, thyme, red valerian, horseshoe and kidney vetch, squinancywort, fairy flax, centaury, eyebright, lesser quaking-grass and many more including, among a rich repertoire of orchids, autumn lady's-tresses. The spine became a sheep-walk patrolled by shepherds and their flocks of Dorset sheep. Mainland ewes were shipped across to lamb early in mild Island pastures.

Long-staple wool was smuggled away to the Low Countries. Though sheep-farming is on the increase, a mere 20,000 animals graze where twice that number were shorn annually at the end of the eighteenth century. Depression and ferment following the Napoleonic Wars toppled the shepherd, the king of the farm, from his high place. New manures, steam tractors, Dig-for-Victory, ploughing grants and artificial demand stimulated by the Common Market all mean that arable land has trespassed further up the slopes than at any time since before the Great Mortality when medieval strip-lynchets terraced the downs' flanks. Then tilling demanded cheap labour which the pestilence wiped out; now it requires one man and a machine. Where the lone shepherd erected temporary hurdles on the hills to protect his crop of wool, corn whitens in vast fenced fields. Coppices, which furnished hazel and ash for writh or wattle hurdles, and withy-beds once kept their stations in the valleys, but since the last war the Forestry Commission's trees have marched uphill. Plough and plantation have usurped the sheep's territory, disowned an inheritance of miraculous turf, flayed the downs' skin and demolished or disturbed about 60 per cent of their prehistoric monuments. What is left must be jealously guarded; by the National Trust, by landowners and by farmers who are now discovering that re-seeded grassland is a paltry substitute for the real thing. If incentives must be offered, then the hill sheep subsidy must be applied to downland. Sheep, by consuming a rich resource, preserve it: they shear the monuments left by our ancestors and present them clean against the sky; their exploitation is conservation.

Where the turf is founded upon angular flint gravel, capping the chalk, it puts up clumps of furze and bramble, and gnarled hawthorn trees that seem petrified in a perpetual gale. A gravelly track runs before Brighstone Forest; below, marl-pits, like those that pock the downs from east to west and limed the land to north and south, display old wounds; and, like all the springs that tap the spine's reservoir, Buddlebrook runs out of Buddle Hole and skirts the site of Rock Roman Villa and the quarry at Combe. Onwards, at Limerstone Down, when I was standing still—scanning the confused swell of downs to the east with their rounded crests and dry-valley troughs, surveying the sheep-speckled Sandrock ridge with Brighstone and the Back of the Wight beyond, and lazily retracing my steps along the backbone to Freshwater and the West Wight—I caught sight of my first hoopoes flirting their head-dresses, fluffing warm brown plumage and flouncing zebra-striped wings and tails. I was hot. Sweating, I pulled off my shirt risking, despite my tan, a severe dose of sunburn. I doubled back into the forest; lined with Corsican pine and stacks of felled timber, the track burned and was simply more humid, but a path under a canopy of beech, sweet-chestnut and pines offered a damp coolness. Birds coasted down the rides or crashed about in treetops. A red squirrel, tufted ears stiff with alarm, seemed to wring his hands and chide me, before scampering away to a high trapeze in the forest's Big Top. I left the highest point of Wight's spine behind me, embedded in trees.

You can exit dramatically from the forest on to a marvellously rounded brow called Gallibury Fields. They fall away to Fern Bottom and Bunker's Bottom, pressed to right and left by the Scylla of Cheverton Down and the Charybdis of Rowborough Down. Depressions lined with flints and sheep-droppings hint at the Iron Age or Romano-British field system that covers them. Pits and ridges that emboss the turf below were dubbed British Villages, and W.H.D. Adams derived Gallibury from "burgh of the Gaels". Newbarn Down's Celtic fields are being erased; oats, barley and winter-wheat gild the once-green domain of mole and rabbit but, though clipped by the plough, Gallibury Hump survives, a Bronze Age bowl barrow, pagan footing for Christian generations' gibbets and most likely root of the name "Gallow-bury". Rowridge is plinth for a television mast, and, not far below, a rare plant raises its head; there, discovered in the 1840s, is the only British niche of the lilac and purple trumpets of *Calamintha sylvatica*, previously supposed to be confined to Switzerland.

The broad crown of Bowcombe Down ripples with dun furrows. The share strikes fire from the cold heart of flints the size of human skulls; skulls like the Saxon ones disinterred, in the 1850s, from the shallows of an ancient and huge bowl barrow, now flattened. A cemetery of eleven mounds was also undone up here to reveal Saxon burials and cremations. They were young memorials, only a millennium old, but they too have been ploughed out of mind. Like a familiar, a hare materializes from its form and thuds across broken ground. Carcases of crows, that should by rights be Danish ravens, hang from makeshift gibbets and hawthorn trees around the field edge, noosed with blue binder-twine. Pheasants strut jauntily over flints and clods where soon they will be plucked ripe from the air by a hail of shot. From here you can see across the *beau combe* to the rumpled patchwork cushion of Garston Down; and beyond, across the Wilderness and the Bowl of the Island to the answering chalk bulwark of the Southern Downs, poised above the Channel. Northwards, the Solent glints like a moat protecting emerald pastures and the deep green lozenge of Parkhurst Forest. Nearer, but far below, smoke drifts like a shroud above a mixed herd of black, white and ruby cattle. In Great Park's fields, where quarry fled hunter in the oldest royal park in Britain, a man with a brand of straw on a pitch-fork is sowing seeds of flame in stubbly furrows. Where, before tilling, a white weft of lime stretched hedge to hedge, now fire lays down its black warp.

Up here, blacker smoke sent up its pall when a German plane crashed during the war: a beacon for Carisbrooke kids in search of souvenirs. Ignoring the village that flows down into Newport, we leap over Lukely Brook that, in its prime, cleft the Wight's spine; we clear the noble Castle of Carisbrooke on its sculpted hill; use Mount Joy and its modern cemetery as a stepping-stone; skip across the Medina valley and set our feet down above the great chalk-pit of Shide. We have stepped from the Hundred of West Medine into East Medine. The primeval Medina would not have been so easily crossed. The golf course on Shide Hill has fairways on a gravel terrace laid down when the river was a great tributary running into the greater Solent River. The bulk of St George's Down is an older, higher terrace, cut by springs into enchanting combes to the north and standing up as a steep escarpment to the south. On its summit, the gentlemen of the Island rode and played, not golf, but bowls in the first quarter of the seventeenth century. The bowling-green was laid out by Henry Wriothesley, Earl of Southampton and Shakespeare's patron, when he was Governor. The gentry dined in a "house of accommodation" from which they could literally supervise the Wight until, five years after Southampton's death of fever in the Low Countries in 1624, the habit died, John Oglander tells us, "for want of company". The nightjar churrs here still, but the Down is a livid wound, dishevelled by quarrying into canyons and mounds, a shifting scenario of other-worldly ochres in which great machines gnaw at the ground on which they creep.

Redundant gravel pits have been put down to poor pasture, and new stabling put up beside the old barns of Great East Standen Manor. It is a deceptively unpretentious house, behind whose eighteenth-century brick-and-flint front and semi-circular slate-roofed porch lurks the ghost of the home of Princess Cicely. Daughter of Edward IV, sister of Henry VII's queen and wife of his cousin Lord Wells, she was retired or exiled here with her obscure second husband, Thomas (or John or Richard) Kymbe (or Keme or Kyme or Keen). The place feels older than its present fabric; an enormous stepped chimney inscribed "WS 1768" incorporates an anachronistic "priest's hole". Great beams in attic rooms mesh according to joiner's roman numerals that might have been cut yesterday. Under roofs haunted by colossal spiders, each October Princess Cicely is reputed to make her presence felt.

Burnt House Lane climbs and switchbacks from Shide to Gallows Hill and Arreton Down, where Saxon graves were superimposed upon Neolithic and Bronze Age relics including a fine grooved "Wessex" dagger and many other bronze weapons. Legend has it that one Michal Morey burnt his own house to destroy evidence of a disturbing murder, but this is not so. What is certain is that, four months after the fatal day in 1736, the stinking and dismembered body of James Dove, Michal's fourteen-year-old grandson, was discovered stuffed into a pair of leather panniers and concealed, with bloody gloves and a bill-hook, in the Arreton wood near their home, the now-deserted cottage of Sullens. Did Michal kill the boy for money left by his father, or because he was late bringing his nammit? Versions vary, but certain it is that, after much hue and cry, Michal was tried and hanged in Winchester. His corpse was then returned to the scene of the crime, and hung in chains from a gibbet erected on the burial mound at Downend, now known as Michal Morey's Hump, while children chanted:

> Michal Morey is dead,
> For chopping off his grandson's head.
> He is hung on Arreton Down
> For rooks and ravens to peck down.

A floor-joist in the Hare & Hounds at Downend is said to be the gibbet-post; Michal Morey's skull, displayed there in a glass case, is almost certainly prehistoric; but the pipe-rack from a Newport inn, tracked down by Roy Brinton, was made from the "chains" that once swung with their gruesome cargo on the crest of the Wight's spine.

Downend Chalk Pit, that almost undermines Michal Morey's Hump, is a luminous landmark from which the old trackway now runs, a ribbon of tarmac, along Arreton and Mersley Downs. Besides the rock itself, water is the great resource of these hills. It percolates through Chalk and Upper Greensand, collects above the Gault Clay and springs out northwards to Wootton Creek or southwards to swell the Eastern Yar. It is garnered in reservoirs that lie in the paradisal nook called Knighton, where a pumping-station sends it through the down and north to slake Ryde's great thirst. On the road, above a handful of stone-mullioned cottages built in the 1690s, two massive gateposts lead to no mansion at all. The gardener's cottage remains beside a walled garden overgrown with magnolias, old roses and lemon balm. A heap of rust in a boiler room once heated a wall where espaliered peaches ripened. Through dense undergrowth there is a spinney of ash and apple-trees that once was a bowling-green; the stone grotto, where folk sat listening to the clack of wood against wood, now hears nothing but timber's growing-pains and the charm of birds. Above is the relic of a terrace and a mound of rubble, long overgrown and planted with tall conifers, the grave of a house called Knighton Gorges which has almost been expunged from Wight's memory. It is a spook-monger's paradise, but I shall not rehearse all the tales of apparitions, poltergeists and ethereal music that cling to the place. It was a large irregular building of grey stone covered with ivy; a buttressed turret crowned a thirty-foot-deep dungeon; the terraced garden fell to a spring and a willow-hung pool; a Gothic window on the east side survived from an earlier house. There Eudo de Morville found refuge and did penance for the murder of Thomas à Becket. His grandson-in-law was the first of three Sir Ralph de Gorges, Crusaders, adventurers and probable Knights Templar, whose shield of arms' field d'or was blazoned with an azure gyre. The third Sir Ralph's daughter married Sir Theobald Russell of Yaverland who, in 1340, engaged the French over the hill at Nunwell and is said to have died of his wounds in the bedroom known as "The Room of Tears", under the portrait of a turbaned Turk. The room was so christened by Anthony Dillington, to whom the Russells sold Knighton in 1565. He was a Poole man who married Joan Hacket of Purbeck, and who, in a letter of 1574 to his son Robert, called Wight for perhaps the first time "the Garden of England". Sir Robert Dillington was knighted by Queen Elizabeth, and when he was later committed to the Fleet Prison for crying "Liberty!", Island gentry petitioned successfully for his release. His nephew, Sir John Oglander, eulogized him as "honest, stout and valiant . . . as full of conceits without offence, and very liberal, that all men loved his company." His "base, proud and miserable" nephew, another Robert, even removed hay from the stable-racks when mounted visitors arrived, and by such thrift bought Mottistone and a baronetcy. His issue squandered his substance, and Sir Tristram Dillington died in 1721 in suspicious circumstances. There are stories of secret rites and Dionysian revelry, of sudden deaths of relatives leading to despair, and of a servant who led his master's body, mounted on his horse Thunderbolt, into the pond; a cover-up for suicide for which he was rewarded with a small farm near Brading. Deviously, Knighton Gorges came down to Maurice George Bisset, who hosted a little Hellfire Club here, and entertained Sir Joshua Reynolds, the Garricks and John Wilkes, as well as Lady Seymour Worsley of nearby Appuldurcombe. Her husband, Sir Richard, sued Bisset for £20,000 but was adjudged privy to the prostitution of his wife and awarded one shilling. Bisset married the daughter of another of Lady Worsley's gallery of lovers, and grew old, eccentric and syphilitic in his glorious estate. He set his face against his elder daughter's marriage to a clergyman and, because the house was entailed on her, in November 1821 he engaged masons to demolish it. So the house died; and he, on 21 December in the gardener's cottage.

High above, on Ashey Down, is a triangular pillar of stone erected as a sea-mark in 1735. Ryde, proliferating along the north coast, was a mere satellite of the manor of Ashey, and Ashey Farm was the site of a cell of the abbess and nuns of Wherwell. In the first Elizabeth's reign, Agnes Porter, widow of this parish, was convicted of witchcraft. The Oglanders of Nunwell can trace their line from 1874 back to that Richard d'Oglandres who came to the Island with William FitzOsbern at the Conquest. There is a design, attributed to John Nash, who built so much and left so little on Wight, for a replacement for the present house which was not even built. Two earlier houses, on a site in Bloodstone Copse, were burnt down in about 1522 and by the French in 1377. The park is decked with magnificent trees, but the surrounding forest's death-knell was sounded when Sir William Oglander cut timber worth £80,000 at the outbreak of the last French war. At the down's foot ash, alder, beech and hazel mask marl-pits like bomb-craters, and giant chalk-white fungi thrive beneath pines clamorous with rooks. Pigeons flee noisily into the thick tops, hares kick up their heels and red squirrels skitter up the backs of trunks.

There is a grand prospect, from the house and from the down above, of the old town of Brading and of Brading Haven, beyond, that was an inland sea before its reclamation. The southern slope of Brading Down faces another world: manicured vineyards maturing in the sun slope down to cornfields, twisting lanes and the old preserve of Brading Roman Villa. Molten lead and glass, charred wood and cherry-stones hint at its fate. Bones of deer, hare, ox and goat with shells of oyster, whelk, cockle, limpet and snail suggest its inhabitants' diet. Shards of crockery include Samian, New Forest and Nene Valley wares, together with fine blown-glass, a mortar of Purbeck marble, turned Kimmeridge Shale ware and vessels and tools of iron. Painted wall plaster boasts an "eagle" and a bowl of luscious plums. Alongside sumptuous mosaics there are prints of a dog's paw and a human foot left in long-dry clay.

We make the final giant step across the Eastern Yar, over a golden field where big round bales are clustered like pieces in an unfinished board game, and up on to Bembridge Down, the spine's last instalment. It is dominated by what seems to be a hill-fort out of the Iron Age, but turns out to be one of Palmerston's elaborate Follies, built in the 1860s against Napoleon III at a cost of almost £49,000. It was a military installation until after the last war, but now its cunningly guarded moat and barrack keep of brick and flint is a secure base for light industry. To build the fort, they uprooted a grand obelisk and replanted it further along the down beyond hawthorn trees, prolific blackberries and a belt of beeches. It commemorates Charles, Earl of Yarborough and Baron Worsley of Appuldurcombe House; from Whitecliff Bay, far below to the north, and Sandown Bay to the south, yachtsmen can look up to it, and to the memory of the corner-stone of the Royal Yacht

Squadron at Cowes.

Culver Cliff drops sheer and white away, leaving you full of admiration for the holy man who is reputed to have made his cell in the Hermit's Hole a little below the brink, and breathless before the long arc of pie-crust cliff, where Sandown and Shanklin teeter on the sea's edge, with the hulk of Dunnose beyond. Culver was haunted by pigeons whose Anglo-Saxon name *culfre* it bears; and hawks too, for Elizabeth I issued a warrant for the recovery of some that had been snared up here, and "for the persons faulty of this stealth and presumptuous attempt". More recently, William Woodnutt had the rabbit-trapping rights, and one war-time morning caught more than he bargained for, the pilot of a crashed Heinkel.

One Christmas holiday, Algernon Charles Swinburne tramped along the beach far below and stared up at Culver that reared before him like a snow-peak. Suddenly he felt the urge to prove himself to himself, and perhaps to his sea-dog father who seemed to scorn his effeminate son. He stripped and doused himself in the icy sea, toning his body and nerving his mind for the ordeal. He dressed, and began to climb, hand over hand, foothold to crumbling foothold. Near the summit he found himself perilously overhung and had, painfully, to retreat. At the bottom he prospected for a better route. He assaulted the white face again; towards the top he heard a sound like an anthem played on Eton Chapel organ; its source, a flock of gulls, rose from a hollow and swarmed about his face. He clung to the turf and hauled himself up on to it. He awoke from a dead faint to the sight of a sheep's eyes gazing into his. With what relief he must have looked over the crown of the down; what joy to be alive, achieved, and looking across Whitecliff Bay to "Binbridge Isle" and the Foreland, the easternmost extremity of Wight. He was safe.

Salvation of a deeper order was Legh Richmond's burden: "As I pursued the meditations which this magnificent and varied scenery excited in my mind, I approached the edge of a tremendous perpendicular cliff, with which the down terminates. I dismounted from my horse, and tied it to a bush. The breaking of the waves against the foot of the cliff at so great a distance beneath me, produced an incessant and pleasing murmur." Down on the sandy beach under the vertical ochre strata of Whitecliff the minister spied, with joy, a disciple of his, a negro servant sitting on a rock reading his Bible. He made the steep descent to the bay. The negro welcomed him and they talked, prayed and wept together in a "new and solemn 'house of prayer'", from whose glistening, samphire-speckled wall sea-birds launched themselves into airs that rose off the sea like the wind of the Spirit.

At night, with a rising tide, Nostrils Caves at the base of the cliff exhale the scent of danger, a refuge that turns deadly trap for unwary adventurers. But our trek, our first excursion along the Wight's equator, ends safely on the cliff beyond abandoned relics of batteries and observation posts, and above the ragged end of the spine that juts out into placid water and a beneficent breeze. Gales can be kind, too. In 1587, long before the *Irex* was launched or the rocket-apparatus invented, a Dutch vessel foundered in furious seas below. She was rent in pieces but, John Oglander recounts, the wind was so strong that five men were blown against the cliff and pinioned there, sea-coats spread against the chalk. Thanks to the storm, they climbed upwards without danger of falling until they reached the top, where they crawled on all fours in search of shelter. "The watch thought they had been sea-devils and a while shunned them," but soon saw they were men and gave them succour. For a month they enjoyed the Island's hospitality before obtaining a passage for Holland. A landfall on the Wight indeed; matter for a lifetime of nightmares and blessed awakenings.

PART TWO

ENCLAVES

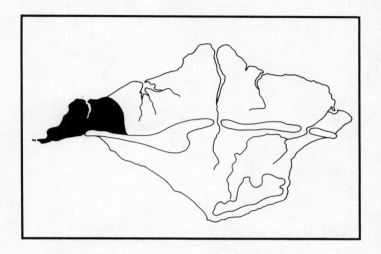

White stacks, a ring of forts turned fun-palace,
crease of Cretaceous Chalk pin-striped with flint,
a turf of miniatures—long undermined
by caverns, tunnels, shafts—crowned with a Cross
since Tennyson made for his beacon there.
His home in the soft heart, the pastel sands
which High Down's green unbreaking wave defends
against the shock of water, clout of air.

Paths lead from chalet-sprawl, up-field, down-copse
to Yar bank and a boatyard's busy hush,
scallop-tiled shop, fish glistering on slabs,
cauldrons to make the armoured lobster blush.
Around the Spit, the Solent sucks at clays,
flesh of West Wight prised from her carapace.

4

THE ISLAND'S ISLAND

... all by myself in my own dark garden ground,
Listening now to the tide in its broad-flung shipwrecking roar,
Now to the scream of a madden'd beach dragg'd down by the
    wave,
Walk'd in a wintry wind by a ghastly glimmer, and found
The shining daffodil dead, and Orion low in his grave.
                         Alfred Tennyson   *Maud*

TENNYSON: Twenty earnest youths from Clerkenwell are in the
    shrubbery; six American professors are in the summer house; the
    bathroom is occupied by the Ladies Poetry Circle from Ohio.
    The son of man has nowhere to lay his head.
                         Virginia Woolf   *Freshwater*

IT IS A sobering experience to stand on the sea-wall and watch the
waves storming in to Freshwater Bay. Each breaker punishes the
shingle and sucks and sighs as it withdraws. Where the bay's chalky
jaws gape, pale rubble eroded from the cliffs tumbles in the tide.
Walls of water compress the air explosively into caverns at either
hand. Freshwater Cave was 30 feet high and 120 feet deep before its
roof fell in the 1850s, and what remained was reinforced to support a
battery of guns above. Opposite, the weather hacked a new stack in
1967; it was christened the Mermaid, and joined the Arched Rock
whose elegant Gothic fragility belies its longevity; and Deer Pound
Rock, so called, we are told, because a deer pursued by Lord
Holmes' hounds came abruptly to the cliff-edge in the heat of the
chase and leapt over on to it to find temporary respite.

Storms have been able to nag their way between the downs here
only because the Yar first carved a gap in the days when the sea broke
on a shore miles to the south. Behind sea-wall and road, a few yards

of gravel car-park lead to the marsh and the stream that is now the Yar's source. This narrow, natural gravel terrace separating salt from fresh water is called Freshwater Gate, for until bridges were built downstream it was the only entrance from the bulk of the Wight into what appears, on Speed's map of 1631, as the Isle of Freshwater. If the men of Newport, the Island's capital, felt themselves to be distinct from the burghers of Portsmouth and Southampton, how much more did the farmers of Freshwater feel themselves to be remote from Newport's life.

The rough magic of the white-walled cove is enhanced by the colours of the small fishing-craft that strain and tug at their moorings against a sea that would dash them on the stones, gulp their wreckage back into its maw and spew the flotsam out again on to the shore. Buoys are scuffled in the foam like a line of orange footballs, but in J.M.W. Turner's sketch of 1795 there is a crude capstan for hauling boats ashore, and those afloat are cunningly secured by ropes and blocks between stakes like saplings, as they are in Newtown Creek today. In those days, The Cabin was the only building at the bay, described by Albin as a cottage where you might be accommodated "in a very comfortable manner, if not in the style of elegance and luxuriousness". The painter George Morland found convivial lodging there, amongst the kind of clientele he depicted in *The Taproom*, for it was a favourite resort of smugglers and fishermen.

Gravels deposited by the older, longer, larger River Yar cap the present cliffs and infill the gap between the downs. Behind The Albion, successor to The Cabin, they yielded up teeth of the Mammoth, *Elephas primigenius*, and a strong whiff of all that prehistory which lies submerged beneath the sediments of later, more articulate times. Part of an Acheulian hand-axe was found in the Marsh in 1920, and other Palaeolithic tools, a Mesolithic tranchet axe and Neolithic flint implements have been discovered up on High Down, together with barbed and tanged arrowheads of the early Bronze Age. Tennyson Down's Neolithic mortuary enclosure looks across to the Afton long barrow, and down to where Moonshill gave up a cache of bronze weapons, and Farringford a hoard of third-century coins.

The Yar seeps from its source, or sources, in a marsh of rushes, reeds, loosestrife and willow-herb, nobly punctuated by dark candles of giant reedmace; where it gathers itself to flow under Blackbridge it flaunts luminous yellow flowers of greater spearwort. The broadening marsh is a congenial lair for otters, and the river runs beneath the Afton road to the Causeway and the site of the mills below Freshwater Church. Boats are berthed on saltings, and from here on the Yar is tidal. On its left bank stand Freshwater Farm and King's Manor, a hint that the West Wight was royal property whose harvests, with those of Whitfield and six mainland manors, went to fund Edward I's daughter, the nun-princess Mary, at the monastery of Amesbury. Where a small tributary from Norton Green and Barnfields Stream feeds the river, you are far enough from any road to feel the remoteness of the Island's island and the importance of the slight, fluctuating ribbon of mud and water in shaping its consciousness. Then, opposite Saltern Wood, where an eighteenth-century salt-house and saltworks thrived, Thorley Brook joins forces with the Yar, river becomes harbour and harbour becomes Solent. A wooden bridge, one vehicle wide, now links Yarmouth with Norton, though there are plans for a bigger one. Here, you can understand both the strength and fragility of insularity, and begin to appreciate the sense of the 1489 Act of Parliament which described the Wight as "desolate and not inhabited, but occupied with beasts and cattle, so that if hasty remedy be not provided, the Isle cannot long be kept and defended, but open and ready to the hands of the King's enemies which God forbid."

The Saxon *tuns* of Freshwater certainly box the compass: Norton, Easton, Weston and Middleton survive as place-names, while Sutton became known as Freshwater Gate. These—and the other satellites, Norton Green, Sheepwash Green, Pound Green and School Green— find an eccentric focus in All Saints Church. The old building is encased in Victorian north and south aisles and a chancel extension. Its fifteenth-century battlemented tower is curiously raised upon a perpendicular arch which gives on to the thirteenth-century work of the west end; but these, and the aisles' twelfth-century cylindrical columns and square abaci, are evidence of earlier enlargements. The core has been re-worked out of all recognition, but it is one of only two Island churches that retain Saxon masonry. It was one of the six that William FitzOsbern gave to the Abbey of Lyre in Normandy. The south chapel belonged to Afton Manor and, in his *History* of 1781, Sir Richard Worsley describes how a slab, with a brass naming the church's founder as lord of the manor of Afton, was prised up to reveal a tomb holding a skeleton with its skull between its legs. Was this a relic of the Norman subjugation of the Island? There is a fine brass to Adam de Compton in the north chapel, and among later memorials is one to Mrs Anne Toppe, sometime of Elizabeth I's Privy Chamber and "in her widowhood by a memorable providence preserved out of the flames of the Irish rebellion"; another mourns Lionel Tennyson, born at Farringford, who died in 1866 *en route* from India where "In haunts of jungle-poisoned air / The flame of life went flickering down". Outside, Emily Lady Tennyson's tomb is delightfully situated at the edge of the spacious graveyard with, as they say, a fine view of the Yar; while the financial adviser to the Kalid of Egypt is flamboyantly housed beneath a large white marble angel who recently suffered amputation of the fingers and daubing with red paint.

The Revd Edmund Venables noted the village of the 1850s as "merely a handful of cottages, with a comfortable inn, the Red Lion, scattered round the quaint old church at the head of the estuary", and in this setting, where the echoes of distant lives and doings reverberate so softly, it is a shock to be confronted with twentieth-century vandalism. But in the bar of the Red Lion, where spirit-bottles' optics wink from under hats naval and caps military, debates and disputes are conducted in the spirit of defiant independence and benign anarchy which characterizes Caulkheads. In June 1982, the Falkland Islands crisis was under scrutiny; an excuse for one beer-fuelled gent to get his nostalgia-needle stuck in the groove of his war-record, but the majority naturally took neither the part of the Argentinians nor of Her Majesty's Government; they were in vigorous sympathy with the islanders themselves. What if the French invaded us? they said. A driver from the tractor-team of the highly mechanized, capital-intensive dairy farms of East Afton and Tapnell was weighing the merits of different silage-cutters and disparaging the tyre manufacturers: "Oi don' think they zeem to consider what Oi got on be'oind. Mind, Oi'm a bugger fer gooin' vull butt, take the tread off on they furrers. Oi don' stop fer no-one, out onto the road, Oi've zid cars use their braykes! Got to git that zilage hooam." Talk concerned with urgent industrial farming, but carrying the tang of the tongue that W.H. Long lovingly recorded in his Dialect Dictionary of 1886.

To my ear, both accent and dialect seem more closely related to

Dorset than Hampshire, and modified by a Kentish twang which, I kid myself, must hark back to the Jutish settlement. Long tells the tale of Manny Young, met early one morning, lerrupen along the road by the withy-bed at Afton Marsh: "The night avore I zed 'en, he'd been helpen to land zome tubs at Totland Bay, and got too much liquor into'n, and slept in a booat on the shore aater they'd clewed up, till mornen." When he woke up, his mates told him they'd sailed back to France. Manny said 'he'd like a look around. "'Where I be?' a zed. 'Why, this es France, edden't it?' 'Why, ye zoat wold man,' I zays, 'thee bist out on't all together, this is Freshwater.' 'If this eeden't the head goo of all I ever zid in my life,' zays the wold feller, 'if there edden't a plaace called the saame in the Island, and 'tes jest sich a plaace as this es.'" Smuggling and wrecking were understandable side-lines, or main-stays in days when farm labourers' wages were intolerably low. Fire, fuelled by the Captain Swing movement that swept across England in 1830, broke out in Freshwater on 29 November, the day after the rector received a "Swing" letter threatening him, the farmers and gentry with summary vengeance if they did not at once agree to pay more. William Cobbett had been in the Island the previous month, but there were many who maintained that the infection, like the brandy and the invasion scares, had spread from republican France. Folk can still remember when men fell greedily on the wreck of the *War Knight*, mined and beached in Freshwater Bay in 1918. It carried provisions, and was gratefully christened the Bacon & Lard Special. Habits and Islanders die hard.

Well-corked brandy for the parson, maybe, but "our *Microscope* informs us that the substance of Cork is altogether filled with air . . . perfectly enclosed in little Boxes or Cells. . . . It seems very plain . . . why the pieces of Cork become so good floats for Nets, and stopples for Viols." The road that runs from Church Place and the Red Lion down to School Green is called Hooke Hill, after Robert Hooke, born here on 27 July 1635 when his father was rector. As a boy in Freshwater he invented curious toys, including a wooden clock and a model ship which fired guns, but when he was thirteen his father died and he went to London. Later he became the first Curator of Instruments to the new Royal Society, and his air-pumps, diving-bells, watch-springs, micrometers and many other devices made him famous. He was, said a contemporary, "of low stature, a crooked body with a sharp ingenious look. Dark brown hair hanging neglected about his face. He went stooping and very fast with a great deal of activity." Some would say that this latter quality was only shared by Caulkheads when they were tub-running. Like them, he worked all night and slept fitfully during the day. He served with Christopher Wren on a committee to preserve St Paul's but, after the first meeting in 1666, it burnt down. However, his most significant claim to fame was published the year before the Great Fire, the *Micrographia*, from which I have quoted, in which he coined the word "cell" as applied to biological structures.

Towards the end of Hooke's life, a farmhouse was built on Hooke Hill. In 1908 its stones were re-used for the building of St Agnes' Church. Their aged appearance, the incised date 1694, the little bell-cote, the quaintly gabled thatched roof and the rustic chancel screen carved by the Revd Devitt deceive many into thinking it a venerable House of God. Lady Tennyson had a hand in its foundation on land given by the Poet Laureate out of his Farringford estate. The estate's deeds refer back to the fourteenth century and one Walter de Ferringford, but the original Prior's Manor, whose tithes belonged to the Abbey of Lyre, long retained a hold on the ground in the form of field-names like Abraham's Mead, Clerk's Hill, Prior's Field and Maiden's Croft. The home farm was sensitively portrayed in water-colour by Helen Allingham. It is probably the only extant long-house, with accommodation for family and animals, on the Wight.

On 11 November 1853, Tennyson agreed with the Seymours to rent Farringford for two pounds a week, furnished, on a three-year lease with an option to buy. It had been built as a small Georgian house in 1806, enlarged to fifteen rooms and embellished with Gothic parapets and wood-mullioned casements in 1810. Alfred approved of that style: "It is like blank verse, it will suit the humblest cottage and the grandest cathedral. It has more mystery than the classic." Emily had fallen for the view, which was mysterious enough when they moved in early on 25 November. When the mists lifted, and the house's glorious situation, with views that then encompassed the Solent, Freshwater Bay, Compton Bay and Blackgang, was fully revealed, in Emily's words, "two of the servants on seeing it burst into tears saying they could never live in such a lonely place". However, the staff grew to comprise a housekeeper, cook, lady's maid, parlour and kitchen maids, a butler, a page, gardeners, grooms and a coachman. Alfred built a shelter of rushes where Emily, delicate all her long life, could lie under the down awaiting Lionel's birth. "Sitting there we heard the sound of the cannon practising for the Crimea"; a prelude for Tennyson to *The Charge of the Light Brigade* at distant Balaclava, and the nearest the poet came to "Cannon to the right of them, Cannon to the left of them." They were happy. One Sunday, Emily "went to communion & afterwards in the garden heard A.'s low whistle & found him lying by the strawberry bed under the trees nearest the wall. We walk in the fields. A beautiful day." Sir John Simeon, a recent convert to the Roman Church, had just inherited Swainston in Calbourne and, despite Emily's sectarian scruples, became Alfred's confidant. He lighted on a fragment of verse in the poet's smoke-filled study, his "fumitory", and by suggesting a narrative framework encouraged the composition of that most experimental of all Tennyson's work, the operatic monodrama *Maud* which he was to render aloud in his driving, rolling, Lincolnshire-tinged tones many, many times after its publication in July 1855, to the delight or chagrin of his hearers in many literary salons.

By 1856 his earnings from his writing alone amounted to more than £2,000 a year. He was able to buy the house, park and farmland of Farringford for £6,900. On 13 May, when the Tennyson's incoming furniture, pictures, boxes of books and antiquities—a jumble of leather, red plush and ornament—cluttered the hall, Prince Albert chose to call. Alfred, summoned from some distant fastness of his new estate, was flustered and forgot to offer a chair. The Prince Consort stood and was charming. He took a large bunch of cowslips back to Osborne for the Queen. "One dropt," wrote Emily, "and I kept it for the children as a memorial. A nightingale was singing while he was here." Much was done by the Tennysons, as by Victoria, *In Memoriam*.

Like his shipwrecked hero, Enoch Arden, on his Island, Tennyson continually described and re-worked his sense of landfall and of loss. Emily vividly preserved moments of their Island life in her *Journal*; the eclipse of the sun in June 1860 provoked this evocative entry: "The sky blackish like a clear moonlight sky. The clouds wonderfully beautiful, dark towards the horizon, white higher up except that now & then about the sun they are amber. The gulls fly slowly &

heavily & there is a sleepy light over down & sea & cape." The next year, when Prince Albert died, they drove to Osborne at once to sign the Book of Remembrance and Alfred worked on a new dedication for the *Idylls of the King*:

> These to His Memory—since he held them dear,
> Perchance as finding there unconsciously
> Some image of himself—I dedicate,
> I dedicate, I consecrate with tears—
> These Idylls.
>   And indeed He seems to me
> Scarce other than my king's ideal knight . . .

The poet had his first audience in April 1863. The Queen noted, "I went down to see Tennyson who is very peculiar looking, tall, dark," but she admired the fine head that the American writer Bayard Taylor had described as that of "a dilapidated Jove". Tennyson's eyes filled with tears the moment the Queen appeared. He found it hard to stand still, and suffered such emotion and discomfort that he could not afterwards recall how Victoria had expressed herself. "I only remember what I said to the Queen—big fool that I was . . . Why, what an excellent king Prince Albert would have made." But she invited him back, and asked to shake his sons by the hand. She would have approved of the way Hallam and Lionel's childhood was cherished and preserved; their parents dressed them in old-fashioned clothes and put off cutting their hair; when, at last, the scissors had done their worst, Alfred and Emily planted some of the dear locks in Farringford's flower-beds. Ten-year-old Hallam described their visit to Osborne at some length and ended with "*Observations*: You must always say 'Mam' when in her Majesty's presence. You must stand until the Queen asks you to sit down. Her Majesty does not often tell you to sit down . . .". Finally, not long before Alfred took his seat in the House of Lords in 1884, with the title First Baron Tennyson of Aldworth & Freshwater, Victoria wrote that she "saw the great Poet *Tennyson* in dearest Albert's room for nearly an hour . . . his eyesight much impaired and he is very shaky on his legs. But he was very kind. Asked him to sit down."

G.F. Watts' portraits of the poet demonstrate the change in him.

The canvas of 1859 captured, in Rembrandt-light, a handsome romantic-melancholic seer with raven-black hair, brows, moustache and beard, his eyes cast down in purposeful reverie. In the red-chalk sketches of 1890 he records the great domed skull and battered features of a monument, with sad, tired eyes. With his friends and patrons the Princeps, Watts built a house in Freshwater called The Briary—burnt down in 1934—where he brought his seventeen-year-old bride Ellen Terry during the brief course of their marriage. Their move, and the consolation and advice for which Ellen fled to the poet, may stand for the constant comings-and-goings of literary lions and notables to and from the Island's island of which Farringford was the focus, and for the demands, as well as pleasures, which were imposed upon Tennyson. The list of Freshwater's visitors and temporary residents during those years is a glittering roll-call, a Victorian Who's Who in which establishment and eccentricity are characteristically compounded. "Nothing could be kinder than both Mr and Mrs Tennyson," wrote the poet Sidney Dobell, "he in his great blind superhuman manner, like a colossal child." Childe Alfred, cast as Arthur of the *Idylls*, a king among knights.

At the time of Lionel's christening, Alfred himself took up brushes and paints—those of Edward Fitzgerald, translator of *Omar Khayyam*—to daub a seascape, of the rocks below the downs, which now hangs in Trinity College, Dublin. Its lack of detail and swirling colour and light show, says his biographer Robert Bernard Martin, how poor the poet's eyesight was even then; it is like a very inferior late Turner. The man who had taken photographs of the Tennyson family in the Lake District called at Farringford in 1859. "W. must have basely misrepresented me," he wrote, "if he said that I followed the Laureate down to his retreat, as I went, not knowing he was there, to stay with an old college friend at Freshwater. Being there, I had the inalienable right of a free-born Briton to make a morning call." The misrepresented photographer was the Revd Charles Dodgson, alias Lewis Carroll. "There was a man painting the garden railings . . . of whom I asked if Mr Tennyson were at home, fully expecting the answer 'No', so that it was an agreeable surprise when he said, 'He's there, sir,' and pointed him out, and behold! he was not many yards off, mowing his lawn in a wide awake and spectacles." Carroll strove to impress upon Tennyson that he was not just a photographer but an author. With permission, he published *An Index to In Memoriam*—3,000 references painstakingly compiled by his sisters—and presented a copy to Julia Margaret Cameron in exchange for a print of her famous photographic portrait of Tennyson, who thought it made him look like a dirty monk. It is fuzzily Rasputinesque, and Carroll, who liked his little girls and other subjects sharply defined, and was, in Helmut Gernsheim's view, "a master of composition, which was one of Mrs Cameron's weak points", commented drily, "I did *not* admire Mrs Cameron's large heads taken out of focus. . . . *She* wished she could have some of *my* subjects to do *out* of focus—and *I* expressed an analogous wish with regard to some of *her* subjects." He must have been jealous of the way in which she had successfully insinuated herself into the Farringford ménage; he, a shy stammerer whose tongue was loosed only in conversation with children; she who, Jowett tells us, had "a tendency to make the house quake the moment she enters, but in this dull world that is a very excusable fault." The imagination which created *Alice* was far from dull, but it seems that his diffident manner did not endear him to the Tennysons; he broke with them, after his request to keep a pirated edition of Alfred's early poems was summarily rebuffed, and abandoned Freshwater for Sandown, and Snark-hunting, on subsequent Island holidays.

Increasingly, Tennyson became impatient with pilgrims and audiences, but he could be touchingly solicitous. When his old friend Thackeray died, his two bereft daughters came to stay in a cottage of Mrs Cameron's; as they sat mournfully before the fire, they became aware of the dark cloaked figure of the Laureate standing motionless in the heavy snow outside, a demonstration of feelings which did not intrude on theirs. When the flamboyant Garibaldi visited the Island in 1864, he planted a Wellingtonia tree which still stands in Farringford's grounds. Mrs Cameron begged him to pose for her; her kneeling posture and her up-raised chemical-stained hands made him think she was an overdressed beggar. She is reputed to have cried, "This is not dirt but art!"

Tennyson loved solitude. He built a wooden bridge that still stands across the lane between his grounds and the farm. He escaped on to High Down. He walked westwards to Warren Farm, where he studied the geology of Alum Bay with Granville Bradley, or to the flint cottage under the down where Shepherd Paul lived. There, discourse with the wise illiterate man who tended the Farringford flock refreshed the poet; the Shepherd Paul Trust, funded from the thrifty man's savings out of small wages, still remains "to give bread to the poor and needy" of the parishes of Freshwater and Totland. Tennyson was a would-be natural-historian and started to compile a botanical dictionary. He maintained that he was a shy beast who liked to stay in his burrow.

If my body come from brutes, tho' somewhat finer than their own,
    I am heir, and this my kingdom . . .

he wrote in *By an Evolutionist*. In June 1860, the professional naturalist Alexander Goodman More, author of *Outlines of the Natural History of the Isle of Wight* and much else, received an enquiry from Charles Darwin regarding the sexual habits of the bee-orchis: "I have been assured that in parts of the Isle of Wight, viz., Freshwater Gate, numbers occur almost crowded together." It was not until July of 1868 that the author of the *Origin of Species* visited Freshwater to recover from the recurrent gastric complaint that had interrupted his work on the *Descent of Man*. Francis Darwin recalled that Mrs Cameron received the family with open-hearted kindness. Her photograph of the famous cranium, heavy brows and haze of white beard was published with its subject's inscription, "I like this photograph better than any other which has been taken of me." But "my head is rather unsteady," he wrote to Joseph Hooker from Freshwater, "which makes my handwriting worse than usual." Two days before he left, he described his Island sojourn succinctly to his collaborator Alfred Wallace as "my nine weeks' horrid interruption of all work."

Visitors were often exactly that to Tennyson. From 1869 onwards his household occupied Farringford only in the winter months. In 1871, a valued neighbour, whose handwriting the poet described as like walking-sticks gone mad, built a new house on the site of Weston Manor. His letters may have been indecipherable, but in character William George Ward was "grotesquely truthful". He was active in the Catholic Revival, and St Saviour's Church at Totland, in whose graveyard Alfred Noyes was buried, is part of his legacy; but just as his house was built exposed to the gales that he loved, he was open to all the intellectual fresh air he could get. He liked

Tennyson, but not poetry. He liked Mrs Cameron too, for he valued people who said and did what they thought, however embarrassing it might sometimes be. The dirty monk and the overdressed beggar arrived at Weston Manor one day, just after Mass had been celebrated in the family's private chapel. She was engaged on one of her last projects—illustrations for a new edition of *Idylls of the King*—and exclaimed, "Oh, Alfred, I have at last found a Sir Lancelot!" She indicated a guest of the Wards, Bishop (later Cardinal) Herbert Vaughan, but Tennyson shook his great head, "No, he won't do, his face is too good-looking. For Lancelot you must have a man with a face seamed and seared by human passions." Squire Ward, as Mrs Cameron called him, earned this salute from Tennyson:

> Farewell, whose living like I shall not find,
>   Whose Faith and Work were bells of full accord,
> My friend, the most unworldly of mankind,
>   Most generous of all Ultramontanes, Ward,
> How subtle at tierce and quart of mind with mind,
>   How loyal in the following of thy Lord!

The poet must have recognized their disparity, as well as their affinity; he himself was vain and hypochondriacal, subject to gout and palpitations, paranoid about blindness and epilepsy. He suffered with bad teeth and continually resolved to give up smoking. He grew more and more fragile in the last dozen years of his life. Mr Thomas Edison's representatives came to Farringford to record him reading on to wax cylinders in May 1890; the voice that still emerges faintly from under surface noise is a mixture of faltering frailty and insistent power. In February 1891, he walked with Princess Louis of Hesse on the down that now bears his name, and raced her to the Beacon whose site is now occupied by his memorial Cross. In the summer he wrote *June Bracken and Heather*, a fine love lyric to Emily, "to you that are seventy-seven". *Crossing the Bar*, that was to conclude all editions of his published works, had appeared. The railway had been extended from Newport, via Yarmouth, to Freshwater. His home would never be the same again and, because of him and Victoria, neither would the Island. On the last day of May 1892, the rector, Dr Merriman, came to Farringford to administer communion before, next day, Alfred Lord Tennyson crossed the bar to the mainland for the last time. It was a sort of last rite.

5

FUN & FIRE-POWER

... the sea was glittering unbearably, like a scaled dragon wreath-
ing. The houses of Freshwater slept, as cattle sleep motionless in the
hollow valley. Green Farringford on the slope, was drawn over
with a shadow of heat and sleep.

D.H. Lawrence   *The Trespasser*

A notice opposite the bar;
The Tennyson & TV Room
—His cloak, his stick, some books. And—ah!—
Grandstand bright through Gothic gloom.

Robert Conquest   *To be a Pilgrim*

IN DAYS WHEN the recurring fear of French invasion was rife,
influential Islanders laid a proposal before Charles I's Privy Council
to provide a safe refuge for their women, children, cattle and goods.
An engineer was engaged to broaden, deepen and fortify the River
Yar, to "cut ye nick of land between ye two seas" and thus to create
of the Freshwater peninsula a real island enclave. The scare passed. It
never happened.

Ironically, the building of the causeway and drawbridge across the
Yar, from Yarmouth to Norton, coincided with the crescendo of
panic over the threat of invasion by the French Second Empire.
Napoleon III and Empress Eugénie had been Victoria and Albert's
guests at Osborne in 1857 and, when the courtesy was returned the
following year, the British party cast a wary eye over the naval fire-
power immodestly arrayed in Cherbourg harbour. A Royal Commission of 1859 recommended national expenditure of £10 million
on coastal fortifications, with £325,000 to be spent on the Island. The
budget was pruned of course, but all around the Wight new defences
were dug in or raised, elderly forts and castles were renovated and

63

the Island & Hampshire Volunteers multiplied more than ten-fold in a year. Men recalled that, sixty years before, during the Napoleonic Wars, Newport and Cowes, Yarmouth and thirty parishes were ordered to muster a defensive force; in 1797 the Wight was one enormous garrison with three thousand natives under arms, and 4,500 mainland troops; one soldier for every three civilians; and no invasion.

Golden Hill is a magical name. It is an Eden of apple-trees, crowned with white walls that in dawn light appear like some celestial city. You approach it on foot through copses carpeted with heath, pill-sedge and spiked sedge, delicately illuminated by pale blue dog-violets. Golden Hill Country Park is an inland retreat for the people of the Island's island. Its summit's white walls are those of a hexagonal fort, built in 1863–7 on a scarp above a wet ditch. The hub of the West Wight's defence system, it had positions for eighteen guns that were never mounted, accommodation for eight officers and 124 men, and hospital facilities for fourteen sick or wounded. It was the Western District School of Gunnery from 1888 until the Second World War; it served then as a barracks, and afterwards was abandoned. Now it is occupied by small factory units, and there have been battles over recent plans to extend the adjoining Golden Hill Industrial Estate into the Park. No one denies the desperate need for new jobs on the Island but, especially when so much factory space is unoccupied, the proposals make a mockery of the fine words spoken by Lord Mountbatten, the late Governor, when he dedicated the Park as a retreat on 4 July 1970: "Today Golden Hill enters a new rôle. It ensures protection against a different enemy—the invasion of urbanization and the population explosion. It becomes one of nature's sanctuaries—a bequest of peace and beauty to future generations . . ."

Below it, Norton Green more or less successfully resists the incursion of modernity. It still has a sense of itself, though chapel and pub have both undergone conversion; with the other houses they are set well back from a street which flows between broad banks. Near where so much masonry and iron was raised defiantly, the sculptor Mignon Jones works in wood and metal and stone; her *Seahorse* it is that enlivens the wall of the College in Newport; her *Meridian I*, of aluminium, wood and pierced and burnished slate, in the Lord Louis

Library; and here, she has translated the eloquent grain of a felled elm
into a vital male torso. Norton Green runs with the Wight's grain;
but Hallet's Shute, the hill that takes you down to Norton Spit and
the causeway to Yarmouth past self-consciously picturesque cottages, detached villas and a Country Club, might as well be in
Surrey. Via the road to Sconce Point you can escape into yet another
world. "Liable to Subsidence" it says, and sure enough it bucks like a
switchback, crazily patched with tarmac where the clays and sands of
this corner of the Island are continually dismantling themselves in the
direction of the Solent.

Sir George Carey built Sharpnor Fort, or Carey's Sconce, against
the Spanish Armada; Sconce Point Battery was installed here about
1800; no trace remains of these, but beyond a disused jetty Fort
Victoria looms out of the 1840s, like two lengths of brick-built
railway arches set at right-angles. It harboured fifty-two guns,
casemated or in open batteries, and an 18-inch-gauge railway
brought supplies from the jetty and fed the batteries with shell. From
emplacements modified in the 1880s to take 10-inch RML guns, you
can see and hear Sconce Buoy's warning and, if the tide is running,
watch treacherous currents rippling the Solent's skin. Walk, leaning
into a wintry westerly wind, along the top of the low fort, and
imagine the prospect facing Charles I as he embarked nearby on the
first day of December 1648: a bleak stretch of water and the
intimidating bulk of Hurst Castle on its spit. Westminster and the
block beyond.

Summer is a better season, and Fort Victoria is a Country Park
with an exhibition, adventure playground and picnic-sites. Part of
the cobbled Military Road to Cliff End is a Nature Trail. Pine and
holm oak, blackthorn and bramble—entwined with clematis, wild
rose and honeysuckle—struggle to keep their footing in shifting
ground. Ferns, bracken and enchanter's nightshade thrive in humid
corners. Ponds collect on the clay below outcropping Bembridge
marl and limestone, and the confused succession of soil types yields a
rich flora: alder and oak, birch and bedstraw, dogwood and Dyers
rocket, hazel and horsetail, restharrow and orchis, sallow and
sycamore, thyme and teazle, willow, wych elm and wayfaring tree.
Above, on Norton Common, Richard Worsley erected a tower in
the 1540s to complement Hurst and keep the French at bay. Lord
Conway demolished it and only the name Round Tower Point

65

remains. From there you can see Fort Victoria's mate, Fort Albert, a monstrous offshore excrescence once bristling with 64-pounders, then an instructional battery and Brennan Torpedo Station; light guns were kept in a state of readiness there until the 1950s, but today its aggressive brick is a retreat for those who own the luxury flats inside. Twin batteries, abandoned on the cliff above after the last war, have fallen into the sea. Cliff End Fort, whose elderly brick was reinforced with concrete in the 1860s, suffered mixed fortunes. The Committee on Heavy Gun Working came to inspect the inaugural firing of new 12.5-inch guns in April 1879, but faults developed in racers, tracks and carriages. In November a repeat performance was staged, but the first five discharges exposed the masonry, and after sixteen the footings were severely shaken. The Fort was rebuilt.

At sea level, freshwater limestones give way to blue clay and the sands of Colwell Bay, a mosaic of spread towels, wind-breaks, lilos, trunks and bikinis from which bright fragments detach themselves and bob in the blue ground of the sea. The cliffs are a colourful and richly fossiliferous succession, alternately freshwater and marine, of clays, sands, marls and limestones that make up the Middle Headon Beds. They slip and slide and torrent down in gouts of mud, making life confusing for the geologist, and the maintenance of the sea-wall a priority. Elegant Venus shells can be picked out of the landslips, and Bramble Chine boasts a fossil oyster bed. In Turner's watercolour there is no sea-wall, just a thatched building from which crumbling steps lead down to a beach strewn with lobster-pots, a makeshift shelter, oars and anchors. Warden Point, then topped only with turf, rears behind in rumpled grandeur, and beyond it, in another sketch, Turner's pencil describes the arc of Totland Bay: duck-boards on the mud lead us into a barely busier foreground of fishermen and boats. The few old buildings that survive at Colwell are roughly contemporary with Turner's visit. Rockstone Cottage was the officers' mess when troops, ready to resist Napoleonic aggression, camped on Colwell Common. Barncroft was a barn then, and served as the canteen. Old people recall Totland as nothing much more than cottages, church, school and farm; the barn's magnificent stone stands proud across the road, once a farmyard track, from the flower-embroidered farmhouse and a granary on staddle-stones.

But these fine old specimens have to be sifted, in the imagination, from the suburban sediment that has settled around them, and from the superficial deposits of holiday camps, flatlets and caravans that cap the cliffs. In the 1850s the Nelson Arms at Colwell was renovated, modestly enough, in the hope of attracting holiday-makers. Now the Colwell Bay Hotel has passed through many hands, bleakly improved and tricked out with amusements. A local man who squatted grimly at the bar, on brief leave from perpetual night-shift on the mainland, mourned not the rural idyll, but the hey-day of the Colwell Regatta when there were more people about and when fireworks burst freely above the packed promenade. A hundred years on from its erection, the pier at Totland is squalidly matter-of-fact in its ambition to part you from your money. It is no longer the pride of the discreet watering-place where, as old photographs show, ladies of quality could parade in elaborate bonnets and parasols, and take the "four thousand miles of ozone constantly pouring upon it" while the sun laid down a blood-red road from horizon to pier-head, and brought a blush to the modest cliffs. A distinguished clientele tested the water from bathing-machines and danced nightly in the grand hotel whose chimneys, gables, balconies and hexagonal tower with a spire presided over the bay. Now it is all rubble. Councillors, worried about population density, squabble over the merits of blocks of flats or bungalows to infill the few remaining vacant lots. Mrs Hammersley's grand house survives, just: decapitated, a bungalow with an interior like an elegant salon. Somehow it sums things up. The man in the pub bemoaned pre-war holiday-camps that would not keep up with the times. But many return happily to flats or bed-and-breakfast year after year, and many are happily settled here. It's a boneyard for old people, he said.

Warden Ledge treacherously divides Colwell from Totland Bay. The *Happy Return*, laden with tin, foundered there in 1827, adrift from Yarmouth where the captain had put in for a doctor to tend a sick woman on board. The crew were rescued but the doctor drowned. Fort Warden, built on the cliff in 1862 and rebuilt in the 'nineties, is a formidable stronghold of fun; a holiday village complete with shops, cafés and amusement arcades where families retreat for a fortnight to fortify themselves against the rest of the year.

From Cliff End you can walk along the newly reinforced sea-wall, beneath Warden Point, to Totland's 1966 sea-defences and the Lifeboat House that sheltered gallant craft from 1885 to 1924. Earlier still, *The Little Dove*, bought by public subscription, was on station here. The first R.N.L.I. boat, the *Charles Luckhombe*, was followed by the *Robert Fleming*, chosen for its task by William Conway. In 1974, fifty years after the last Totland boat saved lives, a memorial to the men who manned her was unveiled in the Parish Hall in the presence of Jack Conway, lone survivor of the crew. Like the lifeboat, Trinity House pilot vessels now work out of Yarmouth, but it was a proud day when the *Landward* of Totland led the coffin-bearing craft *Havengore* up the Thames for Winston Churchill's funeral.

At low tide, you can make on for Alum Bay by picking a way over limestone boulders around Hatherwood Point, taking care not to sink into glutinous mud or slip on mucilaginous wrack. Headon Hill's four hundred feet loom and slump and clamber up above you; kestrels hover and stoop into invisible hollows; then, all at once, the clinically white upright stacks of the Needles come into your sights. But at high water you must take that reminder of past gentility, the Turf Walk amongst Scots pine and sycamore, willow and cherry plum, then briefly climb out of Totland on Cliff Road and up through a tunnel of hawthorn on to Headon Hill. Near the top, limestone is cloaked with turf, but the summit is gravel growing heath, heather and sea-buckthorn, and pungent on hot days with the coconut fragrance of yellow furze.

Totland is "tout-land" or the place of the look-out; a watch was kept to tout for unwelcome customers, and a beacon fuelled ready to flare its alarm along the island chain. Hatherwood Point Battery's footings are a balcony from which to view pacific yachts. From there, or from the top of tumuli, you can look back to Cliff End and Fort Albert, southwards to the Warren and the great wall of West High Down, or south-west to Alum Bay and the great buttressed promontory of chalk that thrusts out and down to the Needles and the red-and-white lighthouse that nightly sweeps its warning beam about the sea.

In the summer of 1917, the ten-year-old Wystan Auden and his two brothers wrote in their diary: "After dinner we walked onto Headon Hill and after we had seen the Tumulus we walked down

The Needles and Scratchell's Bay   Highdown and Tennyson Down

Freshwater Bay

Alum Bay and Hatherwood Point

Colwell Bay and Fort Albert

St Michael the Archangel, Shalfleet

Yarmouth

Newtown Creek

All Saints', Calbourne

Ratsey's sail-loft, Cowes

The Royal Yacht Squadron, Cowes

Warrior figurehead, Spencer (Thetis) Yard

Quarr Abbey ruins

St Mildred's Church, Whippingham

Quarr Abbey Church

Brading Haven

Appley Tower, Ryde

Brading church tower and Wax Museum

Sweetshop, Brading

St Mary's Church, Brading

Princess Elizabeth's memorial, St Thomas's, Newport

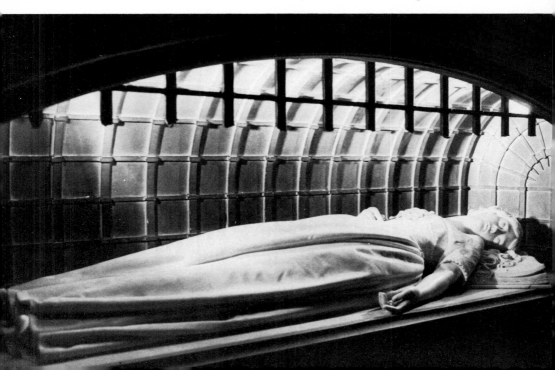

into what looked like an old disused fort but when we got in there an Orderly turned us out saying it was an Isolation Camp. There were two large muzzle-loader guns there. Then we walked down into Alum Bay but it was high tide so we could not go and see the different coloured rocks. Then we came home." Their mother added that the condition isolated inside the fort "was cerebro-spinal meningitis—so felt anxious!". There is yet a third way to reach Alum Bay from Totland, but it is one that I avoid like the plague; the road to a car-park above the cliffs leads you, along with all the other cars and coaches, into the garish shanty-town of shops, stalls, side-shows, snacks and souvenirs called the Needles Pleasure Park. I'd swap Pleasure for Headonism any day!

Guglielmo Marconi is commemorated by a modest monument in the car-park. In the spring of 1897 he co-opted Mr Garlick, the Totland Postmaster, to help set up his wireless experiments. In June, William Preece championed Marconi in his Royal Institution lecture on wireless telegraphy, but Professor Oliver Lodge disputed his claims and ascribed the credit to Hertz—and to Oliver Lodge. Marconi's Wireless Telegraph & Signal Company Ltd was incorporated in July while he was in Italy with his Irish mother. The Government did not applaud this private enterprise, and Preece threatened to cease experimentation until relationships were regularized. The Post Office wrote to the Admiralty on 7 September opining that "as Signor Marconi has now disposed of his rights in the invention to a private company it is thought advisable that . . . the results of these further experiments should not be made public." In November Marconi rented and converted rooms at the Needles Hotel; masts, including one from the Royal Yacht *Britannia*, were planted in the grounds; the sparks that crackled from their wiring were a source of local entertainment. The ex-sailor George Kemp deserted the Post Office for Marconi, and later recalled: "I remember him having to make three attempts to get out past the Needles in a gale before he succeeded. He does not care for storm or rain but keeps pegging away." When Marconi got marvellous publicity by transmitting minute-by-minute reports of the Kingstown yacht races in appalling weather for the Dublin *Daily Express*, the *Evening Mail* issued a supplement which he had translated and published in his home town of Bologna. He told the Irish reporters that "the best results we have obtained were on the small tugboat . . . in very tempestuous weather in the month of November around the Isle of Wight where we had at times about two feet of water in the cabin, and ourselves and all the instruments were practically drenched with sea water. Many of the sailors and engineers of the tug seemed very anxious about their personal safety on that particular occasion." Our intrepid inventor transmitted messages over eighteen miles that day, and in 1898 Lord Kelvin telegraphed friends from Alum Bay. Despite, or because of, the Post Office monopoly on inland communication, provocatively he paid Marconi one shilling a time. On his return from the USA on board the *St Paul* in 1899, Marconi contacted the Needles from seventy miles out at sea.

Overhead cables stretch from the Pleasure Park down to Alum Bay, carrying the chair-lift that swings you out over the fissured cliffs and Alum Bay Chine, the traditional way down to the pebbly beach. Linking Headon Hill's horizontal beds with the leaning strata of the Chalk is the bay's spectacular backdrop of vertical Barton Clays, Bagshot Sands, London Clay and Reading Beds. Laid down variously in marine, lagoon, estuarine, deltaic and freshwater conditions when the once-level land was uprising or downlying, they are rich with evidence of tropical and subtropical flora and fauna. Ages have compressed and tilted them, and weather has sculpted them into the rock-shape of another, more barren and exotic, planet. Turner painted their rugged rainbow, and for as long as people can remember there has been a hut selling glass phials and ornaments resplendent with alternating layers of coloured sand. I have a pencil by me, to correct my typescript, topped with a tube containing Alum Bay's spectrum. You can best appreciate their splendour from a boat out in the bay, after rain, at sunset; then their grey-blues, purplish-reds, yellow-beiges, ochres and blacks are most vivid, stretched like a banner of subtly tinted silk above the sea.

Fine white sand from the base of Headon Hill was shipped to glass factories in London and Bristol, and Josiah Wedgwood experimented with it in the manufacture of porcelain. Nearer the Chalk, the yellow efflorescence on the clays is the alum that gave the bay its name. Richard Worsley was granted a warrant to work alum here in 1561, and we know that there was an alum-works in Parkhurst Forest by 1579. A vein of pipe-clay preserves its delicate record of tropical leaves and fruits, and Mother Larges' Well and other springs issuing from the Chalk have washed out a wild gully whose pink and grey clays exude on to the pebbles.

All that is left of the fine pier where paddle-steamers embarked their passengers are some timber piers protruding from the water below the Chine, but small boats still offer trips around the Needles. From water-level, caverns like Mother Larges' Kitchen yawn; the height and weight of White Cliffs hits you. But, if you are not mesmerized by the detached rock masses with their garrisons of cormorants, you may notice five holes in the base of a chalk buttress; the cliff seems not so solid after all. In 1890 a lift-shaft was sunk, tunnels excavated, and cave positions created for searchlights, QF guns and a Maxim machine-gun. The shaft surfaces 250 feet up in the Old Needles Battery, built in 1861–3 and re-opened for the National Trust in June 1982 by Prince Charles. There you can examine the winch chamber, explosives stores, laboratory, guard room and the gun emplacements in their semi-circular barbettes. There, the first British anti-aircraft "pom-pom" gun practised on a kite towed by a destroyer in 1913. If you are not claustrophobic, you can clamber down spiral stairs and along a tunnel to the 1899 searchlight position which supervises the Needles, and which laid down a Welcome mat of light across the Solent's threshold. In 1893–5 the New Needles Battery was built higher up on the site of a 1781 lighthouse, and at the beginning of this century obsolete 9-inch guns were thrown over the cliff from the Old Battery. There are plans to recover two of them, but when I crawled to the edge of the precipice and looked down into Scratchell's Bay, the sea broke silently over their resting-place; close beneath me, though, were the warm-coloured pinions of a kestrel riding the updraught and plumbing the depths with better eyes than mine.

In the Coastguard Station my eyesight was abetted by binoculars taken as a prize from a German U-boat. Surrounded by charts and pin-ups, coastguards and auxiliaries scan the sea and scour the radio frequencies for distress signals. They alert and co-ordinate rescue services when boats capsize or run aground, when folk get stuck up cliffs or stranded by the tide, and they collaborate with Yarmouth Customs & Excise in tracking vessels suspected of carrying contraband. Here is a place from which to gain a high regard for the elements and a low opinion of human nature. The place is busy enough on fine summer days, but imagine the pandemonium of a stormy winter's night. Imagine too those nights in the last war when a wrecking wind took roofs off huts and men over the cliffs; when mine-laying aircraft strafed the batteries and searchlight beams and anti-aircraft flak wove a defensive net across a dangerous sky.

There should be nineteenth-century ghosts here: men buried in the embanked shell store and cartridge magazine, padding to and fro in rope-soled sandals and calico uniforms with bone buttons, urgently packing powder into shells; fifteen men exposed at each barbette swinging the gun carriage on its pivot, twelve tons of hot barrel rocketing back on its platform at each discharge, to be recharged with fifty pounds of gunpowder and a 256 lb shell rammed down the muzzle; the gun trundling back to firing-position, the lanyard jerked to touch the charge off, rocketing the barrel back again, and again. . . . Pass under the embankment and cross the bridge that was once winched forward and back over the ditch; there, at night, you may meet the only ghost that is said to haunt the place, a bull-nosed Morris that blunders, headlights blazing, from the Old Battery as if trying to make today's mundane solid traffic swerve and crash.

The actor-manager Loraine took off, on a July evening in 1910, from Needles Point Cliff, and his Farman biplane reached Bournemouth in under half an hour. Between 1956 and 1971, more ambitious engines were tested here: above Suncorner there is what appears to be a concrete promenade over an amphitheatre which falls to the cliff-edge. Black Knight and Black Arrow rocket-engines were brought here from Saunders-Roe's Cowes factory and test-fired in huge chambers like ovens or safes. The rockets were actually launched across the world at Woomera, and this massive monument remains *in memoriam* the British rocket-research programme. From it, over a prospect of yellow horned poppies and sea-pinks, there is the best view of the Needles.

In the winter of 1978, snow shrouded the whole headland and could barely be distinguished from the weighty white sky or from the chalk falling far away to the grey waters. But the last time I walked from here to Freshwater Gate, sun raised small scents from the downland flora and mist from the sea; a black-sailed craft, like a ghost-ship, appeared and disappeared to westward; a rash of small rocks lay submerged at the base of the cliff, the swell tossing their heads of black weed, and fishing-boats stitched a course along lines of lobster-pots. Chalk Hill and rarer Adonis Blue butterflies worked yellow-vetch and purple thyme; rarest of all, and confined to the Island, Glanville Fritillaries sunned their modest ochre wings against leaves of plantain. Gulls and jackdaws rose up from the sheer face and plummeted again to their nests; a glorious pigeon, glinting green and blue and purple, allowed me within two feet of it, and I saw that it was ringed, a racer resting between clumps of gorse and hawthorn after its Channel crossing. Rabbits were shyer, scutting away and over the edge, swerving into their burrows at the crest of the cliff.

Ahead was Tennyson's Memorial Cross. Below, to the north, was the bungalow called Largesse, its garden full of immobile animals, gnomes and the turning sails of model windmills. Warren Farm was next, where Tennyson talked geology, now farmed by one branch of the Osman family who settled in sixteenth-century West Wight, far from their Turkish roots. Beyond one of the many chalk-pits that marled the soils north of the downs, the old stones of Alum Bay House stood amongst trees haunted by the missel-thrush. Beside a pit from which pale Headon sands are still dug, and already back-filled with corpses of cars and other scrap, horned black-faced sheep grazed between the cowslips. Bronze Age barrows are easily confused with the bunkers and tees of an abandoned golf-course; and a boundary bank, whose fence hangs off the edge of the cliff, runs north towards a replica of the Nodes Beacon. Past Nodeswell is Squire Ward's Weston Manor, now a home for the mentally handicapped run by the ex-couturier monk Brother Dominic; it was the chapel there, with its ceiling painting of Christ riding a rainbow, that D.H. Lawrence's Siegmund and Helena stumbled across in their doomed quest for pure love. The painter G.F. Watts' studio at The Briary, which escaped the fire that razed the original house, now forms part of a neo-colonial mansion. Middleton Cottage nearby was the Conways' home before they moved to Colwell; Conways and Osmans and the rest conspired to carry brandy tubs up a perilous cliff ascent near the Cross, for temporary concealment in, say, York Farm's pond, and dispersal by, for instance, the carrier at Kippax whose wife's voluminous skirts once concealed a quantity of liquor from the Excisemen. The latter's horses beat a tattoo along these heights, but when I walked there it was joy-riders on horseback who thudded past Tennyson's memorial; hoof on chalk echoed away in the direction of Farringford Hotel, the poet's home, now Pontin's pride and joy.

Tennyson Down's bleached and battered buttresses receded into mist towards Freshwater Gate and the Back of the Wight, and Black Rock with its crew of cormorants looked for all the world like a small craft in peril. Alan Sebrill, in Edward Upward's *The Spiral Ascent*, walked to the cliff-edge here to throw himself off. Fear, he realized, held him back, but "he had been deterred also by the desire—and the sea had made him aware of it—to go on living". The caves below are invisible and inaccessible, but the down declines towards lower cliffs at Watcombe; if you know how, and can make yourself small, you can crawl through a tunnel in the chalk and emerge into the wild privacy of Watcombe Bay, where waves thrash themselves over the rock and sluice back through the pointed arches of its caves. Surmounting the cliff is Freshwater Redoubt whose ramparts and casemated stores surround a *terreplein* on which later dwellings have been erected; originally it could hold seventy men and four officers, and eight 68-pound guns which W.H. Davenport Adams thought would "when discharged, shatter the chalky cliff about the ears of its gallant defenders." Then there is the Bay Hotel where Upward's "poshocrats" danced the night away, and where George Bernard Shaw made his entrance with a gammy foot and a new wife on 10 September 1898. He was photographed on the downs, scribbling *Caesar and Cleopatra* into a notebook and looking, with his peaked cap and trim beard, like Trotsky in plus-fours. On the brink of Freshwater Bay stands the more proletarian Albion, full of overners in the season, but also, as always, of the lore of tides, currents and landing-places or, in my hearing, of the need to improve Inshore Rescue and of the best sources for quality cannabis. Auden and Isherwood merely got mildly drunk there.

A little way up the road towards the thatched roof of St Agnes' is Julia Margaret Cameron's home, Dimbola, whose chicken-house she converted into a photographic studio. A studio reincarnated by Virginia Woolf in *Freshwater*, a satirical send-up of the Tennyson set, privately produced for a Bloomsbury party on 18 January 1935. The play opens with her great-aunt Mrs Cameron (played by Vanessa Bell) washing Mr Cameron's head (Leonard Woolf) while they wait for coffins to be delivered, so that they may at last pack for their exodus to India (in reality, Ceylon). Ellen Terry (Angelica Bell) is on the model's throne, posing to her "Signor" G.F. Watts (Duncan Grant) for *Modesty at the feet of Mammon*. Now, the real Dimbola is divided into two, the symmetry of its central tower and flanking gables spoiled by contrasting colour-wash and a sun-lounge, but in 1926 it was already a guest-house, charging 63/- a week. Saunders Hotel, up Coastguard Lane, then charged 94/6d; but Upward, Isherwood and Auden chose the modest Ocean View, nearer the Bay, where hymns could be sung to Auden's vigorous piano accompaniment. In 1928, after Upward's *The Railway Accident* was written and Isherwood's *All The Conspirators* had been published, the writers returned and chased bits of toilet-paper over the down with their walking-sticks. While Isherwood was still staying there, his cadaverous landlady died as quietly and inevitably as she had run her boarding-house, within a stone's throw of the Bay and of the source of the Yar.

Much has died, much has changed and much survives on the Isle of Freshwater. A victim of its position, it was remote, eccentric and fortified against foreigners. Now its redoubts seduce invading tourists to them; it is a holiday retreat and a retirement refuge. Old cottages encircling greens were enclaves of population in a wild place, but now they are oases threatened by suburban sprawl. However, you can walk and climb and explore here still, and continually be taken aback by scenes of such charm and grandeur that you must conclude how hard it is to exorcize the spirit of the place. Driving back one day on the Calbourne road, I watched the mist coming in like a tide at Freshwater Bay; it flooded the gap between the downs and flowed along the bed of the Yar; it cut off the Island completely like a speeded-up action-replay of a geological trauma. Tennyson Down was submerged, mist melded with sky, and only the dark side of Tennyson's Cross hung in the air. With an old sense of wonder I drove down into the whiteness and across Blackbridge.

6

YARMOUTH & THORLEY BROOK

Yarmouth is much diminished from its ancient consequence.
John Bullar *Guide to the Isle of Wight*

I remember Yarmouth in 1905 when it had about three streets, a
church, a school, a town hall and very few shops. A narrow
dangerous bridge used to cross the river Yar. That has all been
altered.

Eleanor Fernbank *Island Memories*

IT COST YOU sixpence to cross from Norton to Yarmouth by ferry if
you were a gentleman or a lady, and one penny if you were not.
Whatever your station, you had to wait by the Sandhouse, from
which Alum Bay's sand was exported, until the ferryman was ready
to row you across. That was before embankments began to be raised
in 1858 to make causeways linked, in 1863, by the wooden Yar
bridge. The work was to be paid for by revenue from the toll-house
on the east side: 1d for pedestrians, 2d for horses or donkeys and 6d
for carriages or, later, for cars, hearses, litters, omnibuses, stage
coaches and other like vehicles. The Sandhouse now stands in a boat-
building yard, and the toll-house is the headquarters of Yarmouth
Sailing Club.

From the bridge the town appears as a compact, rather Gallic port
in a pint pot, surrounded by sea, harbour and the tidal arm of
Thorley Brook to the south. Confined by concrete banks moulded
like rubber mattresses, the placid surface of the inner harbour quivers
with the reflections of ranked masts, or is lassoed by the swelling arc
of wake from a rubber dinghy whose stuttering outboard motor
swings it round and under the bridge. The Report on Municipal
Corporations of 1835 maintained that "little or no alteration has
taken place here for many years: there is scarcely any trade, and very

76

little importation or exportation . . . Within the last year or two a few visitors have come to reside in the summer." Perhaps it still looks like that, but it is a settlement that has suffered the most dramatic shifts of fortune. The river ran out unconfined over the saltings and the harbour gaped at the Solent; then, in 1843–7, a breakwater in the shape of a tyre-lever was built between Norton Spit and the Castle at a cost of £1,500. Both this and the bridge were bitterly resented by the fishermen, longshoremen and sailors who were also "owlers", working the sea's illicit night-shift. The water was channelled and safer, but their goings-out and comings-in were trammelled and more risky. Arrivals by water used to be transferred to the shore by rowing-boat and disembarked at the Quay, an extra source of income for the boatmen. Then the pier, which still totters out into the water on shaky legs, was opened in 1876 and closed at night by locked gates, which also blocked free passage to the shore during the all-important hours of darkness. The men sold their boats temporarily, so that there was nothing for the Corporation's bailiffs to seize, and chopped the gates to pieces. At last, the gates were re-erected at an angle so that the shore was open to all at all times.

The paddle-steamer that tied up at the Pier used to be known as "The Workhouse", because of the labour needed to keep her brass and paint in trim. A century ago, the port was busy with traffic in coal, slate, corn and thousands of head of livestock per annum, including the ewes conveyed from the mainland each autumn to overwinter and be midwived by the milder climate. Tugs, like the *Jumsey*, and their towboats have gone. The Lilliputian row of buildings that houses the Customs & Excise and the R.N.L.I., whose rescues are commemorated by black plaques on the wall, was recently propped up by timber buttresses against being toppled by the foundation-shaking activity of pile-drivers and heavy plant and machinery employed to extend the berth for Sealink ferries. Sealink and the Harbour Commissioners have spent a million pounds in order to discharge and load pedestrians, cars, caravans, coaches, lorries and container transport in double time. Ramps and docking facilities seem to have grown out of all proportion to the town; mercifully, the car-park is outside the town proper and the roads conduct east-bound traffic around rather than through it, though west-bound vehicles still must queue at the Yarbridge traffic-lights before rumbling across single-file on studded planks into Freshwater

Isle. Another million-pound scheme, to replace the bridge with a new twin-carriageway one a little way to the south and at a better angle for the currents, should change all that. As for the old Pier, change has been vehemently resisted. South Wight Borough Council has been supported by the Department of the Environment in opposing the Harbour Commissioners' plan to demolish it, one of only two wooden piers of its kind left in the country. Since the paddle-steamers abandoned it, it has been an anglers' pitch, a viewpoint, a slalom course for maniacal speed-boat merchants and, some feel, a 637-foot-long white elephant. But where weather and rot and gribble worm have done their worst, the timber will be replaced piecemeal. Whether as folly, amenity or monument, Yarmouth Pier will stay.

Preventive men were cast in a tricky rôle in a town where every other man was a respectable smuggler, "the only honest thief" in Charles Lamb's phrase. They had to come to some arrangement with their neighbours, and much of the town sighed with relief in 1836 when, rightly or wrongly, a court of enquiry held at the George Hotel cleared the Coastguards' Chief Officer and some of his men of collusion with smugglers and accepting bribes. Many of the town's cellars are both ancient and capacious, though nothing much earlier than the sixteenth century survives above ground. There is nothing very grand about Yarmouth—it feels like an overblown model village or a life-size town shrunk to fit its site—but its proportions and its mixture of stone, half-timbering and brick, in which elegant Georgian jostles with rustic cottage or miniature Victorian villa, conspire to make it the warmest and most appealing of Island towns, a slice of old West Sussex on the south shore of the Solent.

Seventeenth-century Jireh House, Saxonbury, the Old Rectory and the Methodist Church with its spire and cottage garden are charming. Eremue Court, a modern block of flats vainly dignified with Yarmouth's ancient name, is not. The National Schools' buildings are fine examples of 1855 Elizabethan, and Alma Place with its eccentric chimneys dates from the time of the Crimean War. From the High Street old walls run down between the houses to the water's edge; Eremue Lane leads to St James' Chapel; Pinings Yard is recent, but set with a grotesque corbel head; The Towers is a distinguished castellated house whose seaward wall has been painted

78

with fake gun-ports since the early eighteenth century; and, next door, the Solent Yacht Club has a delightful colonnade supporting a balcony, now half-roofed and enclosed to the devastation of its proportions and the comfort of Sunday old salts.

The solid grace of the red-brick Town Hall dates from its 1763 rebuilding by Thomas, Lord Holmes. Yarmouth was pre-eminent in the Island and was the first town to receive a charter; it is said that Baldwin de Redvers, Earl of Devon, Lord of the Island and founder of Quarr Abbey, granted it "all liberties and customs belonging to free Burgesses, and quittances from tolls and other customs in fairs and markets" in 1135, though there is reason to believe that one of Baldwin's descendants did the honours in about 1170. Within the arches of the Town Hall's flagged ground floor, the Friday market's wares of meat, butter and other commodities were bought and sold. The Fair was on 25 July, St James' Day, when a stuffed glove on the end of a rod gave its benediction from the first floor and showed that the long arm of the law had relaxed its grip for a day. The charter was renewed several times and confirmed by James I. The town returned one or two members to Parliament until it was declared a Rotten Borough in 1832; though, by our standards, there had been something rotten in the state of local democracy for a long time. In 1601, Sir George Carey desired the burgesses to submit their writ as usual, with a blank space for him to insert names "he shall think fittest to discharge that Dewtie for their Behoofe"; and a later Governor, Lord Cutts, imprisoned a clergyman for voting wrongly, and quartered soldiers in the town when burgesses threatened to act according to their lights. The Mayor and Corporation were honoured with the gift of a mace from Charles II, but the borough was abolished in 1883, and a Town Trust of eleven members has since regulated affairs from the Town Hall.

Many of the "Papers, Writings and Records" of both Town and Church have been irretrievably lost. It is said that a naval guest at the Court Leet Dinner of October 1784, having had too much or too little to drink, resolved to smuggle the Corporation's wine stock back to his ship, but took the Town Chest by mistake. Finding, as it were, no bottle in the drawer of the filing-cabinet, he gave Yarmouth's records indecent burial at sea. Be that as it may, the story of the town's churches is difficult to unravel. The first church of St James is reputed to have been in existence by the early twelfth century, possibly on the site of the Castle; we know that a chaplain from Quarr Abbey was to celebrate daily Mass for the repose of the soul of a benefactor, Alexander Duele, from Michaelmas 1260, in the church of St John the Baptist. This church seems to have been at the east end of the town, where the graveyard now is. Both may have been landmarks when King John stayed here in 1206, while mustering his fleet for La Rochelle, and again in 1214 *en route* for Poitou. Edward III would have seen them when his fleet was gathering to sail on La Hague, but French raids in 1377 left Yarmouth "wholly burnt and made desolate" and the churches "utterly razed and defaced"; so much so that taxes upon the town were waived. Poverty may have precluded repair work, and there is certainly a gap in the list of Rectors of St James' from 1398 to 1621. The French did their worst again in 1524; in 1559 it was stated that scarcely a dozen houses in Yarmouth were inhabited. Though the church bells were all said to have been taken as booty to Cherbourg, a commissioner's report of this period speaks of a silver-gilt chalice in the custody of John Longe and William Younge, together with an old cope of "Redde satten of brege", an old vestment of "Rosset silke", another of "Thered Dormyx wt an Albe to the same", and it adds that one of the bells was taken from the steeple to be sold, but the soldiers of the Castle took it into their charge. A new church had been built to the east of the town, but its footings gave way and it was allowed to decay, finally being demolished in 1635 on the authority of a faculty issued by the Bishop of Winchester to the vicar, mayor and a soldier John Burley, perhaps the same who attempted to muster a force in Newport to rescue Charles I from Carisbrooke. A brief of 1611, the year of the Authorized Version of the Bible, said of Yarmouth that "there remains only the ruinated chancell of one of the churches which the inhabitants of the towne maintained for the exercise of divine service . . . not of sufficient greatness and capacity to containe the inhabitants who resorted thither . . . and the towne being unable from its own rescources to erect and fit a decent church . . . the charitable devotion and liberal contribution of the King's loving subjects throughout the realm is requested towards the new building and re-edifying of the said church of Yarmouth." The inhabitants of Lymington shared the flames of French aggression that flickered across the Solent, and the memory perhaps prompted them to give 32/8d towards the building fund. Soon the present church was erected and consecrated, and many nineteenth-century donors enabled drastic renovations to be carried out between 1831 and 1895.

The small bell, with its *fleur de lys*, that is rung in the entrance under the west tower before each service, is supposed to have been liberated from a French ship in the Solent in Henry VIII's time. Marvin Burley, son of the Royalist Captain, was the first man to be buried in the church, though the large bell in the tower did not toll until 1679, when the fine clock by Matthew Paris was also installed. The stonework of the tower changes half-way up, for it has been given battlements and, as Edmund Venables says, "an addition to its height, with but small increase to its beauty." The architect responsible, Daniel Alexander, was more used to designing the London Docks, Dartmoor Prison, the Royal Naval Asylum, Kent Gaol and Trinity House lighthouses; his tower of 1831 is a bulky monument raised to the memory of his son Henry. Another son William died in 1832, "having, in the last days of his health, with manly love and sorrow, helped to rear the Tower to his brother's memory; now no less a witness to his own." The Alexanders lived in The Towers, as did Captain John Urry, commemorated in the chancel, whose ancestor painted the black gun-ports on his wall; but the most famous seafarer here occupies the south chapel. He is described beneath his effigy as "Robert Holmes, Warrior" and the Latin inscription, in translation, runs: *From his early youth he was given to military glory and therefore entered the Army. On his first outing he fought under the banner of His Most Serene Majesty, King Charles I, valiantly and successfully against the common enemy. Afterwards, with equal courage and renown, he engaged in action at sea, and greatly distinguished himself under the command of the most valiant Prince Rupert* in whose squadron he was an apt student of the piratical techniques employed in the Civil War. *But when he found that the Royal cause could no longer be defended by his service*—a grand way of putting it—*he withdrew and went* as a mercenary *to aid Foreign Princes in France, Germany and Flanders, and became famous there for war-like actions. At length, at the restoration of King Charles II, he was created by him Captain of Sandown Castle and, as a reward for his former merit and courage, he was afterwards knighted.* He was dubbed a notorious duellist and "the cursed beginner of two Dutch wars". Spoils from his harassment of the Dutch off West Africa included the Great Baboon, "much like a man in most things", which Pepys notes in his diary on 24 August

1661, and the gold for which John Dryden celebrates him in *Annus Mirabilis*, "Holmes, the Achates of the General's fight, Who first bewitched our eyes with Guinea gold." His cold-war provocation of the enemy was sanctioned by the Duke of York, and New Amsterdam duly became New York in 1664. *In the year 1666, being appointed a Vice-Admiral of the Red, he entered the Dutch port of Ely with a small fleet, and, having there burnt 180 ships, he sailed to Schelling and destroyed by fire Bradderinum, the chief town of the island*, avenged the next year by De Ruyter's destruction of Sheerness. *For these and several other noble exploits*, and after incarcerating him in the Tower briefly as a sop to the Dutch, *His Serene Majesty honoured him with just rewards for his valour and loyalty, and made him Captain and Governor of the Isle of Wight during the remainder of his life*, that is, from 1669 to 1692.

Beneath an arched canopy supported by Ionic columns of porphyry, the statue of Holmes stands in armour and the posture and accoutrements of a ruler. The coarse face is not unlike that in Sir Peter Lely's portrait of him, but it is rather too large for the body. The story is that Holmes captured the statue and its sculptor from a French vessel *en route* for Louis XIV's court, where *le Grand Monarchue*'s visage was to have been sculpted from life; the artist had to make do with the buccaneer knight instead. The Revd Thomas Pocock, recalling his Yarmouth visit of 1704, wrote less romantically that "this marble was going to France and the ship being cast away at the back of the Isle was made wreck and belonged to this gentleman", for Governors of Wight claimed wreck of the sea. Holmes' nephew Henry erected the memorial, having come from Ireland to marry Holmes' bastard daughter Mary and thus fulfil the terms of his uncle's will. Their son, Thomas, it was who rebuilt the Town Hall; and Thomas' son, Henry, who died aged five in 1751, is still remembered each 11 June when a service is held and the Little Henry benefaction is distributed.

His Serene and Merry Majesty, Charles II, with the Duke of York and Prince Rupert, landed at Gurnard Bay to visit Holmes in July 1671. The governor had had a road specially constructed through Parkhurst Forest upon which to conduct the party to his residence, that had been built by Yarmouth Castle, and to which Charles was to return in 1675. Holmes' house, now the George Hotel, still boasts the oak staircase up which the King made his way to bed. He might not have slept so soundly at the King's Head opposite, though at the Bugle the benign ghostly presence said to haunt it might have nudged him out of dreams of regicide. Now you can sit and drink at plastic tables beside the castle gateway, and beneath the Arms of England and France as they appeared before the union with Ireland and Scotland, and which escaped Roundhead mutilation during Charles I's exile on Wight.

Henry VIII's determination, stimulated by French invasions of the Island in 1524 and 1545, to build castles (in addition to those of 1536 at East and West Cowes) at Sandown, Norton and Yarmouth, was implemented by the then Governor, Richard Worsley. But Yarmouth's was the only one designed after the new style: with squat towers, low heavily reinforced walls pierced by gun-ports, platforms and an arrow-head bastion, all to be erected on the King's land, outside the Corporation's jurisdiction. A carved fragment in the fabric, a hand grasping a cross, hints that the yellow-green freestone was first quarried at Quarr, and then re-quarried from the recently dissolved Abbeys of Quarr and Beaulieu. By 1609, "two buttresses to stay up the walls" were needed to repair assaults of the sea, and by the end of the century the guardhouse had fallen down and the drawbridge over the moat had to be reinstated. Today, the Department of the Environment keeps all in good repair, including the tiny Great Hall, the Master Gunner's domestic accommodation and his circular brick-corbelled powder magazine, once as full of pent-up fury as a beehive, now cool as an ice-house.

Yarmouth has always been paranoid. The painter George Morland, busy with paintings such as *View of the Needles*, *The Castle* and *Freshwater Cave at moonlight, with a group of smugglers* in 1799, was arrested here as a spy in French employ. He, no stranger to paranoia himself, had fled London for Cowes to escape creditors and so that his wife could regain her health; and then from Cowes to Yarmouth to elude the bailiffs on his track. He was staying in the house of George Cole, a rich smuggler, when his sketching was seen as infinitely suspicious and he was arrested, on the orders of General Don, by a lieutenant and eight soldiers of the Dorset Militia, at breakfast time. Amid cries of "Traitor!", he was marched to Newport. They say that a sketch of a spaniel was produced in evidence, incontrovertibly a cunningly camouflaged map of the

Island. In the end he was discharged, with a strong injunction laid upon him to sketch no more.

At about that time, Yarmouth comprised 59 houses. In 1664 the marshes had been embanked, so that not only was it insulated from the outside world by sea, harbour and brook, but also by a drawbridge to the east and four gates that could be guarded: Quay Gate, Outer Town Gate, Inner Town Gate and Hither Gate. A redoubt was thrown up near Thorley Copse. Nowadays you can sketch and photograph the Castle with impunity, but to view the town from the old perspective it is best to walk down Mill Road to the Old Tide Mill. It is now a private house, having fallen into disuse when the embankment of the Newport-Freshwater railway was built through the mill-pond fed by Thorley Brook. Now the railway has gone too, Yarmouth Station is a Youth Centre, and the embankment is a peaceful causeway across the marshes. In Morland's time, when the Mill was new, the south half was the miller's house and the north half housed the mill; tide-flaps still guard the dam wall and, in an extension to the building which probably held a steam-engine, there is the stump of a chimney. Steam killed it in the end, but a mill has stood here, it seems, since before Domesday Book was compiled. Eremud alias Eremue alias Eremuth alias Yarmouth was a Domesday settlement before the de Redvers planned the twelfth-century town or built the Hospital of St Mary & All Saints. A Neolithic axe was found on Yarmouth beach and a polished flint one, southwards at Tapnell. Wilmingham and Afton are Saxon settlements, while eastwards along Thorley Brook is Wellow, where a Mesolithic mace-head was unearthed. Two hundred acres of land there, now farmed like a prairie, was granted by William de Vernon, Baldwin's son, to Quarr Abbey. Later, with Apse and Thorley, it belonged to Christchurch on the mainland, and Baldwin's widow, Lady Adeliza, gave the advowson of Thorley and a tithe of rabbits to Christchurch Twynham. The warren produced 500 rabbits per annum in the days of Edward III, fifty for the tithe and the remainder sold at twopence a head for the King's benefit. To protect the game, the scrub was left uncut; now its cornfields are fertile, sheep crop its meadows, and swans process nobly down the brook.

Before his confinement at Carisbrooke was complete, Charles I visited Yarmouth, and Thorley where Mrs Urry threw a banquet for him. The house where it was held has been replaced by an imposing, and beautifully kept, William & Mary specimen in fine grounds. Beside it, modern farm buildings accommodate pedigree cattle in deep litter; I was concerned when I saw the new block-built sheds rising, but lichen has grown on their roofs and they have been faced, at some cost, with local stone. The land has been planted with conifers, alder and oak, and the place should serve as a model of up-to-date agriculture that respects its context and inheritance. Behind the farm is a walled graveyard raised above the level of the meadows, dark with antique yews and the remains of the thirteenth-century Church of St Swithin. It was rare, because it had a belfry above the south porch; it had been vandalized by "some barbarous church-warden" who amputated its gables and hipped its roof; but that damage has been rectified because only the porch and belfry are left. Equally dilapidated is an ancient sarcophagus, and table-tombs of the Leigh family, one of whose sides had fallen in to reveal, when I looked, scapulae, clavicles and other bones. Most of the church was pulled down in 1871, and the font was transferred to the new church at Thorley Street; the manorial church has moved to where most of the people of Thorley actually live, in pleasant cottages, council houses and an incongruously converted farm. The Street was quite deserted when I approached the phone box there one day; as I opened the door the phone rang. I answered it. I followed directions to a nearby house and rang the bell. After an interval, a small girl in a nightie, clutching her teddy, opened the door. "Mummy's not in," she said. "She's not in," I told the phone. The voice replied, "Oi'll call again, don' matter, 'snot urgent."

Gardens embellished with fruit trees run towards meadows and the brook, and the road back to Yarmouth passes through rich pastures, then above the Green with its prospect of Lymington across the Solent. Yarmouth has spread a little eastwards since Morland's time, but it still preserves its complaisant, almost claustrophobic sense of pride. It is regaled with comfortable pubs, a wine-bar, a delicatessen and a good bookshop; its castle is a squat ornament, and you might be forgiven for thinking that the last excitement to stir Yarmouth hearts was the wreck of HMS *Gladiator* in 1908. Twenty-six lost their lives when she hit the American liner *St Paul* in a freak blizzard. She lay on her side that spring, like a beached whale. Divers in monstrous suits went down to survey her.

Sightseers toured her bulk in hired boats.

By the harbour that has seen so much action, and so much illicit and aggressive traffic, I sat down on a bench beside an old man and his dog. The Yar, shrunk to a trickle compared to the torrent that gouged out its valley, gave way to the incoming tide. The lifeboat in its urgent orange livery rose placidly at its moorings, and a light breeze plucked at the glinting shrouds of densely-packed, highly-strung yachts. Redshank stabbed the mud of the further shore. A party of visitors genially greeted my companion, old salt in blue jersey and aged canvas trousers; his dog stirred, but it was as if he didn't see them, any of us, at all. His eyes registered sky and water and would not be moved to regard us, any more than they would shift for the screaming gulls that swoop on scraps of food, the detritus of each day's small history.

PART THREE

REACHES

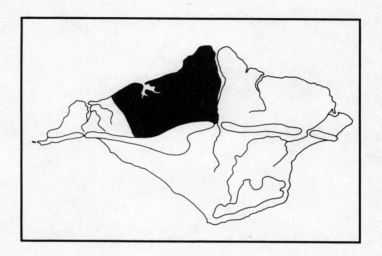

No, lady, it is not quite Alcatraz;
nor one great yacht marina, begging Cowes'
and millionaires-in-gin-palaces'
pardon. Newtown's no place for such bezazz.
Merchants' ghosts stir in Gold Street's swathe of grass,
the Town Hall's lost its town, so careless, yes,
though what's left boasts its Randy. Fairs like farce
vainly preserve old improprieties.

But shall we walk the Wall, see how the Creek
has lost and almost regained Paradise?
We'll plumb Clamerkin's reaches and Rodge Brook
to depths of Parkhurst where no curlew cries.
I'll lead you back to Cowes on seasoned roads
through trees, to bole and keel, to axe and adze.

7

NEWTOWN RIVER

I bunched a hitty, big as a plate
  An' garbed me up a dandy O
To meet my maid by her mammy's gate
  An' away to Newtown Randy O.

Traditional

... The singular creek of Newtown river, a digitated expanse
formed by the union of several dull streams, stained by the clay beds
along which they creep.

Edmund Venables   The Isle of Wight

CHESSELL DOWN, cleared at such cost by earlier peoples, is shrouded
with Forestry Commission trees. Graves in the large Jutish cemetery
there yielded up a rich harvest of trophies to nineteenth-century
excavators, sumptuously celebrated in a recent British Museum
publication; the site should be cleared and re-dug so that the history
of early struggles for the Island can be sifted again. With a bloody
massacre at Carisbrooke, the Jutish Saxons, Cerdic and Cynric,
brought the Wight into Wessex's fold in 530. When Cerdic died four
years later it passed, with fresh slaughter, to his nephews, Stuf and
Wightgar. Wulfere, son of King Penda of Mercia, ravaged the Island
and ceded it to Sussex as a sort of christening present for King
Æthelwald; but not for long, because Caedwalla, with a genocidal
instinct tempered only by Bishop Wilfrid's missionary zeal, retook
Wight for Wessex in 686. It is said that the deposed King Atwald and
his eldest son were buried, opposite the Jutish cemetery, on
Shalcombe Down. There, Saxon burials have been disinterred from
a Bronze Age bell barrow and from another mound, pillaged by marl
diggers, which held two brooches and an iron sword; a third, at
Chessell, gave up sword, spear and beads. Shalcombe Down is

afforested too; the chalk-pit at its foot looks across a track to the lake that feeds a tributary of the Caul Bourne which eventually issues into Newtown River. Water, sprung from the Chalk, is gathered on the Reading Beds and London Clay; it runs along the line of the Osborne Beds, past Little Chessell and Eades Farm to Newbridge, away from the shaded relics of antique cataclysm and onwards to the tidal flux of the last millenium's mixed fortunes.

Chessell was Louis MacNeice's territory for a time, when J.B. Priestley dominated the Island's literary landscape from Brook Hill House. More recently still, one of the barns of the youthful, 300-year-old Chessell Farm has been transformed into a fine pottery, where clay is coaxed into fragile fungal forms. But north of the road it is stone, not clay, on which three square miles of fields are founded. Names like The Quarries, Stony Copse, Stoneovers and Dodpits open your eyes to blindingly white wounds made in the Bembridge Limestone by quarrymen's tools and hydraulic diggers. Churchills Quarry gave up a skeleton in 1933; either Anglo-Saxon or the fruit of some later misdemeanour. The fresh-water stone layers seem to give off their own light, but they have been bed-rock for some dark deeds. Dodpits House is meant to be haunted by a man with an icy touch who hanged himself in a seventeenth-century doorway; and where Dark Lane meets Dodpits Cross, the fingerpost grew into a gibbet on an October evening in 1928, and a young girl was confronted with the cloaked, black-haired figure of a hanging man.

After the Dissolution of the Monasteries, Thomas Hopson exchanged his manor of Marylebone, London, for Quarr Abbey's grange of Shalcombe and land at south Hamstead, together with the Canons of Christchurch Priory's chief Island holdings, east and north Hamstead, Thorley church and the manor of Ningwood. Ningwood Manor House is a gloriously mellow building whose one-room-deep Georgian front, added by Sir John Pinhorn, rates as a modern façade. Its stable-yard rang importantly with the hooves of Hopson's grandson's mounts when he was appointed Captain of the Ningwood Company in 1627, but latterly has allowed old horses a leisurely retirement in the care of the R.S.P.C.A.

Beneath Ningwood, Bembridge Marls give way to overlying Hamstead clays and loams first discovered and delineated by Edward

Forbes in 1852. Northwards the landscape becomes pasture patched with copses of oak, ash and hazel. From the Horse & Groom, you can drop down through a glutinous clay field to the footbridge across Ningwood Lake, a small brook that runs into the Western Haven of Newtown River; then climb between grazing horses to the eccentric settlement of Cranmore. What started as a shanty-town, strung out along a sticky pot-holed road, has developed into a hide-out for plutocratic squatters and gipsies. Luxurious log-cabins and Swiss-style chalets consort with shingled cottages and shacks, some decayed and screened from the track only by tall weeds, others defensively fenced in and patrolled by aggressive dogs. Goats wag their beards among the footings of abandoned sheds and fowls fly up to roost in their wooden houses. Brickhouse Field, Kiln Cottage, Brickyard Cottage and North Kiln are reminders of the industry that thrived here and around Ningwood. Next to the crumbling ruin of Bon Accord is a more surprising product of the heavy clay, Cranmore Vineyard; neat rows of nurtured vines on a south-facing slope mature the vintage sampled by Wight wine connoisseurs in Yarmouth's wine-bar.

Cranmore's special blend of exclusivity and happy-go-lucky make-do-and-mend ends abruptly next to a decayed homestead, when you emerge from a shady copse on to the brink of Bouldnor Cliff above the Solent. You tread a plateau gravel seeded with Palaeolithic tools; below, the cliff's jumbled and tumbled terraces— colonized patchily by foolhardy grasses, furze clumps and scrubby trees—fall away in a cocktail of greens, greys, blues, reds and blacks; laced with molluscs and other fossils of freshwater, estuary and sea, as well as plants like water-lilies and palm-trees, and the bones of turtles, crocodiles and small mammals. Here is a dream of tropical lakes and lagoons overtaken by the sea's inroads, then resurrected and carved by the great Solent river on whose banks Middle Stone Age men left tranchet axes, and where, much later when Bouldnor was known as Bolenoura, medieval men left traces of antler-working, twelfth-century pottery and wattle-hurdling now stranded between high and low water. Bouldnor's battery of the 1890s is derelict, and nothing remains of Hamstead's beacon, as recorded in 1324 and 1638.

From this drastic foreshortening of history and prehistory, the land slopes up towards West Hamstead Farm. Planted conifers, oak and alder scrub, willow, furze, bracken and brambles give way to the domesticity of pasture and ducks on a pond. Seen through the flustered flight of a pigeon flock, the water bears an oil-tanker on its way, and is apparently reflected in the blue highlights of magpies buzzing horses. Pheasants rasp their warning and the hay-scented, silage-sweet, dung-laden air of Hamstead Farm is pierced by the belving of its dairy herd. Hamstead farmhouse had the distinction of being worked on and enlarged by John Nash, prime architect of the picturesque, famed for Regent Street and Regent's Park. He bought three farms here and built up the estate, as recorded in the Hamstead Farm Improvement Book. By 1832, two years after he had fallen into disfavour on the death of George IV, he had created the first railway on the Island: a circular narrow-gauge network serving the farms and the quay. His wife lived at Hamstead after the enforced sale of East Cowes Castle, and the estate was taken over by her relatives, the Pennythornes, who built the Grange. On the death of Miss Rose Pennythorne, the estate was sold and Nash's work decayed or was demolished.

The path drops past woods rooted riskily on the crest of crumbling cliffs and down to the shore where Bembridge Limestone puts in a new appearance as the Hamstead Ledge, over which the ebb boils enough to make any sailor beware. On the descent, the prospect widens and embraces Newtown Bay, Thorness and grim Gurnard with, inland, Shepherd's Hill, Porchfield and Parkhurst Forest beyond. Gorse and teazles raise their hackles and the siren-calls of curlew announce the blunt snout of Hamstead Point. Between dense scrubland and the Dover of ochre pebbles that forms a natural bulwark against the Solent, a green road thick with rabbits runs along to the fleet. A lonely memorial stands at its edge "in loving memory of David Horace Cox Age 22 Lost at sea off Hamstead Ledge with his friend William Patrick Hope Pollock Age 20 On Nov. 27 1932. The Sea Is His. Robin Murray Cox Age 21 Lost at Sea June 2 1934 . . .". On a February day you may find primroses in full bloom, succeeded in the next few months by small-flowered buttercup, sea pearlwort, dyer's greenweed, sea-heath, sea-spurge and henbane. On a calm sea, small boats dredge for oysters, the slight noise of their engines drowned by the grumbling of Brent geese. Shelduck follow the tide's ebb and flow in search of mussels and small crabs; plover dart and bob about the shore, while the cormorant's wave-crest-hopping cruise is interrupted by its reptilian pounce at finny prey, its thrusting underwater action, and the long haul up out of the sea with its silvery prize.

A still cormorant on a post, yellow beak in profile and dark wings heraldically draped, registered my approach with a green eye, flexed its sinuous neck and took to the air reluctantly. On the Dover I saw a man whose presence caused its creatures no concern, a man at one with this world. In a woollen hat, a grimy oiled jersey, ancient worsted trousers and scarred boots, he combed the foreshore for his evening meal of periwinkles, cockles and oysters. I felt indecently elegant in my scruffy walking-gear, guilty about the dinner waiting for me, and soft when I compared the cottage where I live with the small boat on Newtown Creek where he had over-wintered and where the ink had sometimes frozen in his pen. For he was a writer too, a water-borne gipsy whose only necessary connection with the civilization he despaired of was a mooring within walking distance of a post-office, from which he could dispatch articles about the creatures he lived amongst, the fish he hunted and the coastal waters that were his highway. We talked for a long time there of writing and shellfish, of redshank and woodcock, of the greenshank and red-breasted merganser he'd seen here, until I was chilled to the marrow. He liked to talk, he said, with people who knew something. But he abhorred eco-freaks and those who played at self-sufficiency. Mostly he liked to be alone, in the wild. Then he knew where he was; and who he was.

I warmed myself up walking back through white mire, across potched fields where the dying sun reddened lying water, on perilous footbridges over inlets of the creek, and around the saltings towards Lower Hamstead and Creek Farms. The breached basin of old salterns still stands out, but there is little to be seen of Nash's brickworks; its manager, John Lindsay, made a mark though: he emigrated and gave New York a mayor in the shape of his descendant name-sake. One of the older yachts moored on the mud had a green deck and a clinker-built hull painted in yellow, red and blue stripes; across the mirror of the river, the sun set fire to Newtown once again and Parkhurst Forest darkened the horizon. My path made a way through woods full of rabbits, pheasants and red squirrels, past Pigeon Coo Farm, across a twilight field and the bridge over Ningwood Lake, through the pine and beech dusk of

Nunney's Wood, and out on to the road at Hamstead Lodge. There, you feel sentimentally, is a place where it would be easy to live at peace; but across Newtown River and Clamerkin Lake is out-of-bounds territory belonging to the Ministry of Defence; the whole area was used for dress-rehearsals of invasion in the last war; there was a furore here in 1959–60 over plans for a nuclear power station, scotched by an unholy alliance including Friends of the Earth and the Royal Yacht Squadron; and here, in 1980, the more mundane devastation of foot-and-mouth disease ravaged cattle, and Hamstead estate was taboo.

The best way of seeing Newtown River is to pick a hot day and a high tide and sail between spits into the fingers of water that spread and grope amongst the Hamstead clays. Leaving Clamerkin Lake and Newtown to port, and the entrance to Western Haven to starboard, you can make for Shalfleet Lake. Glasswort glistens on the mud-banks, along with sea purslane and the colonizing cord-grasses, of which *Spartina townsendii* was spawned in Southampton Water half-way through the last century as a cross between English twin-cordgrass and a trans-Atlantic species introduced by shipping. Higher up the banks, sea aster, sea lavender, arrowgrass, couch grass and plantain consort with the sailor's friend, the long-leaved scurvy grass. A converted lifeboat is moored near the Scouts' immaculately kept craft. At Shalfleet Quay you can tie up, by courtesy of the National Trust, and take a cooling dip in the temperate though opaque waters. Careful how you dive, though, for it was not called Scealdan fleot, shallow stream, for nothing and you may embed your head in the mud. Where coal was unloaded and warehouses filled with grain, there is only a small boat-yard and all the traffic is of thirsty sailors making for the inn at Shalfleet itself, beyond the point at which the tidal waters of the Lake meet their feeder the Caul Bourne, or cold stream, whose source is the chalk downs at Calbourne.

Cool beer is on tap at the New Inn to wash down delicious meals of local fish, clams and oysters, eaten off scrubbed deal tables set on stone flags; there is no canned music to haunt a post-prandial doze in the chimney-corner, though soot-falls are advertised as part of the fun. No beer is brewed now in the massive stone Malthouse opposite, where William Pinhorn was also the first postmaster in the middle of the last century, and tailor, and sexton. The Manor house is Elizabethan and Jacobean; the Old Vicarage was a clergy-house before Henry VII's time, and retains a portion of fourteenth-century roofing; but by far the most imposing building is the church. Its original dedication, just before Domesday Book, has been forgotten, but the omission was repaired in 1964. St Michael the Archangel it is now, but who is carved on the tympanum under the north doorway's Norman arch is another puzzle: a man with two griffins, Daniel or St Mark with lions, David overcoming the lion and the bear, or, as I think, Adam naming the animals beneath the Tree of Knowledge and the Tree of Life. It is a sturdy, enigmatic piece of stone-cutting which suits the sanctuary it adorns. Among the Purbeck Marble details of the interior is a south arcade inserted when the church was re-modelled in 1270. The south windows are of unique oval tracery, probably seventeenth-century, while the shoddily rebuilt north wall of two centuries later still sports windows with makeshift wooden tracery. Money must have been tight for, when the cupola on the tower decayed, the rhyme tells us that "Shalfleet poor and simple people Sold their bells to buy a steeple". The bells survive, it seems, in Thorley church, but the steeple has followed the cupola into oblivion. Renovators had a difficult time, for when Victorian improvers followed the ill-fated example of their thirteenth-century predecessors and opened the great arch in the tower's eastern wall, new fractures in its fabric added to the old. They too discovered that the tower stands on ten feet of waterlogged blue clay. Now, underpinned, braced and buttressed it stands like a fortress, with five-foot-thick walls tempting the assaults of man. It had no outside door, and a spiral stone stairway still ascends to the watch-tower where a weather-eye could be kept on marauders. It was armed with a three-pounder gun, and was sanctuary for the inhabitants of Shalfleet and its tributary territories who were subject to the piratical and military incursions suffered by the Newtown River in the days of its greatness. It was a block-house of prayer.

Mill Cottage was the bakery, and the Mill with its embanked leat, recorded in Domesday Book, worked later than most in the Island. But upriver, beyond where the Caul Bourne threads the eye of the old railway embankment, Lower Calborne Mill is still in business. The Whillier family from Portsmouth disembarked from a barge at Shalfleet Quay in 1874 and carted their chattels to the mill, where flour was made and bread baked until it ground to a halt in 1967, only to be re-opened by Mr Pretty in 1973. In a deep valley below the limestone bluff on which the village of Newbridge sits, the leat was given head enough, between hillside and stone wall, to enter the mill-house's first floor and drive an overshot wheel geared to dressed stones. The wheel was replaced by a turbine, still driven by a Ruston & Hornby diesel engine when water is low. Grain is nudged into the millstone by a nattering, nagging three-tongued device which has given its name to Mr Pretty's flour: Miller's Damsel. Behind the mill-house, a brick oven is baited with furze and faggots for the baking. The brewhouse there, which produced beer until 150 years ago, has since acquired the equilibrium of a ballet school, and has not yet reverted to type.

Across the Caul Bourne, the chimney of Dowty's brickyard was toppled to deprive the Luftwaffe of a landmark. The bridge was a Newbrygge in 1378, but the core of the present village dates from the seventeenth century. It was an anarchic, independent, non-conformist place. The Methodist Church was built rather grandly in 1836 by the Bible Christians, or Bryanites, for the salvation of a populace whom they found "but little removed from the vilest of the vile". Twenty years later, the Primitive Methodists added their weight to the assault; two years after that, William Way built his infants' school by the old forge; and the Salvation Army garrisoned their barracks in 1892. The Primitive Methodist Chapel was taken over as an Anglican Mission Church, but is now part of a private house; the barracks is a bungalow, and the school has been a Working Men's Club since 1908. There is no pub, Malthouse Green is just a name and I doubt that gin is any longer "to be bought in every house". People can get high in other ways, for one of the Island's leading hang-gliding instructors lives in Newbridge. You can learn to fly powered micro-lights too, though those on the ground are vehement about the buzz they get from them.

Another mill-pond, just south of Normans, is full of rubbish, but upstream at Calbourne Upper Mill ducks patrol the broad leat and peacocks parade on the lawns. The watermill, rolling-mill and machinery, including a silk machine, a hand-mill and a Ruston gas-engine, are picturesquely preserved for tourists in a delightful fold of the Bagshot Beds. Fulling Mill Farm had its eye on the sheep grazing

Newbarn Down, and pummelled body into woollen cloth. The Caul Bourne runs out of Winkle Street where the seventeenth-century sheep-dip was the scene of a famous legal victory for farmers over a lord of the manor who had presumed to charge them for its use. Winkle Street used to be a business-like place, with a butcher's shop remembered in the field-name Butcher's Meade, and a beer-house with a skittle-alley. Now, with its little bridges spanning the bourne's green banks, its thatches and climber-clad brick and stone, it is much photographed; though it might be less so if it had retained its starker name of Barrington Row, given to it by the Barringtons of Swainston. An octagonal lodge built of flint guards the drive up to the classical white façade and ironwork verandas of Westover, where Elizabeth Barrett Browning's younger brother Octavius once lived amongst a gallery full of Holmes and Worsley portraits supervising the staircase that sweeps upstairs; swans drive wedges across the surface of a lake that is the source of the Caul Bourne and of the trout for which it was renowned; horses, White Park cattle, Jacob's sheep and other rare breeds crop grass in the shadow of Celtic fields.

King Egbert of Wessex gave thirty hides of "the hilly places, and woods, meadows, and pastures, and fields" of Calbourne, including Brighstone and Newtown, to the church of Winchester in 826. The charter is mostly in Latin, but the details of boundaries are written in Anglo-Saxon, a practical precaution which the three bishops, three earls and two officers who signed the instrument would have taken for granted; and which William Long, compiler of the *Dictionary of the Isle of Wight Dialect* would have appreciated. Long was born here in 1839 at Grants Cottage, with its brick-quoined stone, thatch and palm-tree across from the pyramidal roof sheltering the iron village pump by Tylor & Sons of Newgate.

Not all of Calbourne's water could put out the fire which lit up All Saints' Church tower like a beacon in 1683. The tower fell and damaged the brass of William Montacute that once graced a fine table-tomb supported by Purbeck Marble pillars. The marble was re-used within the church; the tower was rebuilt in 1752 with a spire which, like Shalfleet's, withered away; and lords of Swainston and Westover, who ruled the north and south transepts respectively, continued to modify the building's thirteenth-century fabric so that the pre-conquest masonry at the west end is only one of many relics of work ancient and modern. Even the square twelfth-century font was chamfered into an octagon; everywhere is evidence of changes great and small. In the chancel there are brasses to the memory of two divines: one, Arthur Price, Rector, who died in Charles I's time, and another, Daniel Evance, Reverend Religious and Learned Preacher, who died fourteen years later but in a different world, that of the Commonwealth.

> Who is sufficient for this thing
> Wisely to harpe on every string
> Rightly divide the word of truth
> To babes and man, to age and youth.
> One of a thousand where's he found
> So learned, pious, wise and sound
> Earth hath but few, there is in heaven
> One who answers, I CAN DEAL EVEN.

—a Puritan anagram for Daniel Evance. His brass is engraved with the severely beautiful figures of Death and Father Time, though the reaper was as likely to have been dogma in those days. Dr Hopton Sydenham, Chaplain to Charles I, was ejected in Evance's favour; and his successor Edward Buckler, Chaplain to Cromwell, was in turn ejected under the Black Bartholomew Act. The church has weathered much, and has presided over the source of the Caul Bourne for perhaps a thousand years. The parish bier that has borne away countless lives from this small settlement still squats under the tower, on whose west wall is the inscription: "I am risen from ye ruins of near 70 years".

Northwards, at Newtown, the Town Hall is oddly isolated as if it was the victim of a time-shift and has materialized in the wrong place. Built of brick and dressed with stone in 1699 on earlier stone foundations, with later Gothic windows and a Tuscan portico, it is a town hall without a town, headquarters of an incorporeal corporation. Inside, however, it harbours all the right props. There is a replica of the silver mace that dates from Henry VII and is mid-way between a battle-mace and a ceremonial one. A plate at its head is engraved with the Royal Arms and, on its obverse, the State Arms of Cromwell: devices useful for coping with reversals of fortune and changes of allegiance during the Civil War. Newtown had learned the gentle art of survival by then. With the rest of the Island, it suffered the depredations of the Danes between 998 and 1009, and is supposed to have been destroyed by Sweyn's men in 1001. It may have been here, in Wiht-land, that Ethelred the Unready over-wintered in 1013, on the run to Normandy from Danish overlord-ship of southern England. If not then, it was soon to become an important place. William de Redvers granted its salt-works to the Abbey of Lyre, and it was called Francheville, free town, when it was created a new town in 1256 by Aymer, Bishop-elect of Winchester. It was reluctantly relinquished to Edward I in 1284; he found its capacious harbour and markets an attractive proposition, and confirmed its liberties and customs the next year, letting the Bishop retain the advowson of the chapel of St Mary Magdalene. The town-plan included 73 strips or furlongs of which 70 were occupied by 1297. Sixty families lived here when, in the oldest extant charter, Edward II granted his son "a market on Wednesday in his manor of Newtown, and a fair of three days." This fair, held between then and 1781—when the Quay could still berth vessels of 500 tons—and revived again in 1920 and since 1973, became famed as the Newtown Randy.

By 1344, Newtown was worth twice as much as Newport; its town seal bears a vessel with one mast, Newport's has two, and Yarmouth's three; its trade, its salterns and its oyster beds enriched it. Maybe it was the Black Death that did for it; it boasts its own Pied Piper legend of the man who whistled the Newtown rats away to a watery grave in the creek, and then, because he was snubbed with a tenth of the £500 reward he had been promised, piped the town's children into the darkness of the woods and oblivion. Often the story continues by asserting that the French heard of Newtown's tragedy and so took their chance to raid in 1377. Newtown and Newport must have suffered the assault of that year, but the only contempor-ary chronicler, Froissart, mentions Yarmouth alone. The French are always blamed for the fate of "Frenchwille De L'Ile De Wyth", as the old crest denominates Newtown, but by 1378 the population had actually grown. Myth and truth are difficult to unravel. The mid-sixteenth-century picture is certainly one of decline; the wool staple had been transferred from Winchester to Calais, enclosures were big business, small holdings were suppressed, and the Island's focus had shifted decisively to Newport. Despite this, Newtown shared the privilege granted by Elizabeth to Yarmouth and Newport, of sending two members each to Parliament: John Churchill, afterwards Duke of Marlborough, 1678–81; Admiral Sir Thomas Hopson, of Vigo Bay fame, 1705; and George Canning, future Foreign Secretary and Prime Minister, at the start of the last century. Ownership of the plots, or burgage tenements, conferred the right to vote, and for long periods these were carved up between families such as the Holmeses, Barringtons and Worsleys. The furlongs' value was thus incongruously and corruptly inflated, and two were sold to Sir Richard Worsley in 1782 for one thousand guineas. The Rotten Borough was disenfranchised in 1835 and the corporate property sold to Sir Richard Simeon of Swainston, who built the present church to Livesay's Early English design. The Town Hall took on new rôles as school, house, hostel and ruin, until it was restored for the National Trust by Ferguson's Gang, a group of quixotic souls known by names like Red Biddy, Erb the Smasher, the Nark, Sister Agatha, Silent O'Moyle, the Bloody Bishop and an architect known as the Artichoke, who delivered money and missives sealed with blood by masked messenger.

Where fairings were exchanged by lovers, where hirings were done, where stock and food and drink, including "kecksey-brandy-O", were sold at the Newtown Randy, all is peace and genteel sobriety. The Francheville Arms, now the Noah's Ark, surrendered its licence in 1916. The village looks much like that plotted on James Mallet's 1768 estate map: many of the boundaries have persisted though the ancient wooden buildings have left no trace; Broad Street leads to something very like destruction; High Street now runs away eastwards into a grassy track called Silver Street in its hey-day; Gold Street, once full of merchants, has hardly a building in it; and a third, parallel street is now no more than a shadowy hint. The neglected, high-shouldered Church of the Holy Spirit, with its symbol of the Dove, has a notice pinned to its door: "Please keep this door closed lest birds should fly in and die of thirst."

But, beyond the church, you can walk into something like peace and paradise; out into the openness of Newtown River, past the site of the old salt-boiling house and the embanked square salterns which ceased production in 1900, and on to the great arc of the sea-wall. The Wall was planned in 1656 and its dykes reclaimed much land for Marsh Farm and Hart's Farm; a fertile field to the east is still called the Promised Land. But on 27 November 1954 the last invader, the sea, broke the Wall's embrace, stormed through a breach and turned pasture back to marsh; an ideal environment for the Nature Reserve set apart by the County Council in 1966 and recently added to by the National Trust. Milk still flows, because cattle graze on what is left and, in a dead tree at the edge of the marsh, wild bees provide the honey. But the main beneficiaries of this promised land are terns and oystercatchers, little grebe and the black-tailed godwit, whimbrel and sandpiper, and all the waders and ducks that either breed here or make it a place of annual pilgrimage.

Beyond Main Marsh and the broken Wall, Clamerkin Lake is now stocked afresh with oysters and, in a new tradition encouraged by the warm effluent water of the power station and oil refinery across the Solent, clams. Cockleshells were brought from Essex for the oysters to spat on, for they fasten on to anything clean, and now the more they catch, the more there is to catch. Nowadays, it is not smugglers grappling for, or creeping up caches of brandy-tubs from the bottom, that are the wide-boys of the Solent; it is the illicit night-time dredgers. Clamerkin Lake snakes eastwards between Newtown and Ministry of Defence land towards the close darkness of copses and the less than idyllic memories that cling unhappily to the rubble-stone bulk of Clamerkin Bridge. There, where kingfishers seem to snatch colour from the carpet of bluebells beneath oak-trees, Preventive men ambushed smugglers tub-running from creek to safety. Flintlock-fire dispatched two of them instantly; others were held at Newtown and transported; but some escaped, with the knowledge of who it was had informed on them. The last act of this particular drama had for its claustrophobic scenario the four walls of a lonely cottage in which his erstwhile comrades took their revenge at leisure, enjoyably, intricately and bloodily.

8

KING'S PARK, QUEEN'S PRISON

West from the Medina a deeply depressing area, which includes
Parkhurst Forest, runs out to the flat land bordering Newtown
River, growing ever sadder as it goes . . .

Barbara Jones   *The Isle of Wight*

. . . breeding every where store of conies, hares, partridges and
pheasants. One little forrest it hath likewise, and two parkes
replenished with deere, for game and hunting pleasure.

Camden   *Britannia*

IF YOU ARE deeply depressed by the terrain, or exhilarated but
exhausted by the pleasures of the chase, you may be revived by a
stop at the Sportsman's Rest at Porchfield, an Elizabethan hunting-
lodge turned brick-fronted pub. Drinking was limited to a small taproom in the corner of the house, now opened out into a congenial
bar. The flagstones were uprooted, and replaced with floorboards
which rotted away; the floor was concreted over, and the walls began
to subside. The old men said it was inevitable after such meddling
with the fabric: it could no longer breathe and had given up the will
to live. Like the fabric of the forest itself, it has suffered many
changes, but it survives. Out of the short season in which life-giving
currency clatters across the bar, you can sit and admire the collection
of stone jars and bottles of every shade of aquamarine, emerald and
sapphire, or yarn with the landlady, interrupted only by the ingress
of a disorderly gaggle of gossiping ducks with an eye to yesterday's
sandwiches. The pub, the lodges and cottages of Porchfield are
strung out on the streamward side of the road, and Rodge Brook is
the thread, shot through a patchwork of pasture, that ties the tree-
hung fringes of Clamerkin Lake to the dense plush of Parkhurst
Forest.

In February 1982, the long nights were lit by a new landmark, a column of lights in the fields of Youngwoods farm, where, after seismic surveys, a rig from the Purbeck oil-field drilled and droned continuously, manned by a small colony of men working twelve-hour shifts and drinking and sleeping the other twelve away at the Wheatsheaf in Newport. Whitehouse Road, used to the desultory bustle of agricultural traffic, suddenly suffered the reverberating onslaught of industrial plant; lorries imported 10,000 tons of hardcore, and transporters bore in the skeletal tower whose steel and diamond proboscis was to probe deep into the earth, feeling after a hoard of black nectar to feed the hives of industry. The promise, or threat, was not fulfilled. The rig was dismantled, the crew disbanded.

Oil did pulse under Forest ground. Lord Mountbatten's plan for PLUTO—PipeLines Under The Ocean—was put into operation in 1944. A pipeline beneath the Solent, SOLO, brought oil onshore at Thorness to a pumping-station near Whippance Farm; a buried artery conducted it across the Forest and the Island to TOTO, a 620,000-gallon tank in Hungerberry Copse above Shanklin. Construction work was done under great tents of camouflage netting, and batteries of pumps at Sandown and Shanklin delivered 56,000 gallons a day under the Channel to Cherbourg, to fuel the Allied advance. In rehearsal for Normandy, the 1st Independent Guards Brigade leapt from landing-craft and scrambled up the mud and sand of Thorness Bay, and Churchill tanks queued to follow in each other's tracks across the beach and into tank landing-craft in readiness for D-Day.

The shores of Thorness and Gurnard, with their remains of Romano-British occupation, formed the northern boundary of the Forest. From them, old tracks—like Whitehouse Road running into Betty Haunt Lane, and Rew Street running into Gunville Street—traversed the wild domain to the chalk ridge which was the Forest's southern fence. George Brannon wrote that "in the time of King Charles II, woods were so extensive that, it is recorded, a squirrel might have run on the tops of the trees from Gurnet [Gurnard] to Carisbrooke, and in several other parts for leagues together." Not that it was uninterrupted trees in all directions, though the word *forest* tends to suggest that now. In 1760, James Lee defined it as "all this that are abroad, and neither domestical nor demean: wherefore *foresta* in old time did extend into woods, wastes and waters, and did contain not only *vert* and venison, but also minerals and maritimal revenues." Wood-crafts can still be purchased in Parkhurst Forest, and woods and wastes have been a resource time out of mind. There were the commons or freedoms of pasture, piscary and turbary; that is, the right to turn out a certain number, or stint, of cattle, the right to fish, and the right to dig turf or peat on common land. There was bote or estovers: rights to take wood for fuel, ferbote; for fences, haybote; for implements and wagons, ploughbote and cartbote; for hurdles, foldbote; and for dwellings, housebote. When Alfred the Great, in his heroic attempt to rebuild English culture out of the ruins left by the Danes, summoned his subjects to pillage all the resources—material, intellectual, and spiritual—at their disposal, in a touching metaphor he urged all able-bodied men to take their wagons into the wood and load them with timber suitable for the work of reconstruction. Men have always done that here; oaks were selected for coopering casks bound with iron or hazel; birchwood was bent into scoops and corn-measures; white-coopering furnished pails and churns for the dairy; and dry-coopering, grain-bins. The mocks or stumps of coppices and withy-beds sprouted wood for weaving; seven-year-old hazel for closely worked wattle hurdles, and older cloven hazel or ash for gate hurdles, the shepherd's temporary enclosures on the downs.

But a forest is more than that. James Lee's definition continues, "when *forests* were first used in England I find no certain time of the beginning thereof; and, although that ever since the Conquest it hath been lawful for the King to make any man's land (whom it pleased him) to be *forest*, yet there are certain rules and circumstances appointed for the doing thereof", and goes on to describe the prescribed perambulation required for the sovereign to stake out his claim. A forest, therefore, is a royal prerogative. The name Parkhurst Forest is revealing and confusing. *Hurst* means an eminence, often wooded, and especially of a sandy nature; from the Forest you can look down through the rides, past Sand Hill, to the low-lying land of Porchfield and Locks Green. *Forest* is unenclosed by definition and, according to Manwood in 1598, is "certen Territorie of wooddy grounds & fruitfull pastures, priviledged for wild beasts & foules of Forrest, Chase & Warren, to rest & abide in, in the safe protection of the King, for his princely delight &

pleasure." But *Park*, in the Oxford English Dictionary, is "an enclosed tract of land held by royal grant or prescription for keeping beasts of the chase. (Distinguished from a *forest* or *chase* by being enclosed, and from a *forest* also by having no special laws or officers)". Parkhurst Forest is a contradiction in terms, but there is truth in the name. Domesday Book notes that the manor of Watchingwell, at the west end of the Forest, had belonged to the nuns of Wilton but was included in the King's Park after the time of Edward the Confessor. So it seems that, even before that addition, and well before 1086, some 350 acres of forest had been enclosed to make the oldest Park on record, known as Carisbrooke or Watching Park. The area between the Solent and the downs, and between Watchingwell and the Medina, was all forest in the broad sense, comprising Park, Forest and, in practice, Commons.

The Lords of the Island enjoyed of the King the right of free forest with the privilege of taking or driving stags or harts. Norman Forest Law was severe. Enclosure or building was strictly limited. Tenants, and their daughters' husbands-to-be, were vetted. They had to fence in their own stock, but walls and banks and hedges had to be low enough to be cleared by a hind and her young. Trespass was all one way, and coverts were hallowed ground. Ferrets and nets were anathema, and dogs were confined and their fore-paws maimed to prevent them enjoying the chase. Laws were relaxed in 1217, and in 1222 the Great Gale uprooted tracts of forest throughout the Kingdom. Edward I purchased the Lordship of Wight for 6,000 marks from Isabella de Fortibus as she lay on her deathbed, and John Maltravers held his lands in Dorset by virtue of attending Edward II for one day at this Castle of Carisbrooke in the buck hunting season. Henry VII was entertained at Brook in 1499, and was so well pleased with his hunting and Dame Joanna Bowerman's hospitality that he gave her his drinking-horn and the grant of a fat buck, yearly for life, from his forest of Carisbrooke. As Captain of the Island, Sir Edward Horsey not only improved the defences, but also re-stocked the Forest and gave it the complexion of a Warren by offering a lamb for every hare brought from the mainland for coursing. George Carey strengthened Wight against the Armada, but offended the gentry by assuming the title of Governor; however, when he was appointed Lord Chamberlain of England in 1596, they were not slow to turn out to the revelry he ordained in the Forest, with a masque and music, feasting and dancing amongst trees garnished with gilly flowers. James I and Prince Charles hunted in the Park and killed a buck, and in 1619 the Prince witnessed military exercises, a "sham-fight", here. Later, when the fighting had become all too real, but before his close confinement in Carisbrooke, some say that he hunted in the royal preserve, then held—as he was—in the custody of Colonel Hammond.

Commoners had their rights too, and exercised them symbolically on the first Saturday and Sunday after May Day. A procession was marshalled to fetch home may from the Forest, and Newport's bailiffs compelled defaulters to forfeit a green goose and a gallon of wine. The crowd was greeted by verderers proffering green boughs in recognition. Hatchets hacked token branches, and Newport was decked "to refresh ye streets and ... to give a commodius and pleasant umbrage to their howses". The Commonwealth reinforced folks' suspicion of privilege, and when the Restoration Governor, Thomas Culpeper, enclosed forest ground, depriving the poor of pasture, a petition speedily prayed redress of the King. Charles II crossed the Forest on Lord Holmes' new road from Gurnard to Yarmouth, stopping *en route* at Great Park. By 1800, the progess from Parkhurst to Yarmouth was the worst in the Wight, crossing a waste of heath and bogs, and impeded by no less than 52 gates. During the years of Napoleon's sea-borne threat, Portsmouth dockyards had exhausted Parkhurst's timber. It was disafforested in George III's reign, the commons were enclosed and cultivated, new plantations were made and the road was metalled. South of it, farm and other names tell the story: Great Park, Newpark, Greenpark, Parkgreen, Park Place ... a revolutionary story, overturning customs that had persisted time out of mind, hedging old freedoms about and ploughing old habits of mind out of the memory.

By the time Alma Lee, tragic heroine of Maxwell Gray's *The Silence of Dean Maitland*, surveyed the landscape from the Carisbrooke to Swainston road, the present pattern was well established: arable on the strip of Reading Beds and London Clay at the foot of, and limed by the run-off from, the downs; and then a transition, represented by the Bagshot Beds, to pasture on the Hamstead Beds. "The grey fallows and wan stubble fields sloped swiftly away from the gate to a bottom of verdant pastures dotted with trees and homesteads;

beyond them were more dim fields, and then a wide belt of forest, principally of firs." Alma accepted a lift home in the carter's magnificent red-bodied, blue-wheeled land-ship, drawn by five cart-horses whose peals of bells chimed at every step, and whose shoes struck sparks from flints in the chalk road. Fire and sparks flew in the Smithy next to the Blacksmith's Arms, a pub at the cross-roads where the smugglers' route, Betty Haunt Lane, dives down into the reclaimed waste, chill with the memory of recent murders and old ghosts. Alma was dropped opposite Swainston, by the hanging wood in which stood the sham-Greek "Temple of Boreas" that was her home. Recently, it has been offered for sale, for some courageous or rich romantic with classical leanings to set up house amongst engulfing trees. It was built as a summer-house for Swainston, which has a better claim than most to be called the oldest house in the Island. Its grand Georgian fabric was gutted by an air-raid in 1941, but the remnants of its twelfth and thirteenth-century buildings, which include a hall and chapel, were left unscathed. It became a hotel and, not long ago, as people dined, the bailiffs moved in for the furniture. For a time the great cellars stood unstocked, where Isaac Ewer buttled for the Barringtons before his translation to Portsmouth as Roundhead Army Commander. The manor of kings, of Montacutes, of the kingmaker Warwick, of false Clarence, of fated Margaret Pole, of Barringtons and Simeons stood forlornly beside a lake whose stream runs north into Clamerkin, in grounds where Tennyson walked under the Cedars of Lebanon and paid his verse tribute to "the Prince of courtesy", Sir John Simeon, *In the Garden of Swainston*. But now it is in business once more under new management. The ruins of North Park are a memorial to Swainston's own sixteenth-century Park; and a house near Upper Watchingwell was a private railway station, built for the Simeons on the Newport to Yarmouth line that casts the long sinuous shadow of a recently dead era across the ancient memory of the King's Watching Park.

Shadow factories were put up in the south-western corner of Parkhurst Forest's camouflage, to back up Cowes' production of war-time hardware. Then Saunders Roe gave way to Ronson's, and to J. Arthur Dixon, the one-time Shanklin printer who made a fortune presenting us with images of England, on the back of which half the world each summer could wish that the other half were here.

Now, recession threatens to push the factories back into the forest shades for good. We could make straight along Forest Road to a much earlier House of Industry; but, since the Forestry Commission opened Parkhurst to the public on their fiftieth anniversary, we can be diverted by their way-marked walks, or by the wayfaring course established by the Wight Orienteers.

In 1815, at about the time that foxes were introduced into the old chase from the mainland "by some sparkish amateurs of hunting", in Brannon's phrase, the plantation consisted of low, unpromising oaks nursed for the dockyards by Scotch fir and larch, and a Parliamentary Return of twenty years later described it as "much neglected, no well-arranged system of management being carried out". In 1856, however, Adams observed that "young lusty firs are shaking their green tops in the wind over three thousand acres". Today, oaks are the proud creatures of the forest; a dozen species of conifer are arrrayed in well-managed stands, along with sycamore, ash and maple, while sweet chestnut is systematically coppiced and split for fencing. Not here, the monotony of a fir-factory whose dark floor allows nothing but fungi to thrive; undergrowth thickens beneath hardwoods and their canopy is alive with great tits, firecrests and many other birds. Walks, rides and firebreaks continually allow fresh glimpses down and out of the forest or deep into its dark interior, and opportunities for losing yourself in a maze that leads to knoll, or marsh, or hide or signal-house. Differing densities of foliage limit and enlarge your vision; clearings open into scrubby expanses of furze and bracken, or cemetery-like arenas of new planting whose young trees are protected from browsers by ranks of white tubes. Some say that the pits and depressions into which you may stumble are of military origin, but they simply mark the places where gravel was dug for forest roads when it was Crown Land. At your feet, gravel gives way to dark humus, springy turf or sucking mud. For me, a forest is a place for deep thought, for dreams and metaphors of life. The visionary—and thus, in England, grossly underrated—poet, David Gascoyne, who lives and works at nearby Northwood, wrote *The Wall* more than 40 years ago. It begins:

> At first my territory was a Wood:
> Tanglewood, tattering tendrils, trees
> Whose Grimm's-tale shadow terrified but made

> A place to hide in: among traps and towers
> The path I kept to had free right-of-way.

And ends:

> Returning to the narrow onward road
> I find it leads me only to the Wall
> Of Interdiction. But if my despair
> Is strong enough, my spirit truly hard,
> No wall shall break my will: To persevere.

It is walls that confront you as you emerge into the light at the south-eastern edge of the forest: the walls of Her Majesty's Prisons of Camp Hill, Albany and Parkhurst. There, in modern fortresses or antiquated buildings dubbed unworkable by many prison officers, surrounded by a metallic wall surmounted by what looks surreally like an endless loop of inner tube, and floodlit like a stadium at night, some of the most notorious men in Britain—Brady, Kray, Sutcliffe —do time at the Queen's pleasure. They are exiled from society, insulated within the Island. Locals regard Parkhurst's top security with suspicion, and fear what its psychopaths and Albany's "hyper-sensitive men with a record of violence" might do if they got out, but very few escape, though "Papillon" MacGillivary did get away from a Camp Hill working-party and row away from his Devil's Island in a dinghy. When escapes are reported, some folk bolt their doors and leave food and drink on their back doorsteps. Prison officers do time, too, in Parkhurst's crumbling riot-damaged wings or Albany's explosive atmosphere, and then pass on to other penal establishments. They are an isolated, shifting community; an unstable satellite of Newport that brings business, but is resented by many Islanders in the way that the troops garrisoned at Albany Barracks used to be.

Albany Barracks' red-brick and timber buildings, clad with brick-like rebate tiles made by Pritchetts' near Kitbridge Farm, were erected during the French Revolutionary Wars in 1798, the year after the French had invaded Wales. It had one of the best parade-grounds in the kingdom but, as Venables wrote, the new erections did "not contribute to the beauty of the landscape, or their inmates to the morality of the neighbourhood", and Keats, the poet, said it "disgusted him extremely with the Government for placing such a nest of debauchery in so beautiful a place." In 1838, the barracks' hospital became the Parkhurst Juvenile Reformatory where moral and religious instruction, together with employment in black-smith's, carpenter's, shoemaker's, tailor's and baker's shops, all performed in silence, aimed to punish and reform; or, like husbandry on the prison farm, to transform ungrateful clay into fertile soil. When Queen Victoria and Prince Albert visited in 1845, she was moved to beg free pardons for the most deserving, and noted that solitary confinement was "triste and lonely". A return visit in 1864, fortified by talks on prison reform with Elizabeth Fry, was hateful to her; there were fewer juveniles, and prostitutes due for transportation begged mercy, or cursed her. She never went back.

The earliest building on ground newly enclosed from the Forest was the House of Industry, or Forest House, of 1770; it anticipated the new Poor Law legislation by more than 60 years, and was established by Act of Parliament "for the maintenance and employment of the poor of the Isle of Wight by a general consolidation of the poor rates". It could accommodate 700 and was governed by a Board of 24 directors and 36 acting guardians. Industry replaced the idleness of the old workhouse system, and Forest House was a prototype of the Poor Law Unions and an example of productivity and comfort to the rest of Britain. A new building went up in 1887, now part of the hospital, and next to the site of a new experiment in self-sufficiency. Radical design, re-cycling of air and waste, energy generation and a thorough re-thinking of hospital needs and resources aim to create an ecologically sound, and cheap, medical unit.

Punitive confinement, military discipline and compassionate rigour have variously characterized Parkhurst's communities. Between Camp Hill and Carisbrooke, the vanished Hospital of St Augustine for Lepers cared for medieval outcasts. Beyond the Agricultural Showground near Clawton Farm, Northwood, the mysterious Confraternity of the Brothers & Sisters of St John the Baptist was founded in 1513 and dissolved in 1536, though what may have been its fabric survived, as Church House, until at least 1690. Crop-marks in the fields show house platforms of the settlement of Northwood that has now drifted towards Cowes, that Cowes which was a junior part of Northwood parish until 1842. Luton Farm is Domesday Book's Levintune; and Chawton, Pallance and Medham—as Caulkstone, Palente and Medeme—all stood in their clearings in the forest when Northwood Church was enlarged in the thirteenth century. Its chevron-enriched south doorway originally gave into the Norman north aisle that was the early church, founded as a daughter chapel of Carisbrooke and contributing to the mother church until 1545. The Norman font was discovered in the churchyard and brought in under the shelter of the roof's plastered barrel-vaulting in 1954. The parish registers are the oldest in the Wight, and the vestry holds a clarionet that accompanied the psalms before the organ ousted it. There are idiosyncratic memorials; one, to Thomas Smith, Rector, died 1681, carved from a block of solid chalk, four feet high and three feet long, and decorated with curious hieroglyphics and the symbols of Death. Northwood's dead were buried at Carisbrooke until 1486, but now the graveyard is dark with yews, heavy with the scent of lilac and haunted by gnats. Among its stones are twin tombs built like brick Nissen-huts, and it is walled on the south side by crumbling ivy-clad farm buildings that shield a rusty-corrugated-iron-scrap-heap of a farm yard; a very different prospect from that in a print of 1794: an uncluttered view of an attractively domesticated church surmounted by a surprising squat wooden tower straddling and overhanging the pitch of the roof. Perhaps it was a watch-tower, with an eye for friend or foe making up-river. It was replaced by an elegant spire.

There is a good viewpoint just north of the church, from which you can gaze across the Medina to the Folly Inn, to the fairy-tale tower of Whippingham Church and, barely visible above the trees, the towers of Osborne House. But what dominates this prospect is Kingston Power Station on the opposite bank, though a house here, glazed with rose-tinted panes, is called Osborne View. Where the Forest's timber was once plundered for housebote, old forest ground has since been exploited for building materials: gravel was dug at Furzyhurst and there were busy brickyards at Werrar, Oxford Street and Hillis. At Hillis Farm, Leslie Long preserves the old tradition of cutting and laying hedges, while the Medina Cement Works of 1840, with its wharf, clay pit and chamber kilns that pioneered the production of cement concrete, is already dead. Calving Close Copse, Waterclose Copse, Sheepwash Copse and Great and Little Werrar Woods are lively relics of the forest that once overhung the Medina's bank. The manor of Werrar was given to God's House in Southampton by Baldwin de Redvers in 1130, when Northwood's

Norman church was probably built at the east end of the Saxon Forest. A coin of Vespasian was found in Pallance Road, and one of Marcus Aurelius in Parkhurst Forest. Six Bronze Age palstave axes were disinterred in Werrar brickyard. Signs of Neolithic life are scattered around Northwood; and brickearth digging at Werrar disturbed numerous hearths and flint tools lying on the Middle Stone Age land surface. Beyond the present Forest, at Coleman's Farm, Porchfield, Stone Age axe-heads have only recently been unearthed; one shaped from stone from Caernarvonshire, such as was used by our distant forebears for lopping elm branches to feed to cattle. These fragments surface like flotsam from the great amnesia; they hint at the human pre-history that the Forest's roots plumb.

The Forest was a retreat for Kings, Lords and Governors, wardens and verderers, foresters and woodsmen. It was a refuge for outlaws, trove for poachers, covert for smugglers and commons for the poor; a place of banishment for lepers, paupers and criminals; of rich resources and wastes, and reclamation. The oil-rig's tower of lights comes and goes, while night after night bright gantries stare down into the prisons. Changes are quick or slow. Trees add to their girth ring by ring, and are clear-felled at last. A tornado struck North-wood in 1876, a house was torn apart and possessions flung abroad into gardens, fields and copses. A local preacher climbed to a pulpit-perch on the naked staircase and harangued the sightseers. The secrets of all hearts shall be revealed, he must have told them; the Great Gale of the world will take us unawares, both the great mansions and our poor houses of clay shall be shaken, the oak and the ash shall be uprooted, yea, even the Cedars of Lebanon shall be laid low.

9

FAT KINE, LEAN KINE

Ther be two new castelles sette up and furnishid at the mouth of
Newporte; that is the onlie haven in Wighte to be spoken of. That
that is sette up on the este side of the havin, is caullid the Est Cow;
and that that is sette up at the west syde is caullid the West Cow, and
is the bigger castelle of the two.

John Leland   *The Itinerary*

It was a rough night in the late summer when the rich are compelled
in their detestable grind to go to the Solent ...

Hilaire Belloc   *The Cruise of the Nona*

BUT FOR THEmetaphorical tornado, the literal nine-days' wonder of
Cowes Week, recent years have seen West Cowes becalmed. Once a
mere seaboard satellite of Northwood, without a church until the
Commonwealth and then only a dependency of a dependency of
Carisbrooke, its first importance was strategic. In 1339, when the
Island had not only been assaulted by storm and flood, but was under
threat from the French and their Catalan and Genoese allies, one or
a pair of peels, palisaded forts, were commissioned to be built at
Shamelord, from the royal forest's wind-felled timber. Cowes' old
name is still preserved in Shamblers Copse south of the town. Henry
VIII's new castles, the West Cow and the East Cow, were stone
guardians of the mouth of the Medina, the broad tree-fringed artery
that fed Newport, the Wight's commercial heart. The twice times
eleven guns never fired in anger from their semi-circular embrasures,
and Sir John Oglander, born in 1585, remembered when "there was
not above three or four houses here", though floating fortresses had
begun to be built from Parkhurst's apparently inexhaustible reservoir
of oak, and the first Elizabeth herself had a small sailing vessel called
Rat of Wight.

A shifting waterfront of yards, quays, wharves and warehouses has since been the substance of, and excuse for, the shambling close-knit settlement that has grown uphill from it. Poised between Forest and Solent, at the mouth of Newport's life-line, it thieved trade from the Island's capital, fattened on its own industry and threatened to shift Wight's centre of gravity northwards. The century from 1815 until the First World War saw Cowes increasingly shaken up as an essential ingredient in the effervescent cocktail of the rich and royal who came, at great expense, to exploit the free elements of wind and tide. Men skilled in working wood and canvas, whose trades were being overtaken by iron and steam, were valued not for the trading and naval strength they engendered, but for the luxury and sport their craftsmanship allowed. Those were the fat years. Though the building of racing yachts and luxury cruisers continues, Cowes' stock-in-trade—the construction and fitting-out of paddle-steamers, lifeboats, torpedo-boats, destroyers, aeroplanes and seaplanes—has declined; the hovercraft which it midwived has never quite lived up to its promise, and the radar and electronics industries are a source of fluctuating hope and concern. Like the lean kine that followed the fat kine up out of the river in Nebuchadnezzar's dream, it is threatened by slow starvation. The fickleness of progress and fashion, followed by recession, make it no threat to Newport now. It can be seen for what it is, an eccentric industrial conurbation, a suburb of the Solent, in the Island but not entirely of it. It is as if it has drifted north and grounded on the Bramble Bank which, for its likeness to a beached grampus, sea-cow or cow-fish, may once have been called the Cow, and thus, by way of Henry's fortresses, given its name to Cowes. There is nothing of bovine placidity in the town's calm; it is a mixture of apathy and quiet desperation, stirred up each year by the forced glamour and hard-headed razzmatazz of Cowes Week. Then, tough questions are asked. Threats of withdrawing the Admiral's Cup Competition have recently been made. The annual whirlwind is preceded by local squalls of self-examination and mutual accusation among Cowes' powers-that-be. Perhaps the contradictions of the place can no longer be borne. In its hey-day, the inhabitants were characterized, like other Islanders, by a kind of carefree sobriety overlaid, at Cowes, by a veneer of serious frivolity. The expression, and the mask, are getting harder to wear.

★

There is a fairy-tale toll-house, called The Round House, where Place Road runs into Baring Road. It is built of stone, with a verandah of branched tree-trunks, a conical roof of ruddy tiles, a picturesque dormer window and a central chimney like a terracotta funnel. It is a relic of the Debourne Manor estate which occupied the most desirable territory between Gurnard, Northwood and West Cowes, and became part of the Wards' Island lands. The Wards' Bellevue was enlarged in about 1840 and, in its French-Italianate-Grecian incarnation, was re-christened Northwood House. Its painted Egyptian lobby and domed Etruscan room housed Benedictine nuns expelled from France before the Great War; then the house became a Red Cross hospital, and was bequeathed to the town and transformed into local government offices in the 'thirties. It is a white elephant whose gracious grounds, now a public park entered through a Doric Lodge, have acquired, by virtue of a subtle bureaucratic magic, an indefinable though ordered bleakness. Schemes are being laid to transform it once more: entertainments, an aquarium, camp-site for yachtsmen, base for Cowes Week activities, maritime museum or community centre. It is hard to think which combination of amenities would least spin the Wards in their mausoleum under the tower of nearby St Mary's Church. St Mary's was plain West Cowes Chapel because it was built during the Protectorate, that piously wished-for communion of saints whose ideal of sacred democracy was offended by hagiolatry. It was tastelessly enlarged by George Ward, and then gloomily rebuilt half a century later, apart from John Nash's incongruous, rigorously Grecian tower. Not far downhill is the yellow brick of St Thomas of Canterbury, endowed by Mrs Heneage in 1796, and thus one of the earliest Roman Catholic churches permitted to be built after the Reformation. Protestant non-conformity used to be represented by a full complement of congregations in more or less distinguished chapels: Independent, Bible Christian, Wesleyan, Free Wesleyan and Primitive Methodist.

One of the most striking features of Cowes is the wall of 1841 marking the boundary of the Ward Estate along the length of Baring Road. It is a good example of Isle of Wight coursing in Bembridge limestone quarried at Gurnard and, though frequently pierced by the gateways of subsequent houses which back on to a golf-course and school, it has been maintained, in accordance with the conditions of sale, as nearly complete as possible. Its stones, and the street names Ward Avenue, Debourne Road and Debourne Close, preserve the memory of the estate that dominated West Cowes. Egypt Hill runs down, between commodious villas and smart 1970s' housing, to the shore at the point where Prince's Esplanade becomes Queen's Road and runs towards Cowes Castle. Egypt Point lighthouse warns vessels off the ledges, where gale and tide combined have battered the sea-defences. Early in the last century the ground between Sir Thomas Tancred's gothick Egypt House and Lord Grantham's villa, nearer the Castle, was invaded by half a dozen elegant cottages, summer residences for the likes of the Duke of Norfolk. The exiled ex-Emperor Napoleon III and Eugénie took Beaulieu House in the autumn of 1872, after staying at the Marine Hotel on the Parade in the previous year. Leonard Jerome was then renting Rosetta Cottage, with its french windows, its yellow roses climbing over the castellations of the porch, its creeper-clad roof, glass-house vine and fig tree. His daughter Jennie remembered the choppy family outing on Napoleon's yacht, the sickness that afflicted almost everyone except the Empress, and wrote, "I can see now the Emperor leaning against the mast looking old, ill and sad ... he seemed to have nothing to live for." The Jeromes' Huguenot ancestors had fled France; the Revd William Jerome was burnt at an English stake in 1540; his descendant, Timothy Jerome left the Wight for America in 1710. Now they were back in style. In Cowes Week 1873, Mrs and the Misses Jerome attended a ball on the guardship *Ariadne*, given by its officers in honour of the Czarevich and Czarevna of Russia. The girls, in their white tulle and flowers, were introduced to Randolph Churchill; Jennie piloted him through a quadrille. The following night, Friday, 13 August, he and Colonel Edgcumbe ate dinner at Rosetta Cottage and, as the girls played duets, Randolph told his friend that he would make the dark one his wife. Later that night, Jennie confided in her sister that she had had a premonition of marriage. Next day, the couple met by careful coincidence on Prince's Green and, after a second dinner, Randolph's proposal was accepted. So began the obstacle course of their romance and marriage.

Jennie Jerome, or Lady Randolph Churchill, recalled those seasons of the early 1870s: "It was delightfully small and peaceful. No glorified villas, no esplanade or pier, no bands, no motors or crowded tourist-steamers. ... The Royal Yacht Squadron lawn did not resemble a perpetual garden party, or the roadstead a permanent regatta. ... The Prince and Princess of Wales and many foreign royalties could walk about and amuse themselves without being photographed or mobbed." Donaldson and Foster painted the Castle and the Squadron members in 1895; the future Edward VII, the future George V and Kaiser Wilhelm II stand on the landing-stage ready to board the Prince of Wales' launch, and the Castle is a bastion of privilege defended by a garrison of gentlemen, apparently united, but in fact riven by rivalry and snobbery. At the Prince of Wales' relationship with Sir Thomas Lipton, whose successive *Shamrocks* and persistent lack of seamanship provoked a wealth of admiration and amusement, the Kaiser could curl his lip and complain that his uncle went yachting with his grocer. J.M.W. Turner's watercolour of a century earlier shows a cutter sailing past a wilder promontory dominated by trees and the flag-flying fortress, with fishermen heaving a small boat up on to a raw beach furnished with lobster-pots, a capstan and a cannon. Soon, capstans were to winch bathing-machines out of the fashionable waters to the west of the Castle, where warm baths were provided; but Turner's picture helps us to imagine the Cowes of a more adventurous age.

In April 1587, *en route* from Portsmouth for Raleigh's Virginia, John White's colony rested here for eight days. In 1633, the *Ark* and the *Dove*, commemorated by a bronze plaque, put in here on their way to found the State of Maryland. Sir John Oglander tells us that Cowes was then full of "prizes and men-of-war which gave great rates for its commodities". Aubrey describes Sir William D'Avenant's plan to carry artificers, mainly weavers liberated from a French prison, to Virginia; and how, on being apprehended by a Parliamentary ship, he was imprisoned in Cowes Castle for high treason in 1650. D'Avenant was Shakespeare's godson, and held by some to be his natural son; he was Poet Laureate after Ben Jonson, and his *The Siege of Rhodes* was the first English opera to be performed. He worked on his *Gondibert* at Cowes, and in a post-script to its first edition he wrote, with the strength and sensitivity of a man of action who was also a poet, "I am here arrived at the middle of the third book. But it is high time to strike sail and cast anchor, though I have run but half my course, when at the helm I am threatened by *death*, who, though he can visit us but once, seems troublesome; and even in the innocent may beget such a gravity as diverts the music of verse." He kept his head, however, though he had lost his nose through disease and caused his friends to fear for his eyesight on account of his lack of a place to prop spectacles, and lived to intercede with Charles II on behalf of the poet Milton.

It was the Restoration which brought the words *yacht* and *sloop* into popular English usage. Charles II came back from Dutch exile with the gift of a 52-foot *jaght*, the *Mary*, whose single-masted rig the Dutch termed *sloepe*. Samuel Pepys reported the first yacht race between the King and the Duke of York on the Thames estuary. Wight's sport derived from less noble and more serious contests between revenue cutters and their prey, the smuggling luggers. Naval vessels competed at Cowes in 1776, cutters raced round the Island in 1788 and, by 1811, the Duke of Gloucester was gambling on the results. A regatta was organized in 1813, for which the gentry chartered professional seamen, and two years later a meeting at the Thatched Tavern in London founded the Yacht Club, soon to become Royal, thought not the Royal Yacht Squadron until 1833. John Bullar enthused: "Cups are annually given by the Club, by his Majesty, and by the town of Cowes, to be sailed for by the yachts, and thus amusement is made laudibly subservient to the encouragement of British seamen, while the emulation of fast sailing gives a useful excitement to the promotion of naval architecture." By the 1840s the Commander, Lord Yarborough, could boast an aristocratic Squadron of 400 guns. In the late 'sixties, 150 members employed 1,500 seamen, on 120 yachts amounting to 11,000 tons; if you possessed a vessel of at least 40 tons, and were not black-balled by members, the entrance fee was fifteen guineas and the annual subscription £8.0.0. Inflation has done for those rates, and while rich men competed for one hundred guineas in those days, two 1981-vintage millionaires raced for £10,000 in sovereigns. Peter de Savary's syndicate unveiled their Dubois-designed *Victory* in the spring of 1982, built for a basic £250,000 but costing nearer £1,500,000 when fully fitted out. Christened by Princess Michael of Kent, she was dedicated to capturing the America's Cup, first won, to the Squadron's chagrin, by the schooner *America* and held by the New York Yacht Club for more than 130 years. She failed. Tons and guns are not the status symbols that they were, though the bronze cannon before the Castle, from William IV's yacht *Royal Adelaide*, fire off twenty-six starts a day in Cowes Week. There was no naval guardship in attendance in 1982, for HMS *Exeter* had been called to the Falkland Islands, where *Ardent* and *Antelope*, guardships in 1979 and 1981, perished in South Atlantic waters. The Task Force Commander, Rear Admiral Sandy Woodward, was to be seen in the Solent soon afterwards on his yacht *Cry Havoc*. He may have spared a thought for the Yacht Patrol of the Great War, one of whom, the *Lorna*, sank a German U-boat, while others were sunk by mines or submarines; for the Royal Yacht Squadron Castle in its days as a D-Day headquarters; or for the pennant of honour presented, in recognition of what the Squadron's yachtsmen had done at Dunkirk, by their Argentinian colleagues.

Henry VIII's castle was built of re-worked stone from Beaulieu Abbey, so that, as Froude writes, "the spoils of the church furnished the arms by which the Pope and the Pope's friends could be kept at bay". Little more than the gun platform survives from that time. Seventeenth- and eighteenth-century modifications transformed it into a residence, and when the last Governor died, the architect Salvin fitted it for occupation by the Squadron in 1858. Nerve-centre for the most prestigious yachting in the world, it is also a small-scale gentleman's club full of marine paintings in gilt frames. After freshening-up in the beautifully appointed shower-room, where hair-brushes are laid out before expansive mirrors, members may relax into salmon-pink chairs in a gold-carpeted and wallpapered room, with Dutch-tiled occasional tables on which refreshment is served from a chipped coffee-pot by a steward in an ill-fitting uniform. These days, the windows provide a prospect of sail-board contests, or of that fifteen-year-old institution, the bath-tub race. The 1920s and 'thirties saw swimming and rowing competitions, and confetti battles on the Esplanade. The lamented Victoria Pier, where paddle-steamers debouched cargoes of sightseers, was the setting for concert parties, prestidigitators, escapologists and cheap-jacks. Now, the motley crew that is the Ventnor Jazz Band stomp along the front and, still, when the sun has gone down on topless sun-bathers reclining on the decks of cruisers, when searchlights pick out tanked-up yachtsmen doing strip-tease at mast-top, when the harbour is a floating shanty-town and every vantage point is crammed with land-lubbers, the blue touch-paper is lit and for half an hour the sky and water of Cowes glitter as they should. The crowds cheer, sound hooters and sirens, and sing long after all the spent fireworks have fallen back, small spouts of steam, into the dark Solent waters.

In the old days, the toffs arrived from Goodwood, and departed for the moors and the Glorious Twelfth, or for European Spas. Landladies or housekeepers, maids and butlers would breathe again and clear and close up their villas while, in the boat-yards, ship-wrights would settle to next season's yachts. Now, when the season is over, you can sit alone in the Copper Kettle Café, once the taproom and press-gang mecca of the Marine Hotel with its unhappily haunted cellars, and watch the only thing that seems to move: the meritorious street-sweeper, partnered by a dust-cart, stepping out in slow staccato along run-down roads that would grace down-town Battersea. There is a picturesqueness about the Cowes waterfront which cannot be appreciated from the High Street: moorings, figureheads, gardens and balconies; the Red Funnel Car Ferry and Hydrofoil terminal, and the Groves and Guttridge Yacht Marina's jangling forest of masts and spars and shrouds. On land, however, the discriminating eye can pick out architectural delights: Prince's Buildings, the tall classical hybrid built for Marvin's the yacht-furnishers; the Royal Corinthian Yacht Club, whose core is a Gothic marine villa by John Nash, where George IV used to put up; the Watch House and slipway of HM Customs & Excise; the metal and glass of the elegant Island Sailing Club of 1961, the most democratic club whose most distinguished member, the Duke of Edinburgh, is the Admiral of the Squadron; Admirals Wharf, town flats built in the same year on the site of the bombed-out George Hotel; stone-built cottages and the Revd Thomas Binstead Mac-Namara's almshouses of 1881; a late Georgian house with attached shop and malthouse; and the nearby Prospect sail-loft which houses Sir Max Aitken's maritime museum. Despite these and many other survivals, the High Street and its continuations, Bath Road and Birmingham Road, have a dismal air. A number of shops are vacant, and you expect the rest to be stocked with junk, old clothes, and bric-à-brac of the Victorian and Edwardian ages which saw the place's prime. Then you notice a disproportionate number of Royal Arms, "By Appointment to . . .", above them; the ultimate trophy of the chase that is the noble sport of shopkeepers. The chemist's is no mere chemist's, it is Beken of Cowes, doyen of maritime photographers. The outfitter's is John Morgan, inventor of the yachtsman's "uniform". The chandler's is Pascall-Atkeys, and the jeweller's, Benzies, with four-figure price tags attached to the very best chronometers and gold brooches, like that of the Royal Yacht Squadron burgee, set with rubies and diamonds. Colin Windsor's shop glisters with sea-booty: up to thirty species of wet fish, including John Dory, gurnard, squid and, sometimes, shark.

Birmingham House was built in about 1752 for Lord Mount Edgcumbe, but long ago split into two: Westbourne House, and Medina House which was bombed in the last war and restored. Uffa Fox lived here, and tells of the vaulted cellars, the generous stabling, and the domed sweet-water well only fifty yards from high water. He removed the archway and keystone and set them up at his new house at Padmore, but a plaque set into decrepit brickwork commemorates the birth here, in 1792, of Rugby's pioneering pedagogue, Thomas Arnold. William Arnold was Collector of Customs at East Cowes; nine years before his famous son's birth, we find him reporting to his Board that smuggling had rapidly increased to an alarming degree, and that it was a good month for the Excise if only a hundred tuns were landed by the free-traders. Later his house became a Mew & Langton brewery, and in 1845 the garden was submerged beneath White's new Medina Dock. How demoralizing, that a good eighteenth-century brick building, and a listed one at that, which so richly represents a slice of Cowes' history, should be allowed simply to decay.

Up Mill Hill Road is the site of Bannister's Ropeworks of 1820, one of the first companies to move from hand-spinning to the use of the American Good's Automatic Spinner, and the first to replace hemp with wire rope in yacht rigging. It was taken over by White's in 1956; much of it has been pulled down, but the offices, saw-mill and part of the rope-walk have been transformed into workshop units for a welder, an upholsterer, a signwriter and others. The name of White looms large around Medina mouth, but now only in the history books and in the permanent display in the Seely Library. White's began in Thanet in the seventeenth century, moved to Cowes in 1802, built the Thetis Yard in the salterns and marshes that then existed between Medina Road and Arctic Road, and took over Nye's yard, famous for its men-o'-war since at least 1696. By the

1850s, the docks, slipways, steam-saw mills, smiths' and engine-shops, mast and block shops employed up to 500 craftsmen. Thomas White's sons, John and Robert, with Andrew Lamb, built the patent unsinkable Lamb & White lifeboats, invented in 1843 and responsible for saving many lives around our coasts. In 1889, the West Cowes site became an engineering works, building steam engines, boilers, turbines and diesel engines. In May 1942, the Polish destroyer *Blyskawica* was being urgently re-fitted at J. Samuel White's, where it had been launched. On the night of 4 May, the Luftwaffe let fly with 200 tons of bombs, a wave of incendiaries followed by high explosives. The *Blyskawica* left her moorings, dropped anchor outside the harbour, and retaliated all night with such vehemence that her guns had to be doused with water, and more ammunition had to be ferried across from Portsmouth. But for her, the 800 casualties and thousands of damaged buildings, including 100,000 square feet of wreckage at White's, would have been far worse. The *Arethusa* was the last frigate White's built, before the yard closed down in 1965. Elliot Turbo-Machinery succeeded to the site, and closed the works again in 1981, with the loss of more than 500 jobs. Something like panic ensued. There were rival bids for the site. A £4 million plan for a marina with maisonettes, shops and restaurants was instantly opposed by the newly-formed Cowes Industrial Consortium, and by other traders, trade unions and Medina Borough Council, temporarily united against a change of use. Another alliance joined forces with the County Council to purchase the site, to alter Medina mouth's grim mien, and to revive industry and employment in J.S. White's old territory.

Faced with Portland stone, White's old offices still stand close to the floating bridge in Medina Road. There, Ratsey & Lapthorne's looms pluck terylene thread off ranks of twitching, turning bobbins to weave sailcloth. The premises which Ratsey's occupied after 1918 were destroyed in the last war, and Egyptian cotton canvas is rarely employed any more; but the firm whose brigs shipped coal from the north and sailed back full of corn, and which, in the person of George Rogers Ratsey, added sail-making to the business in 1790, still pursues this latter trade. In airy lofts, old skills and new materials combine to catch the wind and give boats wings. Thomas White Ratsey was born in the year of the first America's Cup race, but it was his son Thomas who studied the flight of birds, appreciated the pulling-power of a sail's lee side, and brought the art to a new, scientific perfection. In the spreading-loft, where the sails are cut out, a shiny floor is covered with patterns—different-coloured lines and curves—like a lunatic badminton court. Beside this, men sit on wooden stools and benches, wearing leather pads to protect their hands from the needles they wield, finishing corners, eyelets and holes, and sewing on ropes. In another loft, powerful sewing-machines draw material into themselves and spew out immaculate seams. I watched Joe Hampshire sewing the working-jib for a 79-foot yawl; his machine was set at floor level and could winch and drive the material over the glossy floor. He sat in a pit, sometimes seeming to be submerged in the white swell of the sailcloth from which, at intervals, he would rise up to wrench the weight of it around for a new tack. Though larger than most of the sails now made, this one was small beer. There are memories here of the 4,000 yards of eighteen-inch canvas that went into the spread of the old *Britannia*, and of how even the great Medina loft was too small for the mainsail, so that a special platform had to be lowered across the road, and the residents opposite compensated for the inconvenience.

Across the road, today, is the Spencer Thetis Wharf. Harry Spencer served his apprenticeship at White's and went to sea after the last war. His rich experience, energy and sense of humour conspired to make him indispensable when he returned home. Spencer Rigging in St Mary's Road, founded in 1957, thrived by adding innovation to tradition, so that aircraft and hovercraft, as well as pirate radio vessels and conventional boats, could be given their wire control-rigs there. Down at the Wharf, Harry Spencer specializes in square-riggings. Work on the *Dulcibella*, for the film *Riddle of the Sands*, was followed by a £400,000 contract to make rigging, blocks, masts and spars—with Ratsey's providing sails—for an American film company's replica of the *Bounty*, after designs of 1773. The restoration of ships such as HMS *Unicorn*, HMS *Discovery* and HMS *Warrior* has tested and celebrated the survival of traditional skills. I watched shipwrights at work on the Number Three Mast for Brunel's iron monster, SS *Great Britain*. It is a beautiful sight to see the power and precision of an expertly wielded, razor-edged adze thwacking home into the timber with the same shaping technique that John le Shepwricht of Yarmouth would have employed in 1297; though today the adze is chased by the whining power saw. In a corner of the shop, there reared up the head and torso of the *Warrior*'s figurehead, growing out of a three-ton block of yellow pine, itself built of 70 or so blocks carefully glued together in stages. Adze and mallet and chisel were giving delicate body to the great beard, the flamboyant helmet-plume, the chain mail and the artfully wind-blown cloak. The *Warrior* was launched in 1860; powered by sail and steam, with a retractable propeller and telescopic funnels, she was the swiftest, most heavily armoured warship of her day; she led naval designers into new ways of thought, and herself into rapid obsolescence. Soon the pivotal *Warrior*, restored at Hartlepool and rigged at Spencer's, will find a berth at Portsmouth beside her ancestors, the *Victory* and the *Mary Rose*. Jack Whitehead and Norman Gaches, who worked on the replica of the *Golden Hind* and, individually or in collaboration, on many restoration projects, were carving the proud figurehead, that dwarfed them, after old photographs and Norman's lime-wood scale model. As Jack hacked at the warrior's backside, Harry Spencer winked and told me to watch its change of expression; its face did not shift, except into increasingly subtle lineaments under the caress of Norman's chisel. Its eyes stared unflinchingly forward, already filled with memories of stormy waters. At Spencer's there are lessons for Cowes to learn; they look to the future with a weather-eye on the past. And they give the past a future.

Cowes is a divided town. It is up-market and run-down. It is enterprising and apathetic. It is elitist and proletarian. It is High Tech and redundant. It is East and West, divided by the Medina. That division is easily spanned, by two chains—secured at the west side and attached to weights suspended in shafts at the east to compensate for the tide—upon which the floating bridge drives to and fro. Now she is a diesel-driven beast, but earlier ferries were powered halfway by steam and halfway on their own vacuum. Steel rods and copper pipes gleamed to starboard, and boilers gushed steam to port, while huge iron drive-wheels with wooden cogs tugged the chains through. A coach and four fitted her snugly, and its passengers aloft had a clear view up and down river. There were no speed-boats or multi-hulls to be seen, no marinas or trots for the Sunday mariner, but the Medina was a busier place. Steam-yachts, brigantines, schooners and brigs were berthed at each bank. Fully-rigged sailing vessels unloaded coal at the railway jetty, or loaded flour at Medina

Mills where every tide ground corn; they took on cement at the Cement Works opposite, or put off timber into barges at Medham, where the great square-rigged and steam-powered *Valhalla* used to lie. From Medham House's hard, John Samuel White was rowed, by apprentices in a four-oared gig, to and from his empire twice a day and the same water saw Hamilton White noisily stalking water-birds in his steam punt, armed with a funnel and an enormous fowling-piece. By 1858, White's had built 40,000 tons of merchant shipping; 188 ships belonged to the port; and, in that year, 44 vessels put into Cowes from ports abroad, 65 weighed anchor for foreign waters, while 507 sailed to, and 1,328 from, ports in Britain and Ireland; a tonnage of nearly 68,000, not counting vessels in ballast, representing £4,494 in customs dues from the foreign trade. Just before the American War of Independence, up to 50 Carolina rice-ships put into Cowes each year with 35,000 barrels of rice for re-shipment to the continent, and still earlier Oglander recalled seeing 300 ships riding at anchor.

For many years, Trinity Wharf has sent out its vessels to tend lightships and buoys from the Channel Islands and the Eddystone to the Royal Sovereign east of Beachy Head, and it was at East Cowes that the Customs House was opened in 1575, for West Cowes was then the smaller place. Henry VIII's East Cowe had been constructed some years before from the stones of the religious house of Estshamelorde which belonged to Beaulieu Abbey, the grange having been granted to the Abbot by Jordan de Kyngeston and Margery in 1272. Kingston Farm, south of the town, is their memorial; the name of Old Castle Point, past the breakwater and along the Esplanade, is all that is left of the Tudor defences. Visitors are more likely to invade East Cowes in search of that whimsical monument to the *mollusca*, the Shell House.

When *Britannia* lost her mast during a race, the tree-trunk kept in moist readiness in her slipway was immediately prepared. All night adzes shaped it and riggers worked so that it was stepped, inverted and unvarnished, and replete with sail by ten o'clock the next morning. Near where the *Falcon* and the *Waterwitch* were once launched, the new Penlee lifeboat, the Arun class *Mabel Alice*, was fitted out by Fairey's in 1982–3. From the chrysalis of the Gridiron Shed, now owned by Clare Lallow, White's first seaplane emerged in the spring of 1913. Downriver, Saunders-Roe's Columbine Works launched the SRA1 in 1947, the first fighter flying boat, followed by the great doomed Princesses. Sir Christopher Cockerell's invention of the annular jet enabled the SRN1 Hovercraft to be built there in 1959, the year that the company was taken over by Westland Aircraft. The British Hovercraft Corporation's AP1-88, a quiet 80-foot hovercraft now plying the Portsmouth–Ryde route, made her maiden flight in 1982, but at the same time the firm made many workers redundant. The aircraft-building techniques of BHC are expensive; Her Majesty's Fleet boasts two hovercraft, while the USSR has sixty. Now, Air Vehicles are successfully marketing small craft like the Tiger. Fairey-Allday Marine are building them like boats, welded rather than riveted, and the 1980s may yet see the promise of the hovercraft fulfilled. Even in a time of recession, decay is offset by innovative change. Hang-gliders and micro-lights are being built in sail-lofts. Vikoma International has produced anti-pollution craft to fight oil-spills in the Gulf. Cheverton Workboats have launched triple-engined fishery-protection vessels, and airport rescue Tritons. Plessey's are now working on valuable export orders for naval radar, not far from where guests danced to the Savoy Orpheans on board Marconi's yacht *Elettra* in the 'twenties. Progress is ambiguous, and Cowes was recently united in opposition to a plan to moor a 60,000-ton liquid petroleum gas tank offshore; an armada, headed by the steam-yacht *Amazon*, owned by the late Arthur Lowe of TV's *Dad's Army*, was mustered in Dunkirk-style to convey a petition to Southampton. Cowes was divided over the prospect of oil being struck onshore, beneath Bottom Copse; and split down the middle over the feasibility study ordered to consider a £3 million replacement for the ferry, a permanent bridge to link East and West, and create a water park in the Medina.

Two forgotten rolls of canvas were rediscovered at the National Gallery in 1905. J.M.W. Turner asked his father to send him unstretched canvas, in a letter from the Island, undated but certainly written between July and October 1827, when he was staying with John Nash at East Cowes Castle. It seems that sketching sailing and moored boats on paper, in the Windsor and Cowes Sketchbook preserved in the British Museum, no longer satisfied him. His father obliged, and Turner was at once to be seen on shore and afloat, painting directly on to canvas. There are three sketches for each of the paintings that John Nash had commissioned, *East Cowes Castle, the Seat of J. Nash Esq: the Regatta beating to Windward* and *The Regatta starting for their Moorings*, as well as *Shipping off East Cowes Headland, Between Decks* and *Study of Sea and Sky*, the last of which may be the earliest of his oils to sternly luxuriate in those elements that came to obsess him. The Regatta pictures were well received, though the *Repository of Art*'s reviewer cavilled that "carrying such a spread of canvas in the channel in the like breeze would upset some of these yachts; but the canvas being Mr Turner's they are safe"; while the *Morning Herald* of 26 May 1828 complained that "the composition is a cold grey character throughout, particularly the part intended for the sea, which is more like marble dust than any living waters."

White marble featured in John Nash's Paris-Directoire-style drawing-room, which was the subject of two of Turner's drawings in brown ink and white chalk on blue paper. The Long Gallery was shifted bodily from his Regent Street house. The dining-room, with its richly tasselled and curtained cornice, the Moorish billiard-room, the Gothic library, and the Octagon room's radially-fluted ceiling saw the Prince Regent lavishly entertained in 1817. Turner drew the walled garden with its fountains and statues, for which the Castle's finely-jointed ashlar was the backdrop; its round, square and octagonal towers, to which Nash added and subtracted as a hobby, gave the whole a grand and rugged picturesqueness hard to imagine. The Castle of 1798 passed through the hands of a number of owners including Lord Gort VC, commander of the British Army early in the last war, and then fell into dereliction. Palms grew up through the glass roof of the great conservatory, and Black's guide's "tawdry specimen", Shannon's "noble structure", was succeeded by the housing of Sylvan Avenue, Oak Tree Way and John Nash Avenue. The architect is buried in St James' churchyard, just south of his slender tower; the church's foundation stone was laid by Princess Victoria in 1831, but all bar the tower was rebuilt to Thomas Hellyer's designs in 1868. Almost everything that Nash created on the Island has been modified, mutilated or destroyed.

James Wyatt's Norris Castle of 1799, whose grounds fall away dramatically to a sea-wall of Swanage stone, is a mock-Norman stage-set of a place, surviving solidly enough on its massive foundations, its cisterns, ice-houses and cellars. Even the farm buildings and kitchen-garden wall are buttressed and battlemented, for Lord Henry Seymour, who commissioned Wyatt's drawings, meant it all to last. Here is Victoria's bed, where the twelve-year-old Princess slept, closely chaperoned by the Duchess of Kent, on that visit of August 1831 when the most significant foundation that was laid was the future queen's love of the Wight. Here, charming music chimes solemnly from musical boxes and, sometimes, a ghostly butler's servile shuffle and tentative cough are heard. Here broods the Kaiser's metal-hooded bath, and here stands idly a regiment of walking-sticks. Here too, from the windows and the lawns, is the prospect of the Solent and Spithead; a grandstand, in 1982, from which to watch the Task Force making off for the South Atlantic; to stand in the small Princess's footprints, but in a world beyond Empire, uphill from that yet other world of East Cowes, the working town. A town, however, without enough work, where the sight of Britain going to war with a half-obsolete fleet provoked new mixtures of mixed feelings. The 'sixties and 'seventies blitzed Cowes more effectively than the Luftwaffe, and the damage is more difficult to mend. The calm is more threatening than the storm. Anything to bring back the old prestige, to put fat on the lean kine.

PART FOUR

CIVILITIES

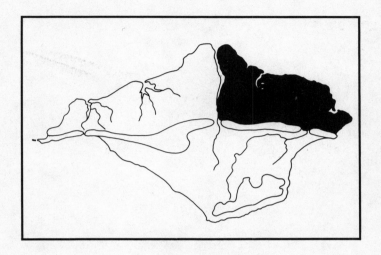

Creeks dammed for mills, streams channelled into leats;
Chillingwood, Deadman's, Blackbridge brooks seep down
from shreds of forest, their rearguard retreats;
wilderness civilized again, again.
Old stone-pits rest under a pall of green
near ruined Quarr, and black monks' praise now beats
against brick spans. The shade of a black Queen
taps out psychic tattoos, entreats, entreats.

Ryde's sprouting spires outsoar her vanity,
her pier leap-frogs mud, while Brading Haven's
spreading lap succumbs to land's advance;
the Fleet's repulsed, rings rust at a lost quay,
the Mayor's Dog baits no bulls. Flats squat, yachts prance
for us—our barbarous urbanity.

IO

RETREATS

On the balcony with Albert
She heard the nightingales.
Here, by royal decree
The past tense shall prevail.
                    Jeremy Hooker   *At Osborne House*

Abbey of Quarre in the yle of Wight. A hedde house of Monkes of
the ordre of Cisteaux beinge of large buyldinge upon the ryvage of
the sees by raporte grete refuge and conforte to all th'inhabitantes of
the same yle and to estrangers traveillinge the seid sees.
                    Sir James Worsley et al, Survey of 1536

HAD YOU STOODin the Princess's footprints on the first day of
February in the first year of this century, a westerly wind toiling
with heavy cloud above Norris's battlements, you would have seen
the Royal Yacht *Alberta*, guarded by six destroyers, passing between
lines of men-o'-war, minute guns firing their last salutes. On its deck
was the Queen's white coffin, made by the shipwright George
Martyn of Cowes, covered by a pall embroidered with the Royal
Arms in white and gold. The gun carriage bearing the coffin had
rolled from Osborne House down York Road to Trinity Wharf,
accompanied by Chopin's funeral march, by members of every
European royal family, and by great crowds who recalled the
slogan displayed in Cowes at the Diamond Jubilee, "Good Sovereign—no change required". In *Give Us This Day*, R.F. Delderfield
comments, "It was as though nobody had ever died before. As
though, to yield up the spirit, and be trundled away in a coffin,
was a privilege extended to the very few, a singular dispensation
by Providence as a reward for spectacular services on earth."
When the *Alberta* left Cowes Roads and turned eastwards, sunlight

split the clouds and lit the vessel on her way to Portsmouth.

Forty years earlier, Victoria had landed at East Cowes on a stormy winter's night, helped ashore by the Duchess of Atholl who described "the *desolate* look on that young face in Her *Widow's* cap!", making for the seclusion of Osborne, that once-blissful retreat, before Albert was in his grave. She had her Consort's clothes, hot water and towel laid out in his dressing-room each night, and for months and years she is said to have slept with his nightshirt in her arms. Queen Elizabeth II at last lifted the blinds, kept drawn so long, in the sitting-room whose balcony had been a box for the night-ingales' royal command performances. Many of Albert's effects lie as he left them; as Victoria ordained they should remain: his umbrellas and walking-sticks in their stand, his writing-desk, despatch-box, and the table for his papers—the treadmill that accelerated his depression and made him compare himself to the donkey in the Well House at Carisbrooke, "who would much rather munch thistles in the Castle moat . . . small are the thanks he gets for his labour". His own paintings hang on the walls, with photographs of the royal children in whimsical tableaux, while white marble effigies of the children's feet and hands rest on velvet cushions.

It was only ten years before Albert's death that the house, apart from the Durbar Room of 1890, was finished. Then, the workmen and their families were treated to a great dinner in the open air, with games and dancing; "not the slightest irregularity occurred". That was in 1851, though the royal apartments had been occupied since September 1846, two years after the old house had been taken for a year's trial, from Lady Isabella Blachford, at a rent of £1,000. Eustace Mann is said to have buried his fortune in Money Coppice during the Civil War, and never recovered it; no-one has yet confessed to digging it up, though a hoard of first- and second-century coins was disinterred in Barton Wood. Mr Mann's grand-daughter married a Mr Blachford, whose son built the house that Victoria bought. All that remains of it is a charming Georgian porch, now set in the nursery garden wall. Prince Albert's vision for their grand retreat, derived from some Sir Charles Barry/Claude Lorrain hybrid, was made incarnate by the builder Thomas Cubitt. Cast iron girders were the bones beneath an Italianate skin. Palladian windows, Tuscan columns, Georgian proportions and two campaniles—the Flag Tower and the Clock Tower—rose rapidly. Not only was the

Pavilion finished in 1846, but the Prince's genius for improvement, in that year alone, extended to the construction of an ice-well and a sewer from the house to the sea, the rebuilding of Barton Manor, the drainage of 50 or 60 acres of land using more than 620,000 specially manufactured drain tiles, laying out the great screen of trees from the nursery to Barton Gate, finalizing the furnishing of the house, the Manor and the Cottage, and planning the Terrace, the Italian Garden and yet more buildings.

In 1853, the Swiss Cottage was brought from Switzerland and erected between the house and the sea. It was complete with a model—in both senses of the word—kitchen, where the princesses could prepare tea for their parents, served in a dining-room undisturbed since those days. The princes learnt carpentry, and all the children had gardening tools with their initials painted on them, still arrayed in a hut like weapons in an armoury of peace. Prince Arthur built the model fortress, Albert Barracks, which so delighted the Tennyson boys. Nearby stands Victoria's bathing-machine, a green hut on cart-wheels with a deep canopy supported by exuberant iron scrollwork, above white steps down which the Queen descended into the waves for the first time in her life, at Osborne Bay on 30 July 1847: "I thought it delightful till I put my head under the water, when I thought I should be stifled." Later, the Landing House was built with its outer staircase, Italianate tower and jetty and, later still, the paved Esplanade and the Queen's Alcove. Recently, the freighter *Gloriosa* was stranded for months, crippled and listing, in Osborne Bay. When the temporarily crippled Prince of Wales moored the Royal Yacht *Osborne* in the Bay, but deliberately out of sight of the house, for the Regatta of 1898, Marconi rigged up a radio link which restored maternal contact with the wayward Bertie. The Queen was offended when Marconi doffed his hat "familiarly". On hearing from the gardener that he should keep out of sight, Marconi threatened to leave. The Queen said, "Get another electrician". Finally, things were explained, and Marconi was granted an audience.

Marconi believed that "this super-set, which is called the human brain, may send out vibrations in the form of prayer . . . the greatest comforter of all," but Victoria and Empress Eugénie indulged in table-tapping séances. The Queen presented a gold watch, "Vicky's Ticker", engraved "To Miss Georgiana Eagle for her Meritorious &

Extraordinary Clairvoyance produced at Osborne House . . ." The reputedly clairvoyant ghillie, John Brown, arrived at Osborne for Christmas 1864 and by all the means at his disposal, including a dram in the afternoon tea, contrived to put "spurrit into the pur wumman". While John Brown gave whisky to his "wumman", and Tennyson presented cowslips to his "dear and honoured lady", Disraeli paid compliments to his "Faery" at her "Sicilian Palazzo with gardens terraces statues and vases shining in the sun," as he described Osborne in a letter, "than which nothing can be conceived more captivating." He would have thought himself, he said, like Proserpine in Hades, had not his Faery's gifts of Osborne primroses reminded him that there might yet be spring; on their account, he told her, "Your Majesty's sceptre has touched the enchanted isle."

The sceptre's touch set Island society scurrying; it brought fleets of impatient or obsequious Ministers and Heads of State, including a seasick Sultan of Turkey, across the Solent; it gave Cowes a bagpipe factory; and, after the Golden Jubilee and the Durbar Room of John Lockwood Kipling and Bhai Ram Singh, it brought the Empress's "Injuns" here. The Munshi, Hafez Abdul Karim, succeeded John Brown in the Queen's affections, in the Household's jealousies, and in the Islanders' speculations. Victoria's sceptre touched off, or at least accelerated, the transformation of the Wight from retreat to resort. Meanwhile, Osborne was a haven, though as early as 1848 it was reported that 40 Chartists had landed at Cowes, on a mission of treason that turned out to be an Oddfellows' Whitsun pleasure-trip. The Fenian threats of 1867 would not prise her from her sanctuary of mourning; the Life Guards and patrol vessels had to be sent to the Wight. It is an odd thought that the summer of 1874 saw both Disraeli's visit to the Queen, when "she was wreathed with smiles and, as she tattled, glided about the room like a bird", and Karl and Jenny Marx's voyage around the Island from their Ryde holiday home and their methodical exploration of the isle's enchantments on foot, as strenuous recuperation from Marx's collapse of the previous year.

Osborne became a convalescent home for officers. The smell of cabbage you may encounter on the back stairs is not the ghost of a royal banquet. In *Goodbye to All That*, Robert Graves recounts how he slept in the royal night-nursery, played billiards on Albert's painted table, sang bawdily in the music-room, drank Rhine wines among the Winterhalters, and walked among the ilexes, deodars, cork-trees, cedars and pines. Sitting on a bench dedicated to John Brown, he opened a letter from Siegfried Sassoon MC containing a newspaper cutting: "I am making this statement as an act of wilful defiance of military authority, because I believe that the war is being deliberately prolonged by those who have the power to end it . . ." Graves hints at the suffering endured at Osborne by officers like A.A. Milne, and is expansive about the spoof club he founded with Vernon Bartlett, "The Royal Albert Society", over which he presided in his regalia of Scottish dirk, Hessian boots and side-whiskers. With its intimate and hyperbolic knowledge of the Prince Consort's private life, the Society would have applauded Lord Ernle's schoolboy exploit. In the year before his death, Albert was standing on the scaffolding of Whippingham Church with the rector and the foreman, supervising the rebuilding of Nash's edifice, when the boy loosed off his catapult at the large target presented by the fat foreman. He missed; Albert cried out, leapt, staggered back and would have fallen had not his companions caught him. Not only does the church contain his monument, marble "erected, under his directions, by his broken-hearted and devoted widow", it is his monument. Topped by a four-square tower embroidered with lancets, enriched with pinnacles, an octagonal lantern and spire, it is a gothick fantasy of enlightened airiness, warmed by underfloor heating and thickly encrusted with memorials. Here is the white marble reredos of the Last Supper, framed in alabaster and presented by Edward VII in memory of Victoria; Prince Henry of Battenberg's sarcophagus surmounted by a sword behind Gilbert's Art Nouveau grille, and the block of decking from HMS *Blonde* upon which his coffin rested during the voyage from Ashanti; an alabaster tablet *in memoriam* 90 Hessian soldiers struck down by typhus in 1794; and tablets to William Arnold, the Revd Matthew Arnold and many others. The dedication is to the Anglo-Saxon St Mildred, and a fragmentary Norman carving of two men on horseback flanking a tree, embedded in the south porch, is all that is left of the church that FitzOsbern gave to his Abbey of Lyre.

The graveyard's notables include Uffa Fox, buried under a stone which depicts one of his parachuted airborne lifeboats, within sight of his beloved Medina. Upriver is Folly Inn, undistinguished now but originally built from the timbers of an old hulk, from which the boy Uffa swam across to Werror to poach swallows' eggs from the brickdrying sheds. This side, goats tangle with brushwood and saddleback pigs nuzzle beneath oaks in a field of chamomile, not far from where Sir T.O.M. Sopwith's wooden hangar spawned Bat Boats and grew into an empire. Downriver, Kingston Power Station's chimneys protrude from behind rising ground. Across the road from Whippingham Church, the gables and chimneys of the Almshouses that Victoria had built for her retired servants flaunt their beautifully restored terracotta; and, beyond, British Hovercraft Corporation's works stand for research and development in the fields of electronics, aerodynamics and hydrodynamics.

The factory gates face Barton Manor's drive. It runs up to wrought-iron gates, worked with Edward VII's monogram, which swing open electronically. Next door to the Manor is the model Farm where Prince Albert assiduously applied the latest in agricultural techniques and, according to an account of 1860, vastly improved the fertility of the gravelly Bembridge Marls "by efficient drainage, deep ploughing and abundant application of manures". Steam then powered machinery for corn and chaff cutting, threshing, grinding, and for a saw-mill. Though the pump-house chimney survives, the engine that lifted water from Barton's lakes up into tanks in Osborne House's towers was given, for its iron, during the war in lieu of gates and railings. "The buildings stand unrivalled for the excellent arrangements of granaries, stables, piggeries, and ox and cow stalls. The granary is a spacious fire- and vermin-proof building erected on brick arches with iron girders." The milking parlour was, and still is, immaculate, though the red-and-blue tiled dairy is now a winery, where grapes from Barton Manor's five acres of vineyards are milled, the mash pressed, the must pumped into fermentation tanks, and the wine fined, filtered and bottled. Ranks of vivid green vines, alternating with wind-breaks of black plastic, run down the south-facing slope from the secret garden to the water-garden, once a pond where the Prince Consort and his children skated. As I write, I am sipping a glass of Barton Manor wine; in its delicious pale gold depths I imagine the mellow reflection of the Elizabethan Court House, "a very ancient moated round," according to John Oglander, "with a drawbridge" and, within an apparently solid wall demolished in Albert's rebuilding, a chapel fitted for the recusant celebration of the Mass. The "Jacobean" restoration is reflected in a lake with a picturesque split-wood and thatch boat-house. Black labradors gambolling on the banks are no threat, unlike invisible foxes, to the black swans whose regal progress in the spring ruffles the reflected glory of an exuberance of daffodils, offspring of 225,000 bulbs planted in the 'twenties. The surface once boiled with rising fish, for Barton's three ponds were monks' stews, regulated by a now-ruined weir of massive stone blocks; the house's ancestor was a retreat for the Black Monks, Augustinians clothed "pallio Hiber-niensi de nigra boneta cum pileo", in the thirteenth century. There is an ancient wall with blocked-up lancet windows to the left of the main door, and above it a plaque discovered in the grounds by Victoria, Empress Frederick of Germany: a griffin holding an open book surrounded by the inscription ". . . *Maris Francisco Corrario Prov Gen* . . .". Barton Oratory was in all ceremonies and in tinkling the bell to follow the use of Sarum, but the intentions of the founders, John de Insula (or Lisle) and Peter de Winton, rectors of Shalfleet and Godshill, foundered under the rule or mis-rule of the arch-priest William Love; the tenements were "ruinoso" and the Oratory, and the endowments that had not been misappropriated, were put into the custody of the priests of Niton and Brading, by order of a commission including the Abbot of Quarr, before being surrendered to Winchester in 1439. History's brew is as murky and unsavoury as today's wine is palatable and clear.

Barton Manor was a kind of annexe of Osborne and, when the kitchens were under pressure, extra food was ferried from here to the House in insulated wagons. King's Quay Cottage and Coburg, a decoratively tiled chalet, both had Queen's Rooms and were retreats from the retreat, embowered in the little Schwarzwald of Albert's planting. The coastline from Barton to St Helen's was thickly wooded, and inland as far as the Island's spine, "the woodlands," wrote Sir H. Englefield, "form an almost continuous velvet carpet of near 10,000 acres, broken only by small farms, whose thatched buildings relieve the tints of the foliage." Streams and brooks garner the waters of the arboreal territory and issue into Shoflet and Wootton Creeks. Between them, Wootton Park's game was confined behind ditches, and by water on three sides, until their preserve was disparked in 1705. The name Shoflet has been lost; King's Quay replaces it, but Wootton is the merest corruption of the consonant Wood Town. Here we are on Lisle or De Insula ground, that once belonged to Edward the Confessor's queen Edith; its fringes, the habitation and resort of fishermen and pirates. Fire ravaged the manor in 1445, though in 1499 the Lisles were able to offer hospitality to Henry VII. Sir John Lisle was a regicide, one of Charles I's judges, assassinated in Lausanne after the Restoration; his widow, Dame Alice, was sentenced to be burnt in old age by Judge Jeffreys, for harbouring Monmouthites; in contrast, his brother William was a royalist who returned from exile with Charles II and is buried here. The austere stone barn of a church beside Wootton Manor Farm is embellished by his monument, by that of Izaak Walton's cousin, and by a Jacobean canopied pulpit, a rood beam sustaining a triumphant carving of Christ the King, and an Early English arch, now blocked, that gave on to a chapel of St Edmund the King. Chimes from a bell-cote call worshippers into the coolness between the shafts and zig-zag moulding of a glorious Norman doorway.

The Jacobean House has gone. Lisle Court, near the mouth of the Creek, is a relatively recent monster, mercifully shrouded by trees. More recent still are the holiday camps, and the expensive detached dwellings of extraordinary pretentiousness. It seems that people who have the desire and the means to live in secluded places also possess a singular talent for cluttering them with tasteless houses. It is a shame that, by the time you emerge from overhanging trees at the water's edge, the delicious flavour of the Creek's mouth is spoiled by the aftertaste of such architecture. Here, at Wootton Hard, are decaying boat-houses, rusting rails running into the water, and rotting piles of old jetties, weed-hung plinths for sea-fowl, protruding from white, pink and green clays. Creek Gardens and Ash Lake were brickworks, and the clays around the inlet make treacherous bedrock. Even houses founded on concrete rafts suffered during the drought of 1976, provoking the hopeful thought that the objects of my wrath may crumble before long.

Across the Creek, £2 million has been spent on enlarging the Fishbourne Ferry Terminal with linkspan bridges that rise and fall with the tide. It now extends a welcome, unseconded by many inhabitants of Fishbourne Lane, to Sealink's Superferries, *St Catherine* and *St Helen*, and their 142-car cargoes. Solent-wards is a derelict lifeboat station and slipway, clay studded with as many oyster shells as pebbles, and the carcases of trees that have taken the plunge as the ground which coddled their gnarled and naked roots was swept from under them. Fishbourne was home to Quarr Abbey's Fish-house, where a gentleman's residence set in an orchard boasts a low-level kitchen, once a boatbuilder's saw-pit. The Royal Victoria Yacht Club has transferred its traditions here from Ryde, while a workshop here spawned a 34,000-horsepower jet-engined car, *Thrust 2*, which gained the world land speed record in the Black Rock Desert of Nevada. The circular village green has an iron seat at its centre, surrounding the great bole of an oak whose branches shade the grass. There, hounds mill around at the annual meet, and an aged butler and maid weave their way between the mounts, handing the stirrup-cup to horsemen and hunt-followers alike.

Back on the Wootton side of the Creek, I made my way along pot-holed gravel roads, past tree-camouflaged shacks and moorings, to where Jack Whitehead's home stands close by the stark though stylish Aquaview Village. His retreat was built with a shipwright's skill. It comprises timbers, including a curved roof-beam and lockers, from the sloop *Veronica* in which he and his family lived for eighteen years. Cabined on the brink of the water, in an interior organized with all the elegant economy of a sea-going craft, he might be afloat but for the fact that he can step out through the garden to his workshop. Its door opens on a sea of faces, a cocktail of costumes, a surreally silent fancy-dress party; for he restores the pride of many a prow, a procession of figureheads ferried, in sad disarray and rejuvenated prime, to and from the National Maritime Museum. Stern sea-goddesses, seductive nymphs, black-bearded turks and noble magi are stripped of sometimes dozens of layers of paint that have clogged and coarsened their fine-tooled features. New wood, newly worked, replaces rotten sections, and fairground colours glisten again on the braided hair, bright faces, billowing robes and voluptuous breasts that braved the seven seas. Out in the garden, Jack shaped a two-ton elm from Horsham into a gentle-faced figure-head for the *Falls of Clyde* in Honolulu. His workshop and creek-side home are rich with mementoes of the craft that has led him a merry dance across the world.

Towards the bridge, Wootton becomes more solidly residential. The bridge was a causeway built for the monks of Quarr, a dam which tamed the tide and restrained the flow of the dourly-named Blackbridge, Chillingwood and Deadman's Brooks. The reflective surface of the Old Mill Pond was grist to the Abbey's exchequer, and spun undershot wheels in the mill that stood beside the Sloop Inn, once the miller's house. The mill, to which the *Silent* used to ply from Southampton, was pulled down twenty years ago; and Fernhill, whose Batty Langley Gothic façade used to preside over the Mill Pond, was burnt to the ground. The Admiral-of-the-Fleet who lived there built a signal station from which he communicated with Portsmouth in the tradition of Woditone's beacon of 1324 and Wootton Point's watch of 1628. The Isle of Wight Steam Railway maintains communications between Wootton Station and Haven-street with locomotives such as *Calbourne*, *Freshwater* and *Vectis*, and rolling-stock including a 1924 Composite carriage. In 1877, a station was built at the northern edge of Fattingpark Copse, called Whippingham, though it was three miles from Osborne. Victoria and Eugénie are said to have used it only once; now it is a private house stranded on the old line to Newport. The private railway steams, like the ghost of the Isle of Wight Central Railway, eastwards through Briddlesford Copse, leaving Firestone Copse to the north and Combley Great Wood to the south. In the old forest's fastnesses is Great Briddlesford Farm, where geese defend the site of the ancient chapel of St Martin, and Briddlesford Lodge Farm, whose hop-kilns stand as a memorial to a pre-First World War crop. The present station at Havenstreet is Southern Railway, 1926 vintage, but restoration work includes a railway museum in the style of Bembridge's blue and red brick station of 1877.

Nearby, the retort house of Havenstreet Gasworks bears the date 1886 and the monogram of John Rylands. He was a Lancashire manufacturer of calicoes and linens, ginghams, checks and ticks, who bought factories squatting fortuitously upon coal seams; he invested £50,000 in the Manchester Ship Canal and applied his gains to charitable causes of all kinds, including English, French and Italian editions of the Bible for free distribution. He spent some of his last years at Havenstreet, and died at Longford Hall near Manchester in 1888. His house here became the Longford Hospital, a tuberculosis sanatorium, and then a women's mental hospital. The Longford Institute of 1885 was a library and reading-room lit, like the rest of the village, by Ryland's gas; subsequently, it played the rôles of

Temperance Hotel, horse and carriage depot, bus depot, nursing home, guest house and presently, The White Owl Restaurant. Havenstreet—the street at the head of the haven—becomes a footpath before climbing to the War Memorial and across fields to Newnham's modernized seventeenth-century farmhouse, whose mill-pond fed the cunningly-diverted stream that filled the ponds of old Quarr Abbey. While Combley was Quarr's largest grange, Newnham was the home grange, and a curious stone image set in the farmhouse wall hints at its pedigree. The path to Quarr crosses the stream, threads through Puckers Copse, and meets the main road at the corner of Elenor's Grove.

The ground hereabouts reeks of legend. Eleanor of Guienne, Henry II's queen, after confinement at Quarr, is mistakenly supposed to have been buried here in a golden coffin protected by strong spells from unholy hands; a passage, closed by a golden gate, is said to run deep underground. In 1857, the *Isle of Wight Observer* reported that labourers making a new road through Quarr's grounds found three small stone cists or chests containing the disarticulated skeletons of "persons of distinction", probably Baldwin de Redvers, founder of the Abbey in 1132, his wife Adeliza and son Henry. Quarraria, daugher of Savigny, with her grey monks, was united to Cîteaux in 1147 and, for almost four centuries, white-habited Cistercians prayed and worked here. Despite, or because of, their other-worldly discipline they held, acquired, exchanged and developed granges and farms, corn-mills and fulling-mills throughout the Island. Their ships sailed from Fish-house, or Fishbourne, and their industry and innovation were responsible for the economic thrift and prosperity of the medieval Wight. The fourteenth century's crescendo of French aggression saw the Abbot contributing to the defences of the Island and crenellating the Fish-house, Wootton Mill and the seaward wall of the Abbey itself. Monkish fingers were thoroughly entrenched in the Island pie. With his eye on rabbit-pie, Brother Hardekyn was caught with three creatures shot in the warren of the manor of Ashey—"*iii cuniculos sagittis transfixit*"—and, shortly before the Dissolution of the Abbey in 1536, the topographer Lambard noted that "although Paulus Jovius wrote that the inhabitants of this island be wont to boast merrily that they neither had amongst them monks, lawyers, wolves nor foxes, yet I find them all save one in one monastery, called Quarr."

In the face of the official attack on French church life, the Benedictines of Solesmes exiled themselves to Appuldurcombe House in the autumn of 1901. Six years later, the black monks bought Quarr Abbey House, a Cochrane residence to which Princess Beatrice and Prince Henry of Battenberg had retreated for their honeymoon. The community's wooden church was moved across the Island, but one of their number, Dom Paul Bellot, was an architect of genius. His masterpiece, the Abbey church, was built in 1911–12 of rough-cast, peach-coloured brick exploited to its full extent. The texture and patterning, the stepped detail and the sweep of its spans, the warmth and grandeur he achieved in Moorish-Expressionist style are astounding. Approaching it down the avenue of polled trees, you might imagine it was a mosque, but the scarecrow in the tirelessly tended kitchen garden puts you right: it is a wooden cross, with a white enamel bucket for a head, draped in a black habit. The long high choir of the church fills with the rich simplicity of antiphonal plainsong. Here, in 1914, Jacques Maritain was the first guest, and here Robert Graves talked at length with the French fathers; "at Quarr," he wrote, "Catholicism ceased to repel me." Visitors are graciously greeted by the Abbot, and wholesomely fed under the pierced brick arches of the refectory, to the accompaniment, the day I enjoyed hospitality there, of a reading from Genesis and an episode from the autobiography of Yehudi Menuhin. After lunch, Dom Frederick Hockey showed me the library, the cloister and the garden in front of the Cochranes' old house. Here, he knew the provenance and life-story of every flower, shrub and tree, common or exotic, as well as he knows the medieval history of the Abbey and the Island which he has so meticulously chronicled. Here is the graveyard of the monks who have entrusted their souls to God, and their bodies to this small plot in the shadow of the great tower under whose aspiring brick they corporately celebrated the Mass.

The bones of the old Abbey lie eastwards, beyond the trees, and have outlasted the elms that were planted there. The ruined precinct walls enclose some twenty acres; the kitchen and infirmary walls, with ragged arches, windows and blind beam sockets, best survived the depredations of John Mill, Recorder of Southampton, who supervised their dismemberment; of his merchant brother, George, who profited from what was left over after the construction of East and West Cowes; of George's son, another George, who with his wife Douzabelle was later to settle at Quarr's ex-grange of Haseley; and of all those who have since taken Quarr at its face-value, and treated the abbey as a quarry. The storehouse, with its tall stepped lancets, still stands as a barn for the eighteenth-century farmhouse; both boast original and re-used thirteenth-century masonry. A five-barred gate, in a wall topped with pennywort and pink campion, gives on to a field golden with buttercups, glittering with the waters that invade it, grazed at the Solent's edge by statuesque cattle set against a backdrop of sea-haze in which, suspended between azure and azure, yachts and steamers silently make their ethereal progress across the abbey's field of vision before retreating behind the trees that crowd the shore on either hand.

As a queen raised Osborne for a private retreat, so a king's public policy razed this retreat. Modern Quarr's prayerful austerity, set within its brilliantly severe shell of brick, consorts oddly with Osborne's elaborate clutter of fine workmanship and execrable taste. Osborne is a grandiloquent morgue; its fascination, however compelling, is a morbid one. Here, among ruins, is an oak tree that has quietly grown up through generations of men. It supports itself by roots like stilts, but its central pillar, its bole, germinated from an acorn lodged on stonework. It grows, flows down, infiltrates the masonry and, amongst ancient footings, taps the soil. There is life here, sap in the stone.

I I

A TICKET TO RYDE

We intend no disrespect to the finest town in the Island in saying
that, generally speaking, people go to Ryde to get away from it.
Ward Lock's Guide

How men, inheritors of all the long passion and experience and
wisdom of ages, could choose to build precisely thus, is indeed a
mystery.

Aubrey de Selincourt   *Isle of Wight*

THE HUMID BREATHof twisted, lithe undergrowth hangs languidly
in Quarr Wood. Years ago, the air wrung with the sweat of sappy
stone and stonecutters. The liquid cries and cacophonous charm of
small birds have long overtaken the barked orders, grunted assents
and work-songs of men, the percussive chime and chatter of iron
tools, the strenuous collaborative effort to disinter the bedrock.
Potency of nature has succeeded urgency of purpose.

Ellery's, stone masons of Ryde, continue an old tradition; it is no
coincidence that Ellery was one of the signatories of the 1651 Charter
of the Ancient Order of Marblers and Stonecutters of the Isle of
Purbeck. There, the everyday word for quarry is *quarr*, retained on
the Wight as a proper name and replaced by *pit*. Between Quarr and
Binstead the pits, scars and spawl heaps are overgrown and
overbuilt. Evidence of the huge energy of an industry is laid to rest
under a green shroud. Only names like Pitts Lane and Stone Pitts
remain.

There is a time to build and a time to let be. Residents of Abbots
Close woke, on a recent Sunday morning, to the aggressive grind of
bulldozers trying to pre-empt a tree preservation order and clear
more land for houses; an injunction stopped them in their tracks.
Growth is set against construction, but is slyly assimilated into the

loaded notion of development. Wildness or wilderness gives way to cultivation, and cultivation with a human face is cast as civilization. Ambiguous civilization, with its civic or urban overtones, has always been set above the pagan or rural, the rustic and the wild. Now, when development threatens to expunge mere growth, when pride of achievement is stifled by the claustrophobia of consequence, we feel the pathos of these words and their derivations. Irony is piled upon irony when, at Quarr, trees are preferred to buildings; the virile bulldozer's destructive-constructive push is halted, temporarily at least, by swift action in support of a passive preservation order. In part, our ecological crisis is a mental crisis; we are led a dance, in circles, on these verbal tracks; we cannot see wood for trees. *Pace* civilization, but not urbanization, I want to see trees here, and the wood unwounded that healed the quarry's wounds. Quarr Wood is a civilized name, if not an urbane growth.

The proud and virile Saxons knew that dust was their origin and ashes their end; they felled timber when they built for themselves, but when their end was the glorification of God they built for Him in stone. They came where the Romans had quarried for Porchester. At Quarr-Binstead they dug limestone, ferried it across the Solent, and carted it within an arc roughly described by Romsey, Reading and Chichester. Under King Edgar, Edward the Elder's Romsey Abbey grew; the Norman kings saw the pits as their prerogative. In 1079, Bishop Walkelyn was granted half a hide here by the Conqueror, and more by William Rufus, for the rebuilding of his cathedral at Winchester. Chichester Cathedral drew fabric from the pits in 1091. Romsey's rebuilding employed Chilmark stone, for Quarr's rock was then ear-marked for an instrument of temporal power, the ramparts of Carisbrooke; though Quarr Abbey was built from it, and Beaulieu and Netley. When the lordship of Carisbrooke and the Wight reverted from Isabella de Fortibus, the last of the de Redvers, to the Crown in 1293, on 20 June Quarr Abbey had to gain a licence from Edward I for quarrying the ground next door. Contrary to what is often written, the Abbot of Quarr never had jurisdiction over the pits. Here, the master mason William de Wynford, working for William of Wykeham, selected stone for Winchester College and, later, for his masterpiece: thus it was that, at the close of the fourteenth century, the Abbot of Quarr was commissioned to cart the stone, some say the last of the good seams, to the sea *en route* for the great new nave of Winchester Cathedral.

The gravels, sands, clays and limestones of the northern half of the Island are a three-dimensional jigsaw puzzle whose published solutions do not hang together. Geologists have not yet fitted all the pieces into place, but recent work shows that Quarr-Binstead stone is not, as was thought, a species of Bembridge Limestone; it is an older rock from the top of the Osborne Beds. From a stonecutter's, as distinct from a geologist's, point of view, the quality of rock within the same stratum may vary drastically within a short distance. It may cleave cleanly and work freely here, and there be fractured and recalcitrant. At Seafield, Seaview, where the pits are now built over, and principally at Quarr-Binstead, there was accessible stone enough to supply several generations of Saxon, Norman and medieval masons. The pits were twenty feet deep or less, and readily gave up their rag and feather: the grey-greenish-to-creamy compact Quarr stone proper, and the paler more fossiliferous and less valuable Binstead stone, whose sparry shreddy texture tends to stun under the chisel or punch. Quarrying went on intermittently well into the last century, but since the Dissolution the best stone has come, not from underground, but from re-quarrying those Abbeys built from it.

It is hard to imagine how many tons of this rich slice of the Island's crust, how many wagon-loads of Quarr stone, groaned their way along rutted tracks; how many oxen, asses and horses perished as they lugged the hard stuff to Binstead Hard; nor how many quarrymen met with accidental death as they man-handled the virgin surfaces, and were buried in the churchyard by the way. More recent graves at Binstead's Holy Cross hold the bones of the giant Samuel Landon of 1844, and of Thomas Sivell "who was cruelly ſhot on board his ſloop by ſome *officers* of the *cuſtoms* of the Port of Portſmouth on the 15th June 1785." Sivell, it seems, was a legitimate ferryman not involved in the illicit running of any sort of hard stuff, mistakenly identified and killed by the hard-pressed Preventive men of William Arnold's time. Under a moulding of conches and scallops, his sloop with full sails set in relief runs before a sun of lichen.

A Norman arch set in the churchyard wall bears, above the keystone, a ram's head upon which squats a grotesque, and bearded, *sheila-na-gig*, hands spreading her sex. There was an outcry, Albin tells us in 1795, from the inhabitants when their "Idol" was removed. It was restored to the church and moved to its present position when the Norman nave was replaced by Hellyer's Early English-style building of 1844, and is now decorously shrouded with ivy. Other more acceptable Norman stones were incorporated in the new work: symbols of Eternity, Sin and, above the porch, the dove of the Sanctus Spiritus. It is possible that the bell-cote of 1925 rings out with the voice, if not the tongue—for the clapper is not original—of old Quarr Abbey; the bell is inscribed with a fleur-de-lys and the petition, in black letters, *Sancta Maria ora pro nobis*, and may be one of two bells noted, along with vestments, candlesticks, a chalice and three cows, in the 1553 inventory of Binstid and Quarr Churchis. A monk of Quarr officiated at Holy Cross until the Dissolution; then Binstead assumed the Abbey's privileges and, for a time, its parsons were styled Bishops of Binstead. But Winchester soon put an end to that; after all, King Ethelred had granted the New Minister the land of Stathe, between Wootton Creek and Binstead Brook, in 982. This was added to King Egbert's grant, in 826, of the manor of Swainston, and given back to the Crown in 1284, along with 2,000 marks, in return for Edward I's favour and the advowson of Calbourne, Brighstone and Binstead. There must have been a Saxon church here to serve the quarrymen, and Tomkins described the old chancel arch as Saxon, but the oldest stones in the chancel's fabric seem to be early Norman herring-bone work. The carved wood is notable—a vigorous Last Supper among the sixteenth-century Dutch panels of the altar, and a strenuous Aaron and Hur lifting Moses' prayerful hands in support of the rector's stall against the Philistines—and was most vulnerable to the fire of 1969. Morey & Sons of Newport made hammer-beams of Sussex oak to hold up the new nave roof; Norman Gaches carved new gaudy bosses for the chancel roof, and the west windows were filled with new glass depicting the Peacock, and the Phoenix risen from its ashes.

Now resurrected to sleep, it seems, amongst the stones and thatch of the old parsonage and other cottages on the margin of Binstead's suburban development, the church and its environs were not always as insular. The stone trade made it a focus of invested effort and spread its influence on the mainland. Again and again, the church registers record the burials of "A man from the Shore (name unknown)" or "A man supposed to be a sailor, name unknown.

Drowned". John Oglander recalled coming here for the funeral of Captain John Gibbons, discoverer of the north-west passage, who died at Ryde and was buried beneath the chancel. On May Day 1803, we are told that "a black man usually called Orenoco was baptised by the name of John Binstead"; he might have been *The Negro Servant* who stimulated Legh Richmond's lines:

> Lord Jesus, Thou hast shed Thy blood
>> For thousands such as me:
> Though some despise poor Negro slaves,
>> I'm not despised by Thee.

As the pits' raw vigour has been masked by luxuriant growth, so, abetted by Victorian restoration and twentieth-century sprawl, have the horizons of an earlier Binstead been trammelled by gentility.

One long-drawn-out September dusk, I turned my back on the numinous stones of Quarr's ruins and entered the chiaroscuro wood where bulky gothick blacknesses and chinks of light betrayed big houses, and the school built by John Fleming, descendant of James I's Chief Justice and "mean tool" who bought Quarr from Douzabelle Mill, owned most of Binstead and gave the family name to the Fleming Arms. Ooze and leaves sucked at my shoes until I emerged on to the road where the church seemed to float, as if merely moored in its boneyard, and the Idol to stir under its still mantle of ivy. I turned to follow Binstead Brook down to the shore when, all at once, lights blazed in a house on the left, a door was flung wide, dogs erupted, two shapes fled across the lighted lawns, vaulted fence and brook, almost knocked me off my feet and disappeared into the dark. The dogs quieted and slunk back, the door shut, the lights were extinguished. I found myself on the shore, near where a Mesolithic hand-axe was picked up and where bones of horse and ox were discovered not far from a fissure in the limestone containing part of a reindeer's skull. Mud and rocks and rivulets stretched to the Solent; a lone lantern silhouetted an unmoving fisherman and glittered yellowly in the shallows. Slapping swell caught the last fragments of the sky's cold light. Shadows shifted in a lighted hut above the slipway, and the trees behind seemed to suck the darkness down in self-annihilation. That night it was easy to imagine signals and Solent assignations, surreptitious landings and immoderate celebrations; easy too to feel the weight of the old stone cargoes bearing down on sled-runners, or on axle-tree, spokes and felloes, down into the rutted track and out on to quay or jetty; or edged down the Hard upon high-wheeled wagons into the water, draught-animals snorting at the chill, men sweating at shifting the rock, block by stubborn block, into stone-boats sinking deeper and deeper into the rising tide that would bear them away to the mainland and the master-builders.

And so to Ryde. Had you followed Lovers' Walk from Binstead to the town 150 years ago, you would have skirted Captain Brigstocke's delightful "cottage" at Stonepits, and the richly planted, spacious grounds and imposing Grecian Lodge of Mr Player's grand white mansion; next, a dwelling recently erected in the old English gabled style, and a pair of commodious lodging-houses; then, the villas of Earl Spencer and the Duke of Buckingham set in wide lawns and embowered by shrubberies, and Westmount, seat of Dr John Lind, late of Haslar Hospital, Portsmouth, where his father's researches into scurvy had put the Navy in his debt. Developments to make an estate agent's mouth water, and names—Player, Lind, Brigstocke—to conjure with; men who conjured a town and a resort out of the humble fishing port below, and the village above the hill, so recently separated by a field of twelve acres called Node Close. In 1780–1, one of the pack-ways linking Upper and Lower Ryde had been laid out as Union Street, with plots for villas; a union which promised to engender a Regency watering-place to rival Brighton.

Not much more than a century before, in 1656, the population of Ryde was estimated at 220. Remains from the Neolithic period onwards—including a late Bronze Age urnfield at Swanmore, hoards of palstave axes at St John's and Haylands, a gold coin of Verica from the Iron Age, and a possible Roman cemetery at St John's—show continuity of settlement. But in medieval times, La Ryde was merely an outlier of the manor of Ashey, belonging to the Abbess of Wherwell near Andover, whose sources of income included revenue from the ferry to the mainland. The northern part of the manor was bounded by Binstead Brook to the west, the Solent to the north and Monkton Mead Brook, the northern reach of Smallbrook, to the east. Six acres of Monks' Meads belonged to Quarr, and then to the holder of their Newnham grange who was entitled to the first crop of hay every other year so long as a stone image there was preserved. The brook ran down into marshy ground and out at the Sandy Duver; now it runs under the town and Esplanade just west of the boating lake. The rest of Ryde and the manor of Ashey were, until 1868, part of the parish of Newchurch, which also included Ventnor on the south coast. East Ashey farm contains portions of the seventeenth-century manor house, has a barn dated 1688, and a large fish pond with smaller breeding and fattening ponds now grown over by trees. A tree-fall revealed a late medieval midden; platforms and earthy undulations, like ripples from long-sunk stones, are all that is left of homesteads, crofts and enclosures that comprised the ancient settlement. Giles Worsley leased the manor from the Abbess for £12 and ten brace of rabbits a year; he rebuilt the windmill at Upton, repaired buildings and constructed a lime-kiln in the Abbess's wood. After the Dissolution he purchased the manor from the Crown for £759 19s 2d on 20 March 1544. Worsleys gave way to Dillingtons and the manor was split up. Henry Player bought Ryde Estate from Sir John Dillington for £3,000 in 1705; his son Thomas built Ryde Chapel in 1719, and his grandson William laid out Union Street and bought Ryde Manor from Lord Mount Edgecumbe in 1789. His daughter, Elizabeth Lydia Player, married Dr John Lind in the same year.

By the turn of the century the population was approaching one thousand. In 1810, Mr Yelf established his hotel and began the commercial life of Union Street. Russell & Bromley's was once the famous Sheridan's Boarding House, and, above ground-floor level, the buildings retain their distinguished mien. Some early shop-fronts have been impeccably preserved, but others, vanadalized by their proprietors, wilfully undermine the character of the street. They are loud-mouthed with plate-glass and gross lettering, while their neighbours' curlicues, mouldings and just proportions gently seduce the discerning through their doors; those of a beautifully furnished outfitter's, for example, and a chemist's still lined with apothecaries' jars and drawers, and warmed by an iron stove in winter.

On 29 June 1813, Elizabeth Lydia Lind noted a momentous event in her diary, "The first stone of Ryde pier was laid." Great timber piles driven into the sea-bed founded the big daddy of seaside piers. Gone were the tribulations of Fielding's time when, in Captain Marryatt's words, "the wherries came in as far as they could, and were met by a horse and cart, which took out the passengers, and carried them through the mud and water to the hard ground." On 4

June 1819, Mrs Lind wrote, "The foundation stone of our house at Westmount was laid by my mother"; it is now Ryde School; and, on 25 July 1820, her daughter "Elizabeth was married ... to Mons. Antoine Beat Albert du Thon." Later, two du Thon daughters were to marry the brothers Edmund and Samuel Peters, grandsons of the painter, William Peters RA, and great-grandsons of Matthew Peters, author of *The Rational Farmer* (Newport 1770), whose family had been Gosport brewers with a monopoly on supplying beer to the Fleet at Spithead. Arthur Peters, farmer and now teacher at Ryde School, showed me the manuscript copy of the 1821 *Population of Ryde*, as returned to the Government by Richard Ellis, Overseer. Suggestive details are given of some of the 2,876 inhabitants: "William Lulloff, Labourer infirm, Keeps the Tollgate ... William Watson, Carpenter, wife straw hat maker Industrious ... John Woodford, Shoemaker, wife attends Bathing Machine ... George Williams, Seaman but mostly works on the Road ... Robert Newnham, Labourer infirm for an Ideot, 2/- per week from Parish ... Thomas Long, Postillion, Industrious neat and clean ... Davy Richards, Labourer does anything catch hares ... Mrs Linnington, Husband in Goal (sells gin) [sic] ... Charles Grinham, Sexton, loves Drink wife very industrious ... Michael Moorman, Himself in Horsham Gaol wife in the house of industry ... Geo Yates, Seaman, wife from him/Children deserted/sent to West Indies for smuggling ... Simon Swartherage, Boots at the Bugle Inn ..."

The next year, Elizabeth Lydia Player was married at Newchurch to Captain Robert Brigstocke. Soon the Pier was extended to 2,040 feet and received "the handsome and commodious vessels of the United Steam Packet Co.". The monumental Brigstocke Terrace, by James Sanderson, outstared new arrivals. The Captain's grandson lived there in grandiose isolation until his death in 1956. Sanderson also rebuilt St Thomas's, of Binstead stone; now the churchyard is a garden, controversially part-paved with broken headstones—crazy graving—and punctuated by surviving tombs, including that of Captain Daniel Malayeef, December 1808, whose ship the *Twerdoy* was part of the Russian Fleet that surrendered to the English on 3 September. The derelict church is to be transformed into a fit setting for the Brigstocke's exotic China Collection.

St James' makeshift medieval shape rose up at the same time. An Act for paving, lighting and watching the town was passed in 1829 and, two years later, John Lind's classical Assembly Rooms and Market—whose wooden cupola has been recently restored—was built to serve a town of, by then, 3,676 souls. Westmacott's Italianate Royal Victoria Arcade opened in 1836; it was restored by Mr J. Homer and re-opened in 1974, after a battle with a Town Council who wanted to pull it down. Gas came in 1838, and much hot air was exchanged about the merits of development. "Houses of a very superior description have been built," wrote one, "Badly built houses especially to the east," a second asserted, qualified by a third as "more resembling a slice of second-rate fashionable London stuck on the side of the island".

So Ryde grew, and grew rich; but the poor continued. William Goff, an ex-servant of the Linds', broke into Westmount and stole £135 on 8 March 1839; he was pursued to Newport and apprehended in Southampton. In July, at Winchester Assizes, he was sentenced to fifteen years' transportation, but died in gaol before sailing. During the next 30 years, more churches provided for the edification of the populace, and the vanity or piety of their benefactors: St John's, Oakfield; the Countess Clare's Baroque Early English Roman church; the Linds' Holy Trinity by Thomas Hellyer; a number of architecturally non-conformist chapels; the "high" and mighty St Michael & All Angels at Swanmore; and the climax, George Gilbert Scott's All Saints, with its ambitious pinnacles and spire puncturing the skyline, garnished inside with marble, alabaster and semi-precious stones, and seating 1,300 souls. It was a symbol of the town's confidence, coinciding with its new parish and borough status of 1868.

Meanwhile, Prince Albert had laid the foundation stone of the Royal Victoria Yacht Club, all Tuscan and Corinthian, with a seaward battery; hilarious scrapbooks record the patrons' schoolboy-ish fights, jokes, quibbles over etiquette and stage-managed dramas. Now it is Brian McDermott's Prince Consort Theatre, a worthy successor to Ryde's Theatre Royal, where Mrs Jordan made her last English appearance, and Ellen Terry made one of her first, as Puck. The Royal Infirmary was built, and a new local Act provided for a waterworks and reservoir of 504,000 gallons four miles away at the foot of Ashey Down. A new Esplanade, coped with Swanage stone, extended 1,200 feet eastwards across marsh, Duver and the un-marked graves of many of the hundreds who perished when Admiral

Kempenfelt's *Royal George* went down in August 1782, mourned by William Cowper's *Toll for the brave!*. When villas in Dover Street and the Strand were built, skeletons were disinterred, but not commemorated here until 1965, when Lord Mountbatten unveiled a simple memorial stone in Ashley Gardens.

The population approached 10,000 in the 1860s. The pier grew to almost half a mile, and was widened to accommodate the Pier Tramway, powered variously by horse, steam, electricity and petrol: it ran across the Esplanade and reached St John's Railway Station by 1871. The railway added another instalment to the pier when the London & South Western and the London, Brighton & South Coast Railways jointly made their own link via Ryde Tunnel—really a roofed-over cutting—in 1880. Now, St John's Road's wrought iron, its workshops and its signal-box from Waterloo Junction, serve ex-London Transport Underground cars which, should you wish to escape Ryde before you've arrived, take you from the pier-head to Brading and on between the downs to Shanklin. In the age of coal, before tube-train and hovercraft and diesel ferries, steam-packet met steam-train at the end of an ambitious timber and iron pier. Amusement machines on stalks and plinths displayed an architecture-in-miniature to rival that of Ryde itself. Pennies, as they dropped, chimed a frivolous Victorian tune, the band's brass brayed in the Eastern Gardens, and sovereigns fell into the laps of hoteliers and high-class shopkeepers. Now Ryde is half-decayed and half-restored. It lacks conviction, not knowing whether to conserve or develop. It quakes as Tesco takes off on its redundant airport and establishes an empire unlike anything Arthur Hill dreamt of in his High Street store. It shivers as Newport, which for so long it threatened to out-class, seduces Marks & Spencer to it. It quivers at the thought of oil-wells in its back yard. Committees argue the case for an illuminated pagoda spelling out "Welcome to Ryde", while the sea defences crumble and threaten to flood the railway tunnel. But, if there is any of the old assured arrogance and gimcrack charm left, Ryde will ride out the storm. It had the nerve to expand, sprawl, explode over the hill. Over the hill? Let's hope it has the guts to survive.

What would Henry Fielding think of it, 230 years on? Of the sand trapped by cunning breakwaters upon his hateful mud, of the rowing-club, the boating-lake, Bicycle Island's races, the amusements, the discos, the holiday flats and struggling hotels? Of the cabin-like room in which he, his wife and daughter were confined, he wrote, "I make little doubt but this apartment was an ancient temple, built with the materials of a wreck and probably dedicated to Neptune in honour of THE BLESSING sent by him to the inhabitants." After that, perhaps the fake half-timbering that lurks under the picture-postcard thatch of the Thatcher's End tourist-trap would come as a relief. Appley House, whose mistress regaled them with welcome hospitality, is gone; a park, golf-course and housing estate occupy the site where David Bryce built his seat upon capacious cellars and the proceeds of smuggling; he furnished it gaudily in the manner of entrepreneurs, filled his library with duplicate books clad, by a perspicacious bookseller, in different bindings, and died, discovered and undone, in the Fleet Prison. A later folly, Appley Tower, was made by the Paymaster-General Sir William Hutt out of fairytale stuff; it served teas to Victorian matrons who braved the walk along the Esplanade; now it sells sea-shell souvenirs, and still bears the motto which present-day Ryde would dearly love to own, *Vouloir est Pouvoir.*

Oak and hazel shade the shore path eastwards. Sand and mud-flats glitter. The Spithead forts squat, like ungainly fat follies, in water serenely ridden by liners and warships alike. Puckpool Point, "resort of fairies", is undermined by tunnels and guarded by a battery where mountings of its 1863–1950s weaponry can be seen, including those of its original 13-inch mortars, designed to pound the decks of enemy ships, and the only English examples of Armstrong Barbette mountings. The only weapon-training I have witnessed nearby was archery on Puck Hill.

Between Spring Vale and Seaview, where the toll-road runs behind the sea-wall, and in front of what is now the Flamingo Park, there was once a haven called Barnsley Creek with a flour mill at its head and Fairy Hill behind. After 1790, James Kirkpatrick's men embanked the Duver, scooped out collecting ponds, salt-pans and sluices, built the boiling house and housed his workers in Saltern Cottages of 1640. Cranes, peafowl, geese, flamingoes, macaws and cockatoos rule the territory around a mini-Niagara Falls. Now, sea-going vessels pass Seaview by, but amongst its bungalows and early Victorian cottages there persists a sort of marine architecture to suit

Rope Walk and Fort Ground: planking, weatherboarding and balconies, as well as solid stone like the double-fronted Georgian cottage that is now Lloyds Bank. The old Methodist Chapel is a boat-building shed, and some of Seaview Electricity Supply's street-lamps survive, with their huge, safe-like bases. Seagrove Bay was a pitch for bathing-tents and, in 1880, Francis Caws extended his elegant iron pier 900 feet out to sea. Four pairs of pinnacled standards plucked up the wire ropes that held its five spans in suspense. Pony-traps conveyed passengers along it from berths used by the Southsea ferry, the East India Company and Trinity House. The handsome, sinuous, quivering creature was totally destroyed by a terrible storm in December 1951. The Pier Hotel changed its name to the Halland Hotel, and was pulled down more than a decade ago. The reclaimed land on which it was founded was protected by sea-walls now shattered to rubble by the waves. Approval, given for an eight-storey tower block, has mercifully lapsed, but it seems that holiday homes of some sort will go up here. If so, let them be strongly and sensitively built. If not, let the breakers argue with the native rock.

Nature wreaks terrible revenge when man's urbanity overreaches itself. Dramatic changes have been witnessed on either side of the Old Fort's site on Nettlestone Point, where the sea once reached inland, and where man once reached out to sea. Construction and decay, development and recession alternately flatter and erode our ambition, like the tides that beat and retreat from the strongest bulwark of all: the tan and beige rock of Nettlestone. Its rag looks like choux pastry, as hard as the Purbeck Burr, but unquarried now. It is shrouded with wrack, and overhung by delicate and durable fronds of tamarisk.

12

BRADING HAVEN, BINBRIDGE ISLE

Eastward of us extended a large river or lake of sea-water, chiefly
formed by the tide, and nearly enclosed by land. Beyond this was a
fine bay and road for ships, filled with vessels of every size, from the
small sloop or cutter to the first rate man-of-war.

Legh Richmond   *The Young Cottager*

I saw them in their rest, a sojourner
Through a whole month of calm and glassy days
In that delightful island which protects
Their place of convocation ...

William Wordsworth   *The Prelude*

HISTORY IS Afragile creature. The evidence can so easily be eroded,
destroyed or abused. It can be exaggerated, exploited, suppressed or
simply lost. And when the evidence is gone, history is as persistent
or as evanescent as memory; and, sometimes, as fertile as the
imagination. Between Horestone Point and Node's Point the sea
jostles and abrades the pebbles of Priory Bay, beneath cliffs of
Bembridge Marls clad with sycamore, birch and fir. The gravels
topping the slopes hold a hoard of Palaeolithic implements, first
observed on the beach in 1886, sea-worn, but recognizable. I
remember walking the arc of the bay in a ferocious downpour, and
watching the frail lace of skeletal sycamore leaves being appliquéd by
storm-force to the stones' contours; the recent past's shadowy
pattern briefly imposed upon a fragmented but adamant bed-rock.
Uphill, above the trees, above lawns and terraces and steps, rain
lashed the vine-hung stones of The Priory: Sir Nash Grose's mansion
with its restored, thatched barn, gothick embellishments and clock-
tower, now an exclusive hotel. I wondered if the Blue Lady of the
Priory walked in this weather: an apparition attached to a 200-year-

old stuffed King Charles spaniel still kept, to quiet her, in a glass case above the stairs; a shade evoked and given an enlarged territory by smugglers of St Helen's. A ghost, real or imaginary, is a useful explanation of night movements and an effective deterrent against their investigation.

Above the massive, fractured sea-wall of Node's or Watch-House Point, there are no reported Old Stone Age spooks at the gravel pit, nor do the beacon-minders, or artillerymen who manned the Battery, haunt the place now. Old stones and ectoplasm have been exorcized by the gaiety of a holiday village. Successive monosyllabic signs on the way out exhort you to "Have ... A ... Nice ... Day". In the first days of June 1944, Nodes Point Battery looked out on the Fleet massing for the invasion of Normandy. They say that you could walk from the Island to the mainland on the decks of ships. Today there are just the four great stepping stones of St Helen's, No Man's Land, Horse Sand and Spit Sand Forts: circular masses of granite and iron founded on artificial islands, honeycombed with chambers and watered by artesian wells. The guns of these Palmerston Follies threatened Portsmouth with self-inflicted wounds, and when an attempt was made to blow them up with dynamite, the blast shook houses and broke glass on the Island. Napoleon III's posture was a false alarm, and not the first. Sir John Oglander of Nunwell noted that, in May 1624, thirty sail of good ships— Hamburgers—lay at St Helen's. A Captain Browne tried to make a prize of one, and had his brains beaten out for his pains. "He told me the day before that he dreamt his nightcap was full of earth and worms." Sir John took horse for St Helen's and met men fleeing inland, with news that a force of 500 or 1,000 had landed. The beacon was fired, Portsmouth alerted, the King woken and the Fleet dispatched "to succour the Isle of Wight, which was reported to be taken and myself and divers others to be slain." William Scott of Bembridge, in his ninetieth year, and five years bedridden, got up and fled three miles. But nothing had happened. No one had landed. Sir John threw the man who had ignited the beacon into Carisbroke Castle prison. There was a lot of explaining to do.

The view was dominated, in October 1982, by the antenna-like arms of the giant floating crane *Tog Mor* which, with an ease which belied the alarms and excursions below, lifted the carcase of the *Mary Rose* from the preserving mud and water of the Solent into the dangerous light of day. On 18 July 1545, a French armada of battleships, pinnaces and galleys neared the Nab, reconnoitred St Helen's Point, and engaged the English Fleet. Admiral D'Annebault's *Maitresse* ran aground and was abandoned off St Helen's. The next day, wind and loose cannon careened the *Mary Rose* over and her gun-ports, open for action, took in water. Anti-assault nets trapped the men aboard. Henry VIII watched her go down. A witness wrote, "And the King he screeched out like any maid, 'Oh my Gentlemen. Oh my gallent men' ... Drowned like rattens, drowned like rattens." The *Great Harry* was also disabled. The French made three simultaneous landings on the Island: near Bonchurch, where the Hampshire militia received a drubbing; near Sandown, where the Island militia under Worsley eventually drove them back to their ships; and at Seaview, where they took Fortground, drove the garrison to Priory Wood, burning Nettlestone as they went ... But we shall leave the last French attack on the Wight in desperate, delicate balance, to return to it, I promise, later in the chapter. In 1488, Sir Edward Wydeville, a supporter of Henry Tudor, who had returned from exile to the Lordship of Wight three years before, embarked at St Helen's with forty gentlemen and 400 stout commoners, to go to the Duke of Brittany's aid against the French king. One boy alone crept home with the news that the rest had died at St Aubyn-en-Cormeilles. Sir Theobald Russell, lord of Yaverland and commander of this military district, lost his life in 1340 when the French landed at St Helen's and pressed inland before being repulsed.

Retreating rapidly into the past, to 661, it may be that Wulfere, son of Penda of Mercia, entered Wight here when he laid it waste and won it from Wessex, ceding it instead to the King of Sussex. Island settlements called Woolverton, including the vanished one near Bembridge, may be a relic of his occupation—Wulfere's towns— though, only fifteen years later, Caedwalla of Wessex brought Wight briefly beneath his heel once more. Bede tells us that Wilfrid of York, Bishop of Selsey, was on the Island then with his clerks, Bernwin and Hiddila, and that Caedwalla granted 300 of its 1,200 hides to the bishop. Thus, tradition has it, the Jutish inhabitants were baptized at Brading before the unbaptized Caedwalla exterminated them. "So last of all the provinces of Britain," says Bede, "the Isle of Wight accepted the Faith of Christ." Henry Fielding added his own caveat:

"Nay, there is some reason to doubt whether it was ever entirely converted."

Nowadays the old church of St Helen's is just a buttressed tower at the north end of Duver. Its landward medieval details are intact, but the sea washes and lashes an east face incongruously shielded by white-painted Trinity House brickwork. A sea-mark with barely a toehold on the land, it was the focus of the twelfth-century Cluniac Priory whose chancel, hall, chambers, culver house and other buildings lay about it, fed by crofts and fields, woods and rabbit warrens nearby. It was a nest of French, and English, monks at the eastern entrance of the Island. It was dependent upon the Priory of Wenlock in Shropshire until, with the other alien houses, it was suppressed and its possessions granted to Eton College by Edward IV. Where monks laboured, fishermen brave spray and cast into the wind, golfers drive off, and resplendent dune and saltmarsh flora flourishes along the Duver, from whose southern tip the ferry makes across the harbour mouth to the sands of Bembridge and shores dark and thick with oak.

"Many thanks My Dearest Fanny for your two letters. From my heart I wish it was peace, then not a moment would I lose in getting to my Cottage." So Horatio Nelson wrote from St Helen's in 1798, "April 7th 8pm, April 8. Noon Wind SW.", urging his wife to take financial precautions. "I have bought a *new* Stockbuckle at double the price of the old one which 18 years past cost 1/6. Just 1 penny p.ʳ year ... You will take care & secure a few hundred pounds for if England to herself is not true our funded debt must fall, and with it who can tell *what*." St Helen's Roads was the ideal place for the Fleet to await a fair down-Channel wind, sheltered from the south-westerlies, before sailing to try and close with the French armada off Toulon in May, but finally catching and dispatching them, in August, at the Battle of the Nile. The previous year, the Navy in Spithead had mutinied violently over victuals and conditions. St Helen's, with its 200 inhabitants, its geese and cattle on the Commons, unknowingly was poised to grow ten-fold in 50 years as a victualling depot, supplying beef, mutton, birds, eggs, beer and especially sweet water. Off it, convict and crimped crews could be worked up to fighting fitness, while on shore a cannon warned local men of the predatory land-fall of the crimpers, the press-gang.

Intelligence had to be good, anyway, for men engaged in the unpatriotic brandy trade with the French. Sailors plundered the Priory ruins for "holystone" with which to scrub the decks to sea-worthy whiteness; they may also have used raw rock from the "very good quarey of fre stone harde by the sea side at Saint Helleyns pointe." By the time Nelson signed off, "May God Almighty protect you is the most sincere prayer of your affectionate Husband", the new church was already nearly 80 years old, though it would be rebuilt in 1831, with a chancel of 1862. It is half-way to Nettlestone, and to get back from it to the village you must cross a wide meadow to the vicarage and hack your way down the overgrown lane called Broomlands, past the Primary School, before you emerge on the Green near the red-brick pub and its delightful stone-built neighbour, The Sailors' Home. Here there is no close-knit, hierarchical, feudal sense of community. Eddington Farm preserves only a memory of Etharin, Domesday Book's name for St Helen's. The Green, with its ancient rights, has a democratic air. Non-conformist chapels gaze at one another across it, and the open space is haunted by less reputable dissenters: free-booters, owlers and Jacks-and-Jills of all trades. A tablet over one cottage door boasts that "Sophie Dawes, Madame de Fouchères, Daughter of Richard Dawes, Fisherman and Smuggler, known as the Queen of Chantilly, was born here about 1792." I should be tempted to add a new detail to the romantic myth—that of William Wordsworth, full of melancholy forebodings of impending war, blessing the baby girl, or Horatio Nelson patting the six-year-old, but already alluring, winkle-gatherer on the head as he went to buy his new stock-buckle—had not Marjorie Bowen systematically blown Sophie's cover in *The Scandal of Sophie Dawes*, and charted her progress from the House of Industry to Covent Garden, from gentleman's mistress to brothel-girl, French officer's wife and lover of the Duc de Bourbon, the last of the Condés. Jean-Charles de Fontbrune claims that her murder of the Duc was prophesied by Nostradamus in the sixteenth century:

> De nuict dans lict supresme estranglé,
> Pour trop avoir seiourné blond esleu,
> Par trois l'Empire subroge exanclé,
> A mort mettra carte, et paquet ne leu.

The compromiser of the restored French court, fortune-hunter and suspected murderess returned to England, a dropsical and pious benefactress; at St Helen's, the gravestone of her nephew, whom she probably killed, was "erected as a mark of affection by his aunt, Madame La Baronne de Fouchères." Dicky Dawes Gut, the channel between Dicky Dawes Banks on the charts, is a more honest memorial to the oyster-catching, lace and brandy smuggling family who made, in Sophie, the illicit big-time across the Channel.

The reclamation of history is a tricky business. An ineluctable tide of forgetting, like the great wave which swept away the ruined chancel of the old church in 1720, threatens to swallow the past. Some features, like the tower, survive; other things, like the bodies of seamen sewn into hammocks and thrown overboard, are washed up fortuitously—such anonymous comings-ashore are frequently recorded in the church registers between 1798 and 1815; most things sink, decay and contribute to the amorphous ooze, the sediment of all that has left no story, no history at all. What the landscape records is often deceptive or ambiguous. You might think that the marshes and fields between the harbour and Brading had always been so, until you notice the canalization of the River Yar, and the embankments keeping the sea out. When Nelson looked at Brading Haven at high tide, it was a great and beautiful lake running inland towards the gap in the downs; at low tide, it was a waste of slime, and folk would have told him that in the old days it was lush pasture studded with sheep and cattle, and that Brading meant "broad meadow". Its flooding was the inevitable result of a presumptuous attempt to draw, by sorcery, a rich but forbidden treasure from the well where it was concealed. The well spewed out a tidal wave instead; or so runs one of the stories. The stones for Stonehenge were said to have been brought to Brading Haven from France, and set up on Arreton Down before finding a home on Salisbury Plain. And, more possibly, the haven was where Alfred the Great's ships took on the Danes in 896, where all were stranded by the ebb and fought a bloody battle on foot, until the tide reached the Danish ships first and enabled the survivors to row away, though two were later cast on shore and hanged at Winchester.

The eastern Yar's source is close to the Island's southern tip. It flows from Niton northwards, under Bleak Down, past Great Budbridge and eastwards to the north of Sandown, where it narrowly misses running into the sea. In 1388, Sir William Russell drained the southern part of the haven, between Brading and Bembridge Downs, and built the Yar bridge and causeway. Thus, his manor of Yaverland was linked to Morton, and what the old maps call Yar Isle or Binbridge Isle could communicate with the rest of Wight. He may not have been the first, for some derive Bembridge from the Saxon for "beam-bridge". As the western Yar isolates Freshwater, so its counterpart, abetted by the erosive sea, almost makes an island of Bembridge's territory. George Oglander and Germaine Richards walled in North Marsh in 1562 and, in 1594, Edward Richards took in Mill Marsh and new land between Yarbridge and Brading so that a new quay at Brading was berth for vessels that formerly had anchored near the High Street. In 1620, Sir Bevis Thelwall took on Dutchmen, directed by Sir Hugh Myddleton, to reclaim 700 friable acres at a cost of ten pounds an acre. A steened well, near the middle of the haven, showed that men had indeed once dug there for water in the days before water was all. Dry land again, it was sown with corn, but a wet season and a high spring tide breached the bank on 8 March 1630, devastating houses, barns and mills. Sir Robert Worsley had new plans, and an estimate of £4,170, prepared in 1699, but they came to nothing. A letter of 1874, written by John Wilson Fardell, the Oglanders' agent, describes how the haven had been bought from the Earl of Yarborough by Sir William Oglander, to prevent its enclosure and thus preserve the watery prospect from Nunwell House; he discusses the bill, then before Parliament, for a bank between St Helen's Mill and Bembridge and a railway to traverse it from Brading Quay; he says that Lady Oglander would be satisfied with £10,000, and glad to relinquish responsibility for sea defences. The year 1878 saw Jabez Balfour's notorious Liberator Company make its attempt. An extra high tide smashed the wall and drowned some workmen, but at least the embankment was completed at a cost of £420,000. A marvellous photograph of 1879, taken from the downs, provides a panorama of the expiring haven, with work proceeding on the raw ramparts. St Helen's Tide Mill, whose mill dams you can walk on still, was then barely a century old, and finally closed in 1931. Its stones were re-used, after incendiary bombs razed it in the last war, for a private house on the site. Scandal surrounded the reclamation, and controversy involving the Bembridge Harbour Improvements Co.

followed the building of a modern block of flats, near the old railway station of 1877, which hardly improves the prospect from anywhere. Eight-wheeled carriages of the defunct Isle of Wight Railway rest on the Duver in their new guise as holiday chalets. The gasworks and St Helen's Quay, both of about 1880, were connected by a narrow-gauge railway. A remnant of track crosses the road by the works entrance.

Upriver at Morton, in the shadow of Brading Down, a merchant seaman by the name of James Thorpe was watching the ploughing in the autumn of 1879, when he caught children scrapping over shards of Samian ware. Sir Henry Oglander's excavations of the next fifteen years uncovered the footings, mosaics and rich pickings of Brading Roman Villa. Just when Brading's decline was being rubbed in by the evaporation of the haven that had made it a port, the backward reaches of its history surfaced in the share's wake. A grey corrugated-iron shed now covers the hub of the Romano-British estate. In Brading itself, the thatched and half-timbered, blancmange-pink shape of Osborne-Smith's Wax Museum asserts its sense of history with hard-headed whimsicality. Wax is malleable stuff and, in the melting-pot of what is claimed to be the oldest—and certainly the most cunningly "restored"—house on the Island, a mix of fact and fiction, history and horror story has been moulded into a titillatingly dressed, flesh-and-gore, show-biz impersonation of the past.

Sober searchers-after-truth should cross the road to the Old Town Hall. The first-floor room is full of town records and memorabilia, charmingly set out in unpretentious disarray. The oldest extant town charter is of 1548, but it refers back to Edward I's charter of 1280; though, as part of the manor of Wightfield, or Whitefield, the Kyng's Towne of Brading seems to have belonged to the Crown long before that. As the capital of the East Wight until the end of the eighteenth century, it was a focus for the people of small fishing-villages, such as Ryde, on fair days and festivals. Some old houses, whose diamond-glazed casements peer dazedly out from dark interiors at the tourist traffic, still retain in their timbering the iron rings from which tapestries were hung on high days. At the junction of the Mall and High Street, like a small Barbara Hepworth sculpture, the Bull Ring is embedded in tarmac, for "it was the custom from time immemorial," says Sir John Oglander, "for the

Governor of the Isle of Wight to give five guineas to buy a bull to be baited and given to the poor. The mayor and the corporation attended at the bull-ring in their regalia, with mace-bearers and constables; and after proclamation, a dog called the mayor's dog, ornamented with ribbons, was in their presence set at the bull."

The Town Hall's ground floor consists of the old stone lock-up, a miserable cell for miscreants, and of open eighteenth-century brick arches sheltering the stocks, whipping-post and, at one time, the Brass Gun inscribed, "John and Robert Owine brethren made this Pese 1549, Brerdynd". When the Reform Bill was passed, townsfolk dragged it to the summit of the down and set it off, but, being a reactionary beast, it burst. To us, it might have seemed a barbaric borough, but its Elizabethan burghers were responsible for paving the main street and for cleaning their own doors at least once a week; 4d was the penalty for ignoring the injunction "that none of the Town ... shall carry into Halfpenny Lane any soil or dirt, nor otherwise to ease their bodies there." Silt accrued in the haven, Ryde arose, St Helen's and Bembridge grew up, land was reclaimed, and at the end of the last century the Corporation was replaced by a Trust. The 1871 Directory portrayed "a very ancient and fast decaying town", but recent reorganization has restored Brerdynd's official town status.

Bishop Wilfrid founded the first Island church here, they say, on a pagan site underpinned by old bones of giant size; but St Mary's fabric is mostly twelfth-century, with later arches supporting a tower containing eight bells dating from 1594 onwards, and a stone spire. The church contains an ancient water stoup, and, amongst its niches, lancets and Purbeck marble pilasters, many delicious memorials. On her white marble mattress, the touching effigy of fifteen-month-old Elizabeth Rollo has slept since 1875. The figure of John Curwen, Constable of Porchester Castle, is incised, and was once inlaid before thieves got at him, upon a slab of 1441. In the fifteenth-century Oglander Chapel, oak effigies of Sir William and Sir John, placed there by the latter's will, sturdily recline upon tomb-chests; their rolled campaign mats, armour and Crusader postures are anachronistic; the seventeenth century romantically adopting the heroic aspect of the fourteenth. The Oglanders' male line died out in 1874, but a cousin took the name, and the present Lady Oglander lives in the converted stable-block of Nunwell House. Where Henry

VIII stayed and Charles I dined, twentieth-century ears have recently been assailed by the din of mock-seventeenth-century battles: sounds that would have seemed discordant to Cecil Aspinall-Oglander, author of *A Nunwell Symphony*, for they implied the selling-out of a family history reaching back to the Conquest.

Legh Richmond, recounter of humbler histories in his *Annals of the Poor*, is commemorated by a brass in the south aisle of the church where he was deacon and priest from 1797 to 1805. The Report of the Tract Society tells us that his improving and inspiring tales, translated into many languages, "led to most beneficial results in Nicodemia, successfully proclaiming the gospel in the city whence Diocletian issued his first edicts against Christianity." In the churchyard is a sundial mounted on a medieval preaching cross, and the soft shadow of Victorian sentiment is thrown across a perfect photograph of a young woman and two little maids contemplating the headstone of "Little Jane" Squibb, Legh Richmond's *Young Cottager*, who died on 30 January 1799 in the fifteenth year of her age. Richmond made her faith a legend, and you can walk, as he did, past the iron pump of 1764 and the Bull Ring, to her brick-quoined cottage of clunch and thatch off the Mall; but not forgetting to call in at the wonder of Brading, while it remains, the High Street sweet-shop with its ranks of sweetmeat jars, its antique counter, its gas lamps and its clutter: one of a species endangered even in my childhood; a relic of sweetness and soft light, surviving in an ancient borough desperately clutching at its last shreds of dignity.

Iron rings in Brading's old harbour wall have long let go of their moorings. Wall Lane leads you out, past the redundant cement-works, to the dry quay and across the inner haven on a breached embankment. Horse-tail, willow herb and osier give way to meadow, glowing with marsh-marigolds, from which larks and plover rise and cross and re-cross the sinuous, glinting Yar. Downriver it straightens, disciplined by banks and weirs, and bisects marshes chiming with reed buntings, reed and sedge warblers, clamorous with redshanks and the coarser cries of duck. Towards Centurion's Copse, great gorse bushes flaunt their lemon flowers and coconut scent, pitches for circuses of wrens. Luminous bluebells, elegant sallows, angular blackthorn flaked with blossom, reed-quills and rush-cushions furnish a kingdom for the imperious missel-thrush on his gnarled oak plinth. At the edge of the dark copse, a spring wells up like a moat protecting prizes of wild garlic, celandine and anemone that glimmer amongst undergrowth and soft, lopped debris beneath a canopy of hazel, oak and ash. They say no nightingales sing here; there is a thickness of atmosphere, penetrated only by the grating of distant pheasant. Here once was "a considerable city" on the banks of the haven, with a chapel dedicated to St Urian, the eighth-century holy man corrupted, by nearby Roman relics, to Centurion. So long as St Urian's well remained untainted, so long would Wolverton thrive, prophesied the hermit of Culver Cliff; one day a pilgrim from the Holy Land laid a palm frond at its lip, and the inhabitants stoned him for threatening its purity; his blood sullied the water, Culver's great bulwark, the Ness, fell into the sea with a thunderous, doom-laden roar, French invaders landed and their firebrands' hungry tongues consumed the town. This last, at least, probably happened in 1340; some stones of the chapel still stood in the seventeenth century, and trial excavations have revealed the footings of a big building, thought to have been the medieval manor house. On the copse's wet margins, orchis and iris are patrolled by iridescent dragonflies going, staccato-fashion, about their everyday aerobatics.

The drone of a light aircraft changes its register and drops to the bright, green expanse of Bembridge Airport, where Dennis Norman and Frank Britten started production of Islanders in 1967. Now, Pilatus-Britten-Norman products fly in every corner of the globe. Our road ignores the phalanx of grounded 'planes, passes between the Propeller Inn and the white bulk of Bembridge Farm's buildings, and makes for the path through Steyne Wood to the Windmill. Now in the custody of the National Trust, the windmill is the only one left on the Island. Atop a 30-foot stone tower, four sails were offered to the wind by a rotating wooden cap, and timber mechanism on four floors ground flour, meal and cattle-feed from the early 1700s to the First World War. When Steyne Wood Battery's embanked warren was manned by artillerymen, the windmill was a look-out. For J.M.W. Turner it was a viewpoint from which to sketch a full haven, with Brading and Ashey Down sea-mark beyond.

John Ruskin, Turner's champion, visited the Island once when he was ten. His tour included Appuldurcombe's art collection, and Nash's East Cowes Castle where his future hero had worked.

Since 1919, the centenary of his birth, Ruskin has been the presiding genius of John Howard Whitehouse's Bembridge School. There, his principles of Sacrifice, Truth, Beauty, Life, Memory and Obedience have been applied to the craft of making men and, lately, women. The Ruskin Galleries and Warden's Library hold the largest Ruskin collection in the world, comprising some 3,000 books, volumes of diaries and letters, and more than 1,200 pictures, from boyhood drawings to the last sketchbook of 1889, as well as works by Millais, Burne-Jones and many other contemporaries. If the school's architecture is informed by the spirit of Bournville and Welwyn Garden City, the rest of Binbridge Isle seems to have aspired, from Ruskin's birth onwards, to the condition of rural or suburban Surrey. Hill Grove, Tyne Hall and East Cliff evidence an outbreak of mansion-mania, and Lane End, creeping housing-estatitis. Respectability ruthlessly outflanked the raw settlements of farmers, fishermen and free-traders, though it should be said that some villas were founded upon less than fairly-gained fortunes. Symbolically, the Bembridge Marls were too slippery for the first church of 1827; they undermined its uprightness and faulted its fabric. The large, lanceted, stone-spired edifice of 1846 went up, and stayed up. Edward Wise, Dame Priscilla Attrill, Colonel Morton and the first vicar, Sir Henry Thompson, contributed to the edification of the peninsula. But when Mollie Downer, whose wise-woman's wisdom embraced every hedgebank and cellar and passage and cave and tub-raft that was receptacle for evil spirits, willed her home to the vicar, it was not well-received. The Witch's Cottage, where Downers had lived since 1558, was exorcized—and with it the unacceptable face of Bembridge history—by the simple expedient of burning it down.

Glass cases, frames and displays in the Maritime Museum are vivid with sea-going sagas, immaculately presented, but contained, confined. New pastel-washed cottages on Kings Road are designed for yachtsmen, not natives. Flats replace the arched blue and red brick of the railway station. The grand Royal Spithead Hotel is an annexe for Greylands International College. A man in the Pilot Boat Inn stoutly maintained that the residents of the big houses used to be "proper gentry, no side; but now they're all one up on the Joneses." The inn itself has acquired portholes in its hull, now that fierce competition for pilotage is extinct. Canned Muzack and the juke box compete with one another where Attrills, Smiths and Wallises once sang:

> 'Twas eighteen hundred and war-time,
>   As oft you've heard folks say,
> The pilot cutter *Amity*
>   Was sailing Bembridge way . . .

Skirmishes with French privateers have given way to wind-surfing; wrecking on the Bembridge Ledges to basking in tamarisk-shade on the wide sands. Multi-hulls oust Redwings, but Embankment Road retains some of the old flavour. On the margin of lake and marsh is a shanty-town of corrugated-iron and timber boat-houses, boat-yards and garages. Across the road lives a floating community in every degree and condition of houseboat: the gay, barge-style picturesque, the blank white hulk, the Fairmile motor-torpedo gun-boats stripped of their Napier engines, the rotten carcases, with flags and washing-lines, gates and little gardens, cats and dogs, caged birds and luxuriant boat-house plants. The harbour, a relict haven, is their parish, reverberating with the setting sun's play on ripples stirred by sail or swan.

Eschewing Ducie Way, Love Lane and Swains Lane, where the shade of native oak consorts with the deep shadow of cedar and fir, and the whine of lawn-mower nearly drowns the pluck of ball on tennis-racket; eschewing the pretentious and the merely comfortable, you can round Bembridge Point and make past Colonel's Hard for Ethel Point and the Lifeboat House, perched on the end of a pier which spans the ledge; home of *Jack Shayler and the Lees*, poised on the brink of its slipway. Joey Attrill, born in 1844, joined the first crew in 1867, was coxswain from 1878–1905, had three sons under his command at one time, and died in 1931 aged eighty-seven. The rock that has wrecked so many vessels was itself split for building; we are told that slabs, or "platenerston", were quarried at Bymbrigge in the fourteenth century. Sand and pebbles are retained by a waste of golden stone, weathered bald or mantled with sombre wrack, pungent swarming grounds for myriads of insects, and feast table for hundreds of martins and swallows. They flock in gusts, break into independent, intersecting trajectories like a hail of flèched arrows, and relentlessly buzz the beach. Above the mounds of weed, a lobster-pot squats on blue clay. The cliff's soft palette of pastel-coloured marls is roofed with marine gravel. But this, the Foreland of la Node, is protected by the hard, easternmost snout of Wight, the wickedly jagged lip of the Bembridge Ledge.

Beyond the coastguard look-out and the Crab & Lobster Inn, the cattle of Forelands Fields and Howgate Farm graze on a raised beach salvaged from the sea in the course of the Island's ups and downs, and defended by the Long Ledge beneath. Land-slips rife with willow and gorse, and patrolled by kestrels, are the plush back-drop for beach-huts and boat-houses, some with neat fences and planted plots. Where the band of Bembridge Limestone climbs the cliff, and therefore lifts its defences, the sea has bitten Whitecliff Bay out of the kaleidoscope of beds that are an eastern reflection of Alum Bay. Here, though, in the Bracklesham Beds, is a seam of brown coal, dug from a trench in the beach towards the end of the last century. The coal's fumey, brimstone breath did not make it a social success and, though the tide sometimes uncovers trench props, the wide beach is given over to pleasure. Holiday chalets on the cliff-top seem, in their frailty, to give back some of the white glare of Culver's chalk bulwark that walls the bay in. It dominates the view, glimpsed and glimpsed again between scrub oaks from the cliff path that leads to it from Bembridge School. As it grows ever more massive, the track dips and dives, hedged with hawthorn and ornamented with blackberries and red necklaces of bryony. It has been reclaimed by student labour, an assault course made passable by stout, elegant timber spans that bridge the chasms. As you climb up on to Culver, through an older, soberer cliff-edge hamlet of chalets, the treachery of the rocks is vividly demonstrated by the wreckage of wooden shacks on the beach below.

From Culver Down's summit, Binbridge Isle lies at your feet. White breakers worry at its south-eastern shore, while the haven that lapped Brading is shrunk to a shining harbour cluttered with multicoloured sails. Below the thatched shell of a cottage on Peacock's Hill, moorhens and ducks monopolize their pacific pond and the quiet road. A herd of 'planes seems to graze the airfield's green. But it was below, at the bay, that the French resumed their attack on 19 July 1545, in a renewed attempt to lure the Fleet from Spithead in unfavourable conditions. Contemporary versions of events, written by Martin du Bellay and Sir John Oglander, differ in their partisan emphases, but it seems that Seigneur de Taix landed his forces at Whitecliff, achieved the top of the down with, if they were like me, little wind left to resist an ambush of men on foot "and some horses mustered up among the carts". Many died, more were taken prisoner, and most driven back to their ships. The French Admiral landed reinforcements. King Henry ordered a strategic withdrawal, to draw them inland to their doom. Skirmishes punctuated their progress to Yar Bridge. The sky filled with the smoke of Bembridge and Yaverland, but the wind that fanned the flames did not come over to the English side; the naval attack could not be launched, so the enemy were once more repulsed. On board, next day, the French commanders sat in urgent council-of-war. They dispatched boats to sound the channels, they calculated winds and tides, weighed up the risk of wreck and the advantage of the enemy on his own ground; they planned fortifications and artillery positions. They could take the Island, and then step across to Portsmouth. But they would need to leave 6,000 pioneers and 6,000 soldiers to hold their Wight redoubt. Autumn was approaching. Instead, they would withdraw to Picardy and block the English reliefs' road to Boulogne. Regretfully, du Bellay wrote, "here was such a chance as had not offered itself for a long time. But God orders things as seem Him best." Sir John noted, "This was the last assault our Island had." How near, then, was a drastic twist in the Island's tale. But for French discretion out-voting French valour, the history of the Wight, and of England, might have been re-written in a big way. It was a near thing.

PART FIVE

AXIS

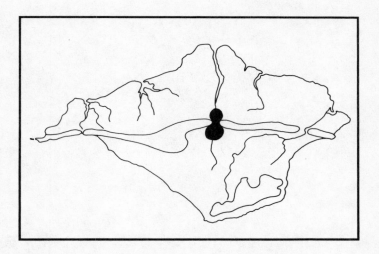

The long view, from Castle keep to Castlehold:
twin torrents once sliced through the Island's spine
and carved Carisbrooke's motte; waters that boiled
now trickle north to annex Newport town
and greet the tides which ride in from the world
to the Wight's heart, trade and war in their train.
All fluctuates, all treasons are repelled
but time's advance, down payment on each stone.

Power's tributaries run to lawlessness
through burghers', clerics', merchants', pirates' ground,
leaving Divine Right stranded behind bars.
Restored, decayed, re-built: the treadmill's round
where nothing keeps or holds, though time allows
the Castle like a trinket on its mound.

13

CAPITAL VERSUS CASTLE

Why, I can mind the time we onny used to goo to Nippert twice or
dree times in the year, wi' a carriage o' corn; and it used to take us all
day to git there and back. . . . There, we used to think ver near zo
much on't as people do now to goo to 'Merriky.
W.H. Long *Dictionary of the Isle of Wight Dialect*

I intend to walk over the Island East-West-North-South. I have not
seen many specimens of Ruins—I don't think however that I shall
ever see one to surpass Carisbrooke Castle.

John Keats *Letters*

THE YEAR 1545 did not see the French ruling the Island's roost from
Carisbrooke. Neither did 1377, though then they besieged the castle
and were repelled by Sir Hugh Tyrrell's men. Tradition holds that
they were also ambushed on Node Hill, now Upper St James Street
in Newport, and in Deadman's Lane; that the *Node* place-names on
the Wight are connected with the French, corrupted from "noddy",
meaning an idiot or a dead body—a term of abuse, or a title given to
places of slaughter. Or should we hark back to some long-forgotten
wave of Celtic invaders from the land of Nod, who imported the
veneration of Nodons, god of healing, patron of fisherfolk? Who
knows? The French left Carisbrooke Castle intact and withdrew
from the Island, paid off with a thousand marks to refrain from
further destruction—or paying 10,000 marks, according to a more
patriotic account, for safe conduct—leaving their dead and three
ravaged boroughs of Yarmouth, Newtown and Newport in their
wake. Exchequer records note the "entire burning, wasting and
destroying of the town of Newport, so that no tenants were resident
for upwards of two years." A hoard of 5,000 fourteenth-century
silver pennies was dug up in 1850, presumably hidden by someone

who did not live to recover his loot.

Newport, with Carisbrooke one mile to the south-west, is the centre of the Wight, the Romans' Meda; Richard de Redvers' "Novus Burgus meus de Medina" in its first charter of 1177; a New Port for Carisbrooke; "a town," as Camden wrote later, "well seated and much frequented populous with inhabitants, having an entrance into the isle from the haven, and a passage for vessels of small burden unto the key." The names were almost interchangeable; Newport River was Medina town's lifeline. Mount Joy swells up south of the town, gravestones speckling its flank like a petrified flock; and Carisbrooke's masonry stands proud on its mound, like a grandiloquent memorial. To east and west, the spine of the Wight is pierced by the Medina and by Lukely Brook; they define the town's site and make a small harbour where they meet at the river's tidal limit. A situation made for a commercial capital, overlooked and overseen by the castle's keep and curtain walls and bastions, the seat of power.

As the streams run on either hand, so my tale must run: here swiftly, scouring its bed; there sluggishly, relinquishing the burden it carries, the sediment of history. The story would fill many books and, as always, most of what I have seen and learned must remain unrehearsed. From Blackwater the Medina runs between hills, between redundant railway and busy road, between Marvell Farm and West Standen where stood, respectively, a college of secular priests and the free chapel of St Leonard. At Shide gapes the white wound of the great chalk-pit that supplied the Medina Cement Works. Larger earth movements were measured at Shide by Professor John Milne in the 1870s; his observatory pioneered the study of modern seismology. Bats roost in Shide's tunnel, and there are plans to make the pit a nature reserve. Prehistoric migrations and settlements, from the Palaeolithic to the late Bronze Age, left a legacy of implements and weapons at Great Pan. On the west bank, around Medina Avenue and Queen's Road, late Iron Age or Romano-British pottery sherds and a hut-site are a precursor of the Roman Villa complex, much of which lies under the houses and gardens of Avondale and Cypress Roads. The villa, discovered in 1926, seems to have been begun in the late second century on the site of a fire-razed predecessor. Its bath wing and furnace, mosaics and hypocaust heating, fragments of decorative plaster and Bembridge Limestone roof tiles, bronze bracelets and a woman's jawless skull, are evidence of the century-long rise and fall of the habitation. Saxon life left less evidence, though Domesday Book records seven mills in the manor of Shide alone. A mill house still stands there, as does Pan Mill on its own leat; and Ford Mill stood beside the pyle, or ford, at the bottom of Pyle Street. Roads have overtaken waterways, and the river, quay and harbour are overshadowed by the high-level Medina Way, by the huge roundabout at the bottom of High Street and, soon, by the relief road that will skirt Pan Mill and cross the river to link up with Medina Avenue. Concrete and tarmac have severed Newport from the sense of its site, but barges and boats still bustle modestly at the waterfront, and the water, its power untapped now, flows on.

Lukely Brook rises at Bowcombe Farm and runs through the beautiful valley, the Beau Combe. At Clatterford, the issue of Froglands' springs joins it, and helps to fill the mill-ponds and leats between the village and castle of Carisbrooke. Creeper-shrouded shells and Water Authority buildings now succeed to the titles of Castle fulling-mill, Kent's mill and Priory Mill, where cloth shorn from flocks on the flanking downs was bleached and bodied, and where bountiful harvests were grist, ground slow and small, to powers temporal and spiritual. At the western boundary of Newport, the brook is punctuated by Westminster, or Crocker's Mill which fulled cloth before it ground corn; Home Mill, where Unigate Dairies now dominate Mill Street; St Cross Mill, the "maltmelle" across the stream from the powerful St Cross Priory whose relics are buried beneath the remains of the railway; and the brewery site, from which barges laden with barrels were poled through a tunnel to the quay beside the reclaimed land of Little London. Like the Medina into which it runs, Lukely Brook is powerless now. Patronized by mallard and moorhen, it is an ornament to the lawn of the Eight Bells at Carisbrooke; a deep, dank drain channelled between concrete slabs for much of its passage through Newport's outskirts, though even there it provides a series of secret oases, at the backs of buildings or overridden by roads, where grass and moss and willow keep a foothold, and the occasional kingfisher and otter find a haven.

Carisbrooke Castle's oldest stonework is Roman, they said, until recent excavations showed that the lineaments underlying the Norman works are those of a Saxon burgh, or fortified settlement.

Pagan Saxon burials there, including that of a woman with her purse and bone comb, take the imagination back to the hardly imaginable time when Cerdic and Cynric fought, at Wightgarasburgh, for domination of the Island. There are badly preserved remains of an aisled Roman villa in the vicarage garden, signs of a Roman building under the fields at Clatterford, Romano-British roof-tiles and window-glass from a midden at Bowcombe, and Roman pottery and tiles disinterred on Bowcombe Down. Up there, we have already met Saxon burials, but Sir Edward Clarke, a Newport solicitor who helped Worsley with his *History* of 1781, submitted that Wightgar himself was buried in the valley bottom below the castle, in or near a pagan temple whose site Bishop Wilfrid sanctified, after Caedwalla's conquest, with a church dedicated to St Peter. Early in 1066, Earl Tostig and his fleet, closely followed by King Harold, his brother, had provisioned themselves with the fruits of the Wight before meeting, in opposition, at Stamford Bridge. The Conqueror, William the Bastard, came to Carisbrooke in 1085; his half-brother Odo, Bishop of Bayeux, had gathered a following here and planned to go to Rome and proclaim himself Pope. William arrested Odo in the royal hall; the latter's own guard carried him off to exile, leaving the king with the spoils. "Many of his bags were taken up out of the bottom of a river," wrote John Speed, of Lukely Brook perhaps, or the Medina, "where they were hidden, full of gold ground into powder." Even the mills of Carisbrooke could not make gold dust of Bowcombe's harvest, although it was the richest of the Island's seven royal manors. Two shepherds tended 689 sheep at Michaelmas 1269, and six permanent ploughmen worked 232 arable acres. Extra workers were needed at times, and meals were provided for 163 harvesters and for 41 ploughmen. When the ploughing match was held at Bowcombe, in the autumn of 1981, it was tractors rather than oxen that filled the valley, and many men intent on the same old, shortest, straightest trip between the forelands.

The Priory of St Mary at Carisbrooke and the Priory of the Holy Cross in Newport were hard at work and prayer before Newport streets and burghage plots were laid out. Domesday Book's Bowcombe church is supposed to have been superseded by St Mary's in 1120, but William Pavey noted, in 1719, "on the steeple, cast on the old lead, this date—1064. The sacristan told me that there had been an old bell in the steeple, with a Saxon inscription, and every letter crowned ..." The monks added the south aisle, with its massive circular pillars and cloisters to the north, in 1190. The chancel was destroyed in 1570, and the sanctuary before the old chancel arch was brilliantly re-designed by Seeley & Paget in 1967, on a base of Portland stone. Under the nave's rugged roof-beams is commemorated Sir Faithful Fortescue, warrior of Charles I, gentleman of the bedchamber to Charles II, who retired to the Island to escape the Plague, died at Bowcombe Manor in 1666, within sight of his old master's prison, and lies within hearing of the soberly decorated, and rare, Commonwealth pulpit. William Keeling, East India Adventurer and discoverer of the Cocos-Keeling Islands, was interred under the aisle in 1619 and celebrated, next to Lady Margaret Wadham's canopied stone tomb of a century earlier, by a picturesquely painted board:

Fortie and two years in this Veſſell fraile
On the Rough seas of life did Keling ſaile
A Merchant Fortunate, A Captaine bould,
A Courtier gratious, yet (Alas) not Old ...
Faith ſervd for Sailes, the Sacred Word for card
Hope was his Anchor, Glorie his Reward.
And thus With gales of grace, by happie venter,
Through ſtraights of Death, heavens harbor he did enter.

In the Lady Chapel, a blithely sublime modern Madonna and Child by John Skelton stands in an ancient niche, overlooking the thirteenth-century tomb of Aveline Passelewe, and the grave-slab of a monk with a crozier, perhaps an Abbot of Lyre. The lower half of this, weathered and defaced, was rescued from Priory Farm's pigsty in 1937. It reminds us that the monks here administered William FitzOsbern's gift to Lyre of the richest Island churches: Arreton, Whippingham, Newchurch, Godshill, Niton and Freshwater. Sixteenth-century graffiti, on the outside of the north wall, were inscribed by pupils of the village school that was run in the choir vestry. Old arches, half submerged now, led from the church into the Priory buildings. Coursed stone and flint, a pond with moorhens in their black habits, the names Priory Road and Priory Farm Lane, humps and bumps in orchard and field, and a convocation of crows in the wood are all that is left. St Cross, a cell of the

Abbey of Tiron, is even more thoroughly expunged. Its endowments included property in Newport, Hunny Hill, Shide, Brading,
St Helen's, Gatcombe, Shorwell, Northwood and Mirables. Its hall
and prior's chamber, pantry and kitchen, bakery and larder, granary
and barn, stable and plough-shed, dairy and wool-house made way
for St Cross House, quarried from their ruins. That was flattened, in
its turn, by the Freshwater, Yarmouth & Cowes Railway Company.
Names, like dying whispers, reach us still: St Cross Lane, Holyrood
Street and Lower St Cross Farm.

The Priory was founded in about 1120, not all that long after the
motte and bailey of Carisbrooke Castle were reared upon the Saxon
burgh that the Normans had strengthened for their first fortification.
Baldwin de Redvers, who had confirmed the grants to both Lyre and
Tiron, opposed King Stephen at Exeter Castle and then retreated to
the Wight in 1136. "Baldwin had a castle in it," wrote the chronicler
of the *Gesta Stephani*, "very finely built of stone and very strongly
fortified, from which, assembling a huge pirate fleet, he was trying
to weaken the king's power." He held out until Carisbrooke's water
supply failed, exiled himself to Anjou, then returned to hold Corfe
Castle against Stephen, and took part in the siege of Winchester. It
was his several-times-great-granddaughter, Isabella de Fortibus, the
last of the de Redvers, who restored and reconstructed the castle, and
encouraged the "new borough of Medina" with a fuller charter. If
the castle was father to Newport, and the priories mothers, the town
was a child who took almost half a millenium to grow to maturity.

"In digging lately in the beast market for stone to pave the town
with," Tomkins wrote in 1791, "a large reservoir was discovered,
and several pipes have likewise been found in the road from
Carisbrooke." Baldwin's supply, presumably the abandoned well
still to be seen in the Keep, may have dried up, but Carisbrooke was
Newport's surest supply of sweet water. The Town Well, now
paved over, was sunk at the junction of High Street and Pyle Street;
and other wells, like that recently uncovered beneath Castlehold
Baptist Church, are shown on a survey of 1611; soon afterwards,
Andrew James attempted to plumb the town with elm-trunk pipes,
like that in the Castle Museum, but water-carts continued to make
their trek from Carisbrooke for a century or more. Newport's
church was as old as the town, but it too was dependent, first upon

the Priory and then upon the Church of St Mary. Carisbrooke was the source of water and authority. The part of the town known as Castlehold had been retained by the de Redvers, and the bailiffs had no jurisdiction there; it became a sanctuary for ruffians and, in Sir Edward Horsey's time, for pirates. From the Black Death onwards, Newport suffered repeated plagues and pestilences. In the second week of May 1584, after 300 victims and many deaths, "God of his mercy, toke ye plage from the Towne to our great comfertt"; God's Providence House, now a restaurant, is on the site of the dwelling where the plague paid its last visit. This pestilence, and the jamming of the Carisbrooke Road with plague-carts, prompted permission for the town to open its own burial ground. The old Archery Butts became Church Litten. The water of life and a place for the dead were granted from above.

The 1620s saw Charles I reviewing John Oglander's muster and billeted troops on Arreton Down; and they saw more pestilence, including smallpox, imported from London. Newport was for Parliament from the start of the Civil War. Moses Read, the mayor, inspired by Harby, the Puritan minister, led the Newport train bands and 400 naval auxiliaries against the castle. The Countess of Portland, wife of the Royalist Governor, with her five children and her brother and sister-in-law, the Custodian, Colonel Brette, and his twenty men were besieged. The Countess appeared on the battlements, and offered a fight to the death to Moses Read and a lighted match to the cannon. Easy terms of surrender were at once procured; the Countess removed herself from the Island, and the Parliamentarian Earl of Pembroke was welcomed as Governor. A report drawn up for him by the Deputy Governor, Sir John Dingley, refers to the incorporation of the town by James I, and is eloquent regarding the burghers' mood: "But now they have gotten a charter to be a mare-town and have justices, a recorder, aldermen, &c., which ye other two mare-towns have not, as Yarmouth and Newtown; they will not be governed as those two mare-towns and ye rest of ye island are, which is very prejudiciall to ye country, and I wish it might be regulated. And in that town of Newport ye captain of ye island is clerk of ye market, and hath ye ordering of ye country; this town, notwithstanding, will take ye power to themselves, and hinder men from buying and selling at their pleasure." The view over the battlements was of a jumped-up town full of merchants too big for their boots. In September 1647, it became Colonel Robert Hammond's viewpoint, if not his point of view; though neither his nor the townsmen's positions were unambiguous. In November, as Hammond conducted Charles I to safe custody, it is said that one, Frances Trattle, offered the king a damask rose outside the Rose & Crown. A Christmas visit by Parliamentary Commissioners fuelled rumours of regicide, and Captain John Burley drummed up support for an attempt to free the king; Moses Read braved the crowd, mostly women and children with at least one musket, and reclaimed the town drum. Security was increased, on the Island and in the Solent. Burley was hung, drawn and quartered at Winchester on 3 February for, paradoxically, treason.

The regal coach, shipped across the Solent to the Islanders' wonderment, had swayed and pitched along Wight's tracks and highways to Nunwell or to Thorley. Now, the king was close confined, the garrison stiffened with crack troops, His Majesty's attendants purged. Kingship was in cold storage, divine right in suspense. The castle squatted on its source and stopped the well-spring of its power. It was the passive fulcrum for the see-saw of the English Revolution. "Here, where a donkey treads an endless water-wheel," Winston Churchill wrote of Charles, "he dwelt for almost a year, defenceless, sacrosanct, a spiritual King, a coveted tool, an intriguing parcel, an ultimate sacrifice." Intriguing indeed: Firebrace, Page of the Bedchamber and code-named "D", whispered through a hole behind the wall-hanging; Mary, under-laundress and code-named "B", transmitted messages in cipher. In March 1648, "L" (Richard Osborne) and "Z" (Edward Worsley of Gatcombe) waited with horses at the outer wall to convey the king to John Newland's "lusty boat". From the south end of the Norman hall, they heard the king groan as his body would not be extruded, where his head had passed, through the bars of his chamber window. In April sunshine, he played bowls with Colonel Hammond and Major Oliver Cromwell, his adversary's nephew, on the green made for his pleasure in the eastern bailey. In May, files and *aqua fortis* tried the bars of his new, secure lodging in the north curtain wall; bribed guards beneath his window proved fickle; his accomplices were ambushed; he closed the window on the darkness, and the freedom, outside. He read, he prayed, he wrote. Hammond, in his room, desired mightily to resign, and sweated under the burden of conflicting duties—to

Parliament, to the Army, and to the care of the king's person. September saw the king move to Sir William Hopkins' house, now the Sun Inn, in Newport, for the protracted negotiations misleadingly called the Treaty of Newport. The Commission was based at the Bull Inn, now the Bugle. The Royalists, whose cavalier behaviour provoked disturbances, caroused with forced confidence at The George, long ago demolished. The town was in ferment. Charles touched some for the king's evil and, in a parody of the panoply of state, tried to preside over the proceedings proper in the 30-year-old Grammar School. Escape plots, finally rejected by the king himself, came to nothing. The Army grew impatient with the extended charade and, at last, on 30 November, Charles was summarily roused and hustled to Sconce Point and Hurst Castle. The Solent had been, ironically, a *cordon sanitaire*, a moat. Exactly two months later, the neck that had strained through the bars lay on the block at Whitehall.

Andrew Marvell's *Horatian Ode* says of Cromwell that:

> ... twining subtile fears with hope,
> He wove a Net of such a scope,
>   That *Charles* himself might chase
>   To *Caresbrooks* narrow case.
> That thence the *Royal Actor* born
> The *Tragic Scaffold* might adorn.

Bronze figures of Charles I and James I had been removed from Winchester Cathedral and sold during the Commonwealth. They were buried in an Island garden, but at the Restoration they were repurchased and restored. Moses Read sent the Newport Corporation maces to London, to have the Commonwealth arms replaced by the Royal insignia. The town was granted a new charter by Charles II.

The plague hit Newport in 1665, despite the Wight being declared a protected area. Farmers abstained briefly from market, but in general business boomed. Upward's, provision merchants, set up in 1650 and, as Messrs Upward & Rich, celebrated their tri-centenary in 1950. Francis Searle, of the Brewers' Company, was one of the traders to issue trade tokens—"Ye Isle of Wight 1670 halfpenny F.I.S."—before Charles II issued official copper coin in 1672, and "The Candlemaker to His Majesty King Charles I", in Carisbrooke, was another. Mew Langton's Royal Brewery was to make its fortune from the 10th Regiment quartered, in 1799, at Parkhurst Barracks, John Keats' "nest of debauchery"; it supplied British troops as far away as China and, towards the end of the last century, sent India Pale Ale east in screw-top cans.

When Keats, staying at Canterbury House off Carisbrooke Road in 1817, began his *Endymion*, Nash's Town Hall was brand-new stuccoed brick: its great portico, pediment and Ionic colonnade, raised on the site of the old Town Hall and Cheese Cross, were not yet unbalanced by the Victoria Tower of 1887. St Thomas' Square, with the flesh and fish shambles at the north side, was the Cornmarket. Two hundred and more wagon-loads of grain rolled groaning in to every market, for export down the Medina, for flour, malt, starch and hair-powder manufacture. St James' Square, dominated from 1819 by the ashlar-faced Guildhall, was the beast market, crammed with pens, farmers, dealers, the staccato chanting of auctioneers, the bleating of sheep and belving of cattle, until it was moved to South Street in 1927. Folk can still remember the Spanish onion-sellers, the organ-grinder and his monkey, the knife-grinders and washerwomen, the base of the prosperous pile, represented by a monument in Church Litten Park, "To the memory of Valentine Grey The Little Sweep Interred January 5th AD 1822 In the 10th Year Of his Age". Mill Street was Horsemonger's Lane, and hooves clattered down Holyrood Street and on to the cobbles of Read's Posting Establishment where, now, hearses glide in and out of the stable-yard. Opposite, Yelf's printing-presses still chatter and sigh with the weight of words. Other things have lost their currency: James Kirkpatrick's signature, that I saw on a £50 Isle of Wight Bank note of 20 December 1891, was worthless ink after his bankruptcy; clay tobacco-pipes were made in Newport from 1654 to 1931, and lace-makers spun their webs in Pyle Street and at Coppin's Bridge, while, out at Broadlands, Messrs Nunn & Co.'s Manufactory established a world-wide reputation for machine-made French blond lace and employed 700 workers. After the oyster mortality of 1870, the Oyster Fishery Company brought an action in chancery against the borough, for discharging more sewage over the beds. Charter House's heavy-handed brick once sparkled as the mineral-water works of John Gould & Company; in the 1920s, it merged with Hibberd's of Ventnor and Randall's of Ryde, and moved to its Church Litten premises in 1931; it has since been acquired by

Beecham's. With it went the intricate terracotta moulding that was its trade-mark: the donkey on the tread-mill in the well-house at Carisbrooke Castle, winding sweet spring-water up into the light.

The nineteenth century saw Lord Palmerston, the Duke of Wellington and George Canning representing Newport in Parliament. It saw fortunes made and lost by merchants and lawyers. It saw balls and pageants, market-day excursions to view the farmers' daughters and, before Michaelmas, three Bargain Saturdays when farm servants were hired for the year, men in the beast market and women at Gape Mouth Corner. The successful drank to celebrate, and the rejected drank to exorcize the spectre of the House of Industry, or Forest House. This fête was followed, in November 1830, by fire-raising at Rookley and Newport, and a "strike" by unemployed labourers. The following year, farmers from Gatcombe were greeted derisively at a Reform meeting in the Cornmarket with cries of, "Dree cheers for the Forest House puddens!" "Why be we Forest House puddens?" "Because ye ha'n't got no raisins in ye."

The pious face of radical dissent showed itself in the proliferation of non-conformist chapels, though today the oldest church in Newport is the Roman Catholic, St Thomas of Canterbury in Pyle Street, whose red brick was given by Mrs Heneage in 1791. The Anglican church of St Thomas à Becket was pulled down. Its thirteenth-century stones, some blackened by French fires, were replaced with £12,000-worth of Victorian Early Decorated masonry. Prince Albert laid the foundation stone in 1854, it was completed in 1856 and, in 1858, it gained its independence from St Mary's. Traditional love-feasts, and unhappy disputes, between the town and its Carisbrooke vicars were at an end. The colours of the Royal Bombay Fusiliers hang, like soiled net, in the chancel where they were deposited in 1871, after 26 years' service. In the south chapel, the effigy of Sir Edward Horsey reclines on a woven mat with a horse's head at his feet. He died, at Haseley Manor, in 1582 in the arms of Douzabelle Mill, Captain of the Island, friend of pirates, Throckmorton Plotter, Privy Councillor and plague victim. His epitaph concludes, "And as he lived holily so he executed holily his particular duties." Elizabethan hypocrisy is counterpointed, in the north chapel, by exalted Victorian morbid eroticism: Marochetti's monument to Princess Elizabeth, "erected as a token of respect for her virtues, and of sympathy for her misfortunes, by Victoria R.

1856". The second daughter of Charles I, she died in captivity at Carisbrooke, and her lead casket was discovered by workmen, in 1793, under the old chancel floor. She lies now, healed of her deformities, beautiful and sensuous in white Carrara marble, with her hair spilling over the pages of her father's bible, within a niche like a casket of carved bars. An iron portcullis threatens to fall and trap the curling fingers of her outstretched hand.

Castlehurst, a listed building above Carisbrooke, blazed and smouldered and flared up again in 1982, only months after the Department of the Environment had refused the owners permission to demolish their derelict mansion, and roundly reproved Medina Borough Council for allowing its dilapidation. Newport still boasts its medieval street plan. Stone walls and footings of timber-framed buildings have survived centuries of ravaging and renovation, demolition and development. Pyle House, Chantry House and the Worsley Almshouses stand for old stories that cannot be told here. The Victoria Methodist Church's plum-coloured brick of 1804 is now, inside, the purple and gilt setting for the Apollo Theatre's dramas. But many listed buildings have been erased, much historic detail eroded and replaced by cheap rebuilding and raucous shop-fronts. The Troopers' Rest rests in peace. Hazards House, a contemporary of the Castle Inn, and its ghost were laid beneath the boring County Hall of 1938. More recently, a supermarket was left stranded opposite the desert of the bus-station. Commercial life is essential for the town's health; it has restored a sense of pride which should reflect itself in appearances. Marks & Spencer's has come to town and, taking a leaf out of Chiesman's book, must learn to live in tune with the street-scape. The award-winning Lord Louis Library has proved that adventurous building can consort harmoniously with the old. Pressure from the Isle of Wight Society, and practical restoration and re-selling of property by the Historic Building Preservation Trust, have given Newport ideals and examples to follow. Its late re-assertion of primacy in the Island, and the lack of 'sixties-style development, are now seen as blessings in disguise. Lugley Street and Crocker Street demonstrate that the response to decay should be to salvage and to rebuild sympathetically, rather than to demolish.

Medina Council's imaginative treatment of the Brewery site has shown how successful this approach can be: attractive flats ranged around a sheltered garden with two restored cottages and a malthouse have, by respecting the old, given new life to two acres beside Whitbread's depot and the Brewmaster's house of 1734. Quay Street's width and its mixture of small-scale Georgian and Dutch-gabled houses, of stucco and red-and-blue or grey-and-red brick, lend it an air of modest grace. Seal House is the only substantial merchant's house left on Sea Street, and five riverside warehouses of the eighteenth century were pulled down not so long ago. Hurst & Son's new buildings and walls sport iron grilles in traditional style, such as are retained by the old warehouses which have been transformed into the Quay Arts Centre, opened by Sir Hugh Casson in 1982. Vision and voluntary effort, aided by hard-won support from the authorities, have been rewarded at last with a focus for the arts in which the Island can rejoice. The opening Bill Brandt Retrospective exhibition was followed, appropriately, by a show entitled "Art and the Built Environment".

Beside the quay, Lukely Brook trickles on through decaying sluices, over debris including the obligatory old boot, and joins the Medina in the shadow of a fly-over. There, steam-trains used to wheeze across a sliding-bridge, that let vessels through from the brewery, to the lost station on the site of the lost Priory of St Cross. One remaining derrick shelters under its iron umbrella on the quay's stone expanse. Barges, dredgers, cruisers and fishing-boats lie up where the double-ended ketch, *The Bee*, built before Trafalgar, berthed well into this century; and where Shephard Brothers' Cowes Ketch, *Arrow*, sported yellow spars in support of the Liberal Party. When the sap rose in the forests, Smith's coppiced oak for the tannery and for export to Portsmouth; once, his horses shied back, and their wagon-load of bark dragged them off the quay, on to the barge they were loading, and into Medina mud. The river runs past a Squash Club now, and down to Dodnor's Medina Valley Centre and the Water Park by the redundant cement-works. Bicycle Island's cycleway runs parallel, from River Way, across Dodnor Creek and on to Arctic Road, Cowes. Across the river at Binfield is a fourteen-acre marina, the Medina Yacht Harbour, whose pontoons are cluttered with leisure craft and where the paddle steamer *Ryde Queen* glitters at night and throbs with the rhythms of its floating disco.

★

William Wordsworth and his friends were conducted around the ruins of Carisbrooke Castle, in the summer of 1793, by an old soldier who, promising them the sight of a still greater curiosity, doffed his hat. The poet recognized him as the man bearing up the dying General Wolfe at Quebec, in the painting by Benjamin West that had caused a sensation by depicting contemporary dress in the context of a pietà-like composition. The aged guide thrilled with his immortality. J.H. Reynolds, immortalized in Church Litten as "The Friend of Keats", listened to lines that his friend had been wrestling with, as they sat in "a delightful place I have set my heart upon, near the Castle". Keats drew breath, and began, "A thing of beauty is a joy for ever . . ." He had written to Reynolds that "the Keep within side is one Bower of ivy—a colony of Jackdaws have been there for many years. I dare say I have seen many a descendant of some old cawer who peeped through the bars at Charles the First." Since that time, the castle's strength had seeped away, with the brook, to Newport. Its grandeur was romantic; past power had become the present picturesque. A queen was yet to come with her sceptre and touch the enchanted isle, but no king or lord, warden or governor, captain or custodian, no Prospero with his staff ruled the Island as of old. Keats' ivy has gone, but the grandeur that Turner painted remains. The castle has moved from the sphere of pragmatism into the sphere of art; it enthralls, but no longer holds in thrall; it is a thing of beauty which the Department of the Environment strives to maintain as a joy for ever. It dominates the Island as a sculpture dominates a garden: Gianabelli's outworks and arrow-head bastions, that Sir George Carey commissioned against the Spanish threat; the twelfth-century curtain walls; the drum towers of the gatehouse, topped by Sir Anthony Wydville's work, but deprived of their fifteenth-century oak doors since 1966; the Elizabethan well-house where donkeys tread water up for tourists; and the ruins of the north range. The chapel of St Nicholas de Castro was probably founded in 1070, rebuilt in 1738 without the armoury that had been its attic, dismantled in 1856, reconstructed by Percy Stone, when Princess Beatrice was Governor, on the 250th anniversary of Charles I's execution, and decorated as a War Memorial in 1919.

The Governor's lodgings have undergone many renovations. Isabella de Fortibus installed a chapel in the Great Hall, and an inquisition taken shortly after her death in 1293 describes "a house in the same castle, to wit, one hall, four chambers for straw adjoining the hall, with a solar; one small church and another great church, which churches are supported at the expense of the Abbot of Quarrera; one large kitchen; one chamber for the constable, with a solar to the same; one small chamber beyond the gate, and another under the wall; one great chamber with a solar; one house which is called the Old Chapel; one larder; one great house which is called 'the bakehouse and brew-house', in which there is a granary at one end; two great stables for corn and forage; two high towers, built with the chamber for straw, and two other towers built under the wall; one house with a wall for a prison; one chamber near the same. Richard le Porter hath the custody of the prison in the castle; and of the castle gate, for the term of his life, by charter of Isabella, formerly Countess of Albermarle, and receives yearly, from the manor of Buccombe, his pension." Here Piers Gaveston, favourite of Edward II, briefly lorded it before his terrible death at Warwick. Here, a fourteenth-century Captain dug a tunnel from the house to the keep. Here, Richard Worsley kept his armoury of five iron slings, fowlers and double-basses, 140 hagbuts, powder, bows, arrows, javelins and bills, ready for the French; in the second year of Elizabeth's reign, men with land to the value of twenty shillings were required to provide one arquebus, and Worsley installed an arquebus-maker in the castle to maintain them.

On the Field of Arms, the adventurers Sir Edward Horsey and Sir Robert Holmes reviewed their garrisons, though they lived, respectively, at Haseley and Yarmouth. Between their incumbencies, parade-ground had become bowling-green and, in 1906, it was the scene of a great market mounted to raise money for the restoration of Carisbrooke Church. In 1965, Queen Elizabeth II installed Earl Mountbatten as Governor amid colourful pageantry, and September 1979 saw it full of mourners at his memorial service. In the days when they had power, Governors were not necessarily so popular. Thomas, Baron Culpeper and John, Baron Cutts both enraged seventeenth-century Islanders by exceeding their powers, interfering with the corporations and casting subjects into the dungeon. Culpeper neglected the defences and his kinsman plundered vessels at Cowes, but Cutts made a pact with the Island gentry and became popular, with them at any rate, through his lavish hospitality. Both men repaired and reappointed the Governor's residence. Now, it is a museum full of the history of the Wight: you can ascend Baron Cutts' staircase, set in Isabella's old chapel, to see John Nixon's paintings of the Island in Napoleonic times; you can check Chessell Farm's eighteenth-century accounts, and Tennyson's effects; you can see a crouching-man corbel beam from the old George Inn, and relics of Charles I—a cipher letter to Edward Worsley, a bible and prayer book, a lace cravat, a nightcap, and a locket of his hair donated by Queen Victoria.

In the chambers that the king first occupied, I talked with Jack Jones, the museum's curator and author of the vivid, and scrupulously documented *The Royal Prisoner*. The sun had been shining gloriously, but as we talked of the crisis once embodied in the room where we sat, the sky darkened dangerously, golden light turned to gloom, and the heavens opened. When I left, the long worn flight of steps climbing the motte seemed to stand for the sorry progress to the Tower, and the summit, crowned with a decapitated keep, for regicide. I was drenched before I reached my lodgings, near Keats', in Carisbrooke Road.

William Jones, chaplain to Shakespeare's patron, the supposed Friend of the Sonnets, mourned the death of his master with poems entitled *The Teares of the Isle of Wight, shed on the Tombe of their most noble, valorous and loving Captaine and Governour the Right Honourable HENRIE, Earl of Southampton* . . . Elizabeth had imprisoned him for treason. The performance he had ordered, of *Richard II* at the Globe Theatre, treated too starkly of the toppling of a monarch for her comfort. James I released him, and gave him the Island to govern. His castle made its début as a theatre in 1982, when Theatre Set-Up produced *The Tempest* in the courtyard. Here, Prospero ruled the Island, and Trinculo, seeing Caliban sprawled under his gaberdine, exclaimed, "This is no fish, but an islander, that hath lately suffered by a thunderbolt." Stephano was king in his fantasy, and drunkenly held sway. And Caliban grumbled rebelliously at Prospero, "I am all the subjects that you have, which first was mine own King: and here you sty me in this hard rock, whiles you do keep from me the rest o' th' island."

PART SIX

RICHES

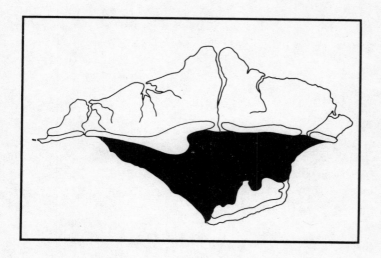

I clamber down the canyon of Whale Chine
to the red apron of the Bay of Death.
The tide worries at hulks of fossil pine,
withdraws with bones of reptiles in its teeth
and shifts old ballast towards Rocken End.
My head silts with sad tales, and tales untold
of legendary cargoes, foundering land
that tumbles at my back, panned, drowned Wight gold.

Inland, riches outcrop between the downs:
luminous fields like emeralds and ores,
clusters of boom-time Jacobean stones;
broad road to shores crusted with villas, bars
and neon piers on pins, whose antique pride
still takes the treacherous waters in its stride.

14

VILLAS & VULGARITY

We seem to have been more fortunate than you, having had almost constant sunshine since we arrived at Sandown. . . . This place is perfect, reminding me of Jersey, in its combination of luxuriant greenth with the delights of a sandy beach.

George Eliot *Letters*

Our joys are ended oversoon;
Short is the breathing time for laughter;
Bless Shanklin for your honeymoon!
And let the children love it after:
So when the daytime fades to night,
And hope alone is in our keeping,
Our home will be the Isle of Wight,
And Spring will bloom while we are sleeping.

Illustrated Sporting and Dramatic News

WHEN THE GREAT Plague made its progress through Newport's streets, taking its terrible pleasure in the inhabitants' flesh, Lady Richards of Yaverland determined to escape the smell of putrefaction and a pestilence which was no respecter of persons. She left her town house with her handkerchief clutched at her mouth, breathed freely on the downs above Arreton, Ashey and Brading, descended to the bridge across the Yar and came home to Binbridge Isle. Yaverland was a haven of health, its cool stones and green crops rooted in red earth above the azure arc of Sandown Bay. The manor house's stately gables were not half a century old then, built on "beer-money", Gervase Richards' victualling of the Fleet at St Helen's; window mullions and transoms glowed with the pride of workmanship; Lady Richards would pass thankfully between the caryatids, nick-named Nero and Cleopatra, with which the wood-carver had adorned the inner door, up the grotesquely magnificent staircase, and go to her rest unplagued by mortal fears. The house in the land of boars, Evreland, incorporates fragments of its early twelfth-century ancestor, and the story goes that its chapel, the church of St John the Baptist, was removed here, whole or in part, from Centurion's Copse. Its south doorway, with a grinning monk's head, and the chancel arch enriched with chevrons, are late Norman too. A workman digging a trench for the new north aisle, in 1889, uncovered a cooking-pot of the period, now on display. The Norman church squats before the Jacobean house, and the group is completed by grand farm buildings, including a barn which cries out for doves to perch in its wind-holes. Lady Richards' homing flight did not have a happy landfall. Her tenants may have been in awe of their lady, but they were more in awe of the pestilence raging in far off Nippert. They had no use for it. Lady or no Lady, she might as well have been a leper. They barred her way.

The population has slipped away from Yaverland. The ground slopes to the marshes north of Sandown and, in the cliffs, is displayed the complete declension of the Cretaceous, the repertoire of rocks which comprise the southern half of the Wight. The Chalk of Culver cliff tops the bill, supported by the Upper Greensand, or Island freestone. Then comes a gully of Gault Clay, the "blue slipper" which keeps so many Island landscapes on the move. The gritty, clayey, sandy, pebbly browns of the Carstone are followed by the white and yellow Sandrock series, and all the deep ochres, laced with green and grey and blue, of the Ferruginous Sands upon which the most fertile soils are founded. Next, Atherfield Clays and Perna Beds lie upon the Wight's oldest rocks, the murky rainbow of the Wealden, lately called the Vectis and Wessex Formations; the Shales are a sandwich for the Beef-bed, Oyster-bed, Cyrena-bed, and bands of iron- and sandstone, while the Marls beneath are most famous for bones of great reptiles which they give up to the tide. Many, including an almost complete iguanodon skeleton, have been sent to the Natural History Museum at South Kensington; others, like the skull fragment of the small dinosaur Yaverlandia, are displayed in the Museum of Isle of Wight Geology at Sandown; and too many are excavated surreptitiously and smuggled out to European museums that will pay high prices for such prizes.

The Wessex Marls drop to sea level. Holiday-makers paddling on the canoe lake are protected from the waves by a frail embankment comprising Culver Road, the sea wall, and sands trapped by a garrison of groynes which prevents the invasion of the marshes and the marriage of the Yar with the English Channel. All seems secure on a pacific summer's day, but stand there in the teeth of a south-easterly and you will see the anger of which Sandown Bay is capable: breakers beating at masonry, the roadway awash, and spume lashing the lake's surface. The defences were breached in the 1820s, the marshes transformed into a salt-water lake, and thousands of tons of pebbles pounded inland. It is a vulnerable place, subject to sea-borne attack and hostile landing.

Sandham Castle is a model built for child's play in a prospect of putting and bowling greens. Henry VIII's original, quadrangular with four towers, had an establishment of two dozen men equipped with eleven brass and iron pieces, 78 hagbuts, bows, arrows, pikes and bills. Less than a hundred years after it was built, Sir John Oglander supervised its demolition, before the sea did the job first. He and Sir John Dennis advised that its successor should be well inland, but the engineers insisted that eighty yards from the shore was far enough. Its moat and corner bastions repelled a force of privateers during the American War, but could not keep the sea at bay. The waves undermined its foundations and demolition began in 1901; a ditch that fed the moat's north side is all that is left. St John's, Yaverland, had long been a garrison church when, in the 1860s, Bembridge Fort's raw white ramparts were raised, and when Redcliff Battery and Yaverland Fort were built. The Battery, near first-century remains of a possible Roman fort, saw service as an anti-aircraft gun-post in the last war, before falling into ruins on cliff-top and beach; and Yaverland's red brick is now submerged beneath a holiday camp. Sandown's last fort was built of interlocked granite and armed with ten heavy guns in 1866; it proved impossible to demolish, and its present denizens are kept behind bars or glass, for it is the Isle of Wight Zoo. Where great reptiles grazed the swamps, small ones now blink at sightseers and big cats prowl. Jack Corney, the custodian of the fort, regularly takes the air along the esplanade with his puma on a lead.

Fantastical cages and cunningly designed pens for poultry and fancy breeds of birds were constructed at Sandown towards the close of the eighteenth century. Not that the name Sandown was then known; Domesday Survey's Sande had become Sandham, a small settlement of cottages between Royal, or Ryall Heath and the sand; the domain of sheep that lived off the commons. The 1801 Ordnance map names only three buildings: first, Sandham Fort; second, Sandham Barracks, built on the heath for 300 men during the Napoleonic Wars, replaced about 1850, with accommodation for twice that number and a military sanatorium, and now transformed into the South Wight Leisure Centre, opened by Prince Michael of Kent in 1982; and third, Sandham Cottage, which the radical John Wilkes called his villakin. George III chose Weymouth as a watering-place; his enemy, "Liberty" Wilkes, arch-agitator against the *ancien régime*, chose to resort to Sandham from 1772 onwards, as a change from the Tower, the King's Bench Prison and exile in France. Sixteen years later, he leased his villakin and set about adorning it in excruciatingly elaborate style. The Tuscan Room bore a tablet, "Fortunae Reduci et Civitati Londiniensi, P. Johannes Wilkes, Quaestor, 1789"; the sitting-room was dedicated "To Filial Piety and Mary Wilkes"; and a Doric column in the shrubbery, after Virgil's tomb, was inscribed to his friend, Charles Churchill, and kept stocked with the finest port in the poet's honour. The Knightsbridge Floor-cloth Manufactory provided material for pavilions disposed among a profusion of flowering shrubs and fruit-trees. The dramas of his London life over, Wilkes created a stage-set here, a local sensation whose chief actor was himself, in his old-fashioned metropolitan costume: blue and gold, or scarlet long-coats, frothy with lace and ruffles, adapted to the country with down-to-earth long boots reaching above his knees, and his powdered queue tied in a bag. He was a wonder of the Wight, strutting between Sandham hamlet and Shanklin village each summer, playing lavish host to sophisticated visitors and buying as many birds as the local urchins could catch, to stock his aviaries and dove-cotes.

When Wilkes died in 1797, the land backing up from the broad bay was marsh and heath, with farms at Yaverland, Sandham, Black Pan, Cliff, Merry Gardens—from *merise* or cherry—Nineham, Hyde, Languard and Shanklin Manors. Sandown, with its military installations and fishermen's cottages, carried on as before. In 1845, Christ Church, with its unusual northward altar, was built to serve the barracks and the village. The next decade or so saw all traces of Wilkes' vulgarity erased; Venables says that "some of the villas which have recently been erected along the cliff, nestling in their low plantations, are in excellent taste", though water was still carted from the Yar. Until the mile-long Esplanade gave the town its front, the gardens of villas ran down to the sands. In 1867, Henry Maund, MD, MRCS, extolled the virtues of the air and the low mortality rate, a theme echoed repeatedly in newspaper reports by the Medical Officer of Health. Lodging-houses sprang up. Four European monarchs resorted here in 1874. Across the road from where the independent Library and Geological Museum was to be built in 1905, the little Gertrude Chataway stayed in the summer of 1875. She watched her neighbour emerge on to the adjoining balcony, imbibe the sea breeze and briskly step down on to the sands. He was Lewis Carroll, and it was his third summer at Sandown. They fell for one another, and Carroll conjured endless stories for her as they sat on the steps between garden and beach. He was writing *The Hunting of the Snark*, in which the Bellman identifies the Snark's five unmistakable marks, of which:

> The fourth is its fondness for bathing-machines,
>   Which it constantly carries about,
> And believes that they add to the beauty of scenes—
>   A sentiment open to doubt.

Fifteen years on, when he wrote to invite Gertrude to Eastbourne, he enthused, "It would be like having my Sandown days over again."

The year 1878 saw the Sandown scene dramatically augmented. The pier was opened, and the 900-ton 26-gun frigate *Eurydice* went down in a squall on her return from a West Indian training cruise. Gerard Manley Hopkins mourned her:

> Too proud, too proud, what a press she bore!
> Royal, and all her royals wore.
>   Sharp with her, shorten sail!
> Too late; lost; gone with the gale.

Of the crew of 300, only two were saved. Fletcher and Cuddiford pose resolutely, but with haunted eyes, and clutch a cork float and life-belt, in the photograph they presented to the Ventnor doctor who revived them. Seven of the drowned were buried at Christ Church. The pier, with its elegant gatehouses and elaborate iron seats, was lengthened in 1895, and given a grandiose pavilion and a landing-stage for steamers. It became a place, not for simply enjoying sea and scenery, but for amusements, stalls, concert parties and excursions or, in Percy Stone's words, "an undesirable accommodation for nigger troupes and hungry trippers". Station Road gained its Art Deco Rivoli Cinema in 1921, and the 'thirties saw the monstrous Pavilion Theatre straddle the sands.

More recently, the uncompromisingly barbaric pier façade, with bars and amusements, has been added; to reach the pier proper you have to make a claustrophobic, ear-shattering, purgatorial progress through some sort of unholy marriage between Soho and Mission Control. Once outside, sun and wind and sea somehow conspire with the stalls, pink elephants and multi-coloured fairground rides to make more innocent gaiety. On the concrete prow of the pier, below the glitter and forced glamour, men and boys let hours and days unreel. They cast baited lines over and over again into the shining bay, hoping for an answering tug from pollack, grey mullet or pout, weaver, garfish or bass, and that gratifying instant when shimmering fins and scales break surface. The sea seems sated. It eases itself in and out over the sand. Today is calm and bright, and it is merely regaining its appetite for the bite-sized mouthful of gastronomic delight which the bay lays out before it: the light meringue of Culver at one end of the board, the Dundee cake of Dunnose at the other, the long coffee and chocolate and caramel layer-cake that is the cliff between, the white-iced hotels and flatlets, and the villas like coloured fancies.

In winter, the town looks battered, shop-soiled and sad. The souvenir emporia are closed, cluttered with gaudy, unseasonal fruit; many are 25 years out of style. Ice-cream signs are jaded, and café menus are curled and faded, shutters and galvanized padlocks belying offers of half-price tea to OAPs. Grey and blue-rinsed heads cluster behind the plate-glass picture windows along the front, taking advantage of off-season rates. Their eyes look yearningly at the breaking sea, and uncomprehendingly at the rainbow-headed, steel-accoutred, brass-studded young ones who traipse and strut along the sea-wall. Neither they nor the place find anything to do. As Edward Thomas advised, "It ought to be packed up and stowed away somewhere for the winter." Like Wilkes' floor-cloth pavilions, perhaps. For those who actually live here the perspective is different. Out of season, they can reclaim Sandown from the grockles. The radical writer, Edward Upward, revered by Auden and Isherwood, lives in a solid house near the station, and talked to me there of his

Carisbrooke Castle

Quay Street, Newport

The *genius loci*, Luccombe Bay

The Crab Inn, Shanklin

Luccombe Bay

Compton Bay

Shanklin Pier

Stubble and
vineyard,
Adgestone

North Court

The Long Stone

St Peter's Church, Shorwell

Below Brook
Hill

Appuldurcombe
House

Godshill
Churchyard

The Chalet Hotel, Ventnor

The Manor House, Ventnor

Maple Cottage,
St Lawrence

St Lawrence Old
Church

Isle of Wight
Glass

Reeth Bay

St Catherine's Point

love for the place. "Nowhere else I have ever been has seemed more beautiful to me than this house and this town," he wrote in *No Home but the Struggle*. "The air here and the sea may not have quite the marvellousness they seemed to have in my boyhood, but my sense of well-being is steadier, if less exalted than then."

Where post-chaise horses used to graze on Lake Common, 'planes, including crop-sprayers and micro-lights, take off from Sandown Airport. Lake itself, once a hamlet in Blackpan Manor, has become a runway between Sandown and Shanklin, and been obliterated on those maps which designate the conurbation above the bay Sandown-Shanklin. Lake got its first church secondhand from Gatten; the corrugated iron edifice arrived on a farm cart. From Battery Gardens, you still get the impression that all is trees and cliffs and expansive sands towards Little Stairs and Gallows Hill. Despite an appeal by the Island's MP, a century-old landmark on the cliff-walk, a Monterey pine with giant cones and a preservation order on it, was wantonly felled in 1983. Nothing came of Edward Penruddock's petition of 1661, for a lighthouse at Dunnose, so that the romantic grimness of that, the furthest headland, is undiluted. Dr Fraser, physician to Charles II, is supposed to have discovered Shanklin's chalybeate waters, but it was not until the second quarter of the last century that the concentration of housing increased, above and below the cliff, to the dilution of the picturesque. Hassell remarked, of the cottages and cottagers, that "the habit of living among fine scenery had given a taste and an eye for the picturesque to the lowest classes". He meant that he had an eye for the vulgar, in its best sense; overners imported the very notion of the picturesque. Keats began by liking it in 1819: "Our window looks over house tops and Cliffs on to the sea, so that when the Ships sail past the Cottage chimneys you may take them for weathercocks. We have Hill and Dale, forest and Mead, and plenty of Lobsters." He worked hard at *Lamia, The Pot of Basil* and *The Eve of St Agnes* in his "little coffin of a room" at Eglantine Cottage, but, he wrote to Fanny Brawne from Winchester, "I began to hate the very posts there—the voice of the old lady over the way was getting a great plague ... I am getting a great dislike of the picturesque."

William Colenutt built the Fisherman's Cottage at the mouth of the Chine, and catered to commoner appetites by cutting a path up beside the stream and the waterfalls that had carved the cleft. He cultivated its wild beauty and charged people for the privilege of enjoying it. A *Punch* writer was to report, in 1873, that "you wander on under overhanging trees, and by the side of glistening rocks, you shudder at the depth below, and you gaze enraptured at the glimpse of blue sky through the fretwork of foliage above, and you soliloquise aloud to yourself . . . and at this moment my eye lighted on a young and lovely brunette standing pensively by a rustic bridge gazing out toward the sea. . . . She said—'Yes, there ain't a many people 'ere today, and I ain't done much. It's sixpence is the regular thing, but it's what you like to give the gal, Sir.' I shuddered. The romance had vanished." Hollier's Hotel was built in 1824. Longfellow left a lively sketch of it: "Our windows look down upon the quaintest little village you ever saw. It is all like a scene on the stage. The landlady is a portly dame; the head-waiter, a red-faced Alsatian; and when the chambermaid appears, you expect she will sing instead of speak." He also left his doggerel on the fountain:

> O traveller, stay thy weary feet;
> Drink of this fountain, pure and sweet;
> It flows for rich and poor the same . . .

Some hope. The lifetime of George Tullege, Shanklin Farm's shepherd, who was born at the beginning of the Napoleonic Wars and died in 1877, saw a transmogrification of his world. His cottage was demolished in 1874, to make way for the Upper Chine, and a studio portrait shows him with staff and smock and sidewhiskers, looking benignly bemused. The census return of 1831 reports a "continual influx of strangers . . . capitalists, bankers, professional and other educated men." Dickens sends the mutual deceivers from *Our Mutual Friend* on honeymoon here: "Mr and Mrs Lammle have walked for some time on the Shanklin sands, and one may see by their footprints that they have not walked arm in arm . . .".

Francis White Popham, the lord of the manor, stipulated that "only single or semi-detached villas were erected and that a portion of the ground was reserved for a garden or lawn", but his excellent intentions were to be overtaken by watering-place mania. Villas, little grand houses and *cottages ornés* sprang up on the cliff-top, though set back a little from what is now Keats Green and the Eastcliff Promenade, to give free rein and a fast gallop to Excise officers trying to keep up with the import trade at Small Hope or the Chine or anywhere in between. The Royal Spa Hotel, at the bottom of Osborne Steps, annexed the central of the three chalybeate springs in its own Grotto. Cows and piggeries in the lower town were outlawed, and Gatten's iron church was rebuilt with freestone drawn in great blocks by five-horse teams from Cowlease, for the railway station's environs had to give a good first impression. Cowlease's spring water was supplemented by a supply piped through from Wroxall Cross. With every convenience, the picturesque could properly be enjoyed. The Old Village's thatch and stone was crimped and preened. The *Shanklin Weekly News & Fashionable Arrivals List* claimed ever new conquests, including Russian nobility with whom the resort was a favourite. Its vulgarity had a well-fed complexion now. And a healthy one. Keats claimed that hot air and damp stagnated here, "an idiosyncrasy altogether enervating and weakening as a city smoke", but folk flocked to breathe its ozone, to plunge into Sampson's brine baths, to drink of the Spa, to bathe in the sea, and to take invigorating walks upon Knock Cliff or upon the downs, the town's southern backdrop.

The fire-engine of 1866, christened *Nil Desperandum*, did not have hose enough to save the Chine Inn, and was replaced in 1890 by a Merryweather engine drawn by horses hired from Bartlett's stables when fire broke out. Shanklin Pier was opened in 1891, and the next year the Lift began to take the sweat out of climbing the cliff. Now it costs 5p to descend the concrete shaft of 1956, and 10p to ascend. The Pier Pavilion was destroyed by fire in 1918, and its iron girders went to build the Playhouse Cinema. Two fires were raised, in 1913, at the Manor House, Shanklin's original power-base now isolated across the cricket green on the outskirts of the town. Nearby, St Blasius' Church had been rebuilt in 1852; it contains the powerfully carved chest of "Dominus Thomas Silsted Prior" dated 1512, Flemish pulpit panels of the same period, Purbeck grave-slabs of the Popham family and some relict fourteenth-century masonry in the chancel. In Shanklin's hey-day, the newly restored church, no longer subservient to Brading, was resplendent with the gaudy silks and satins, the violets, greens, crimsons and yellows, the stripes and ribbons of the Victorian devout.

On a May night in Shanklin Festival time, I stood on the cliff above the eastern end of the Esplanade. All at once the strings of lights, like coloured baubles, were extinguished; the rides and sideshows below went dark. Electrical rainbows were succeeded by a more primitive incandescence, by fireworks' sizzle and roar, by fountains of sparks and by the whine and thunderclap of rockets. It could have been the 1880s. The two-tier town dissolved in darkness. The air below and above was filled with light and smoke. The cliffs bulked large from moment to moment, glowing ruddily. The obsidian mirrors of the sea's swell were fired to glittering crystal, viridian and ruby. Next day saw bright, frail craft riding the Island's airs, and the town was full of cars with hang-gliders on their roof-racks. Old timers recalled the first air pageant, at the new aerodrome at Apse Manor Farm, opened in 1930 by Sir Alliot Roe. A hangar, once a sea-plane base at Bembridge, was erected on the Esplanade in 1923, as a summer theatre, and is now a refuge for Space-Invaders. The walks and steps and raised iron-railed pavements of the town still bustle in the season, and one species of vulgarity succeeds another. Near the elegant Early English-style St Saviour's Church, Keats' Cottage is a red-brick bungalow. The original International Stores' Egyptian Hall is faced, at ground level, with standard plate-glass, though the Regal Cinema still sports its green and gold stained-glass canopy. The covered market sells secondhand books and records, as well as fruit and vegetables. Barney Powell's Shanklin Emporium has, for years, been a sort of one-man show behind glass: high quality binoculars and telescopes mixed with curiosities, junk and a multitude of verbal and visual puns. The Magic Box hawks tricks and jokes, while Madame Zara's soiled Tarot cards and dusty crystal ball are bait for the credulous. At the end of the season, the dark streets of the Old Village and the town are lit by the moving lights of floats: beauty queens, fairy-tale lorry-loads, troupes of clowns, jazz and marching bands, Keystone Cops' sham-fights, a pirate-vessel on wheels, and all the fun of the Carnival processing past Hollier's, the Crab Inn, the Rock Shop, Daish's Hotel and down the High Street; a cacophony of colour, kazoos, bugles, trombones, drums and coin-laden collecting-tins.

More quietly, you can pay your money and stroll down the Chine, whose waterfalls and foliage are illuminated by floodlights; the gels attempt to conjure more romance out of the deep sandstone ravine than it can bear, and succeed only in making it another part of the fairground. A tape-recording recounts the war-time tale of PLUTO, whose green-painted pipeline surfaces here. You can revive yourself with a pint of Burt's Ale or a glass of mead under the vine at the Chine Inn, 300-year-old resort of fishermen and smugglers. You can escape the night breeze in ornate Victorian shelters on the front, where kiddies' trampolines take a rest from the day's pummelling, where pedaloes are beached for the night, and the latest sand-castles are being inexorably erased by the tide. Or you may be seduced, by the mellifluous tones of an organ that overrides the waves' plash, into the warmth of the Pier Pavilion. Under its glorious roof, in dim lighting, elderly patrons sit around tables of plastic "wrought-iron", watching a slide-show of the Island's beauty-spots, everything they missed seeing from the coach convoys that creep around the Wight by day. They sing along to all the old songs and, packing up their troubles, take a turn around the floor for old times' sake. As if to make up for what Shanklin has become, the Council nightly dispenses buckets-full of free nostalgia to those who holidayed here in their childhood, in what seemed like simpler, more gracious, more carefree days. On the same pier, today's young are accumulating their own sort of memories in a cavern of winking, blinking, bleeping, machine-gun-chattering pleasure. Vulgarity is sophisticated now, but its High Tech is sustained by superannuated boards. The stately pleasure-dome and the fun-fair are set upon old timbers and spindly iron legs above the sometimes stormy waters of the bay.

Early in the morning, when the silent pier rides out of the mist like Leviathan, if you are lucky you can buy fresh mullet, bass, gurnard and sole from fishermen who land their catch on the beach. At low tide it is a great delight to walk southwards under the glowing gingerbread of Knock Cliff, past Horse Ledge and Yellow Ledge, to Luccombe Bay and real wild grandeur. Alternatively, the Ventnor road climbs and winds and sweeps around Cowlease, past the woods, old quarries and rushing underground water at the foot of the down, out to the viewpoint above Luccombe village and around the amphitheatre in which Luccombe Farm is set, to a car-park at the east end of the Landslip from which steps and paths take you down to Luccombe Chine.

But my favourite route runs past the Priory, to Luccombe Common. The footpath skirts modest fantasies with elaborate gardens and ponds, villas with planted columns and steps and statues, and eccentric unclassifiable edifices—the Low-Key Bizarre of Mediterranean Surrey. Here is a lurid confection moulded, it seems, from marzipan; here, a garage with picture windows; and here, a naked white marble boy decorously turned away from a lady walking her dogs up through the tunnel of trees. Here is a white blackthorn blossom, dark clusters of ivy fruits, tangled willow, hawthorn and bramble, ash, sycamore and elder, gorse, broom and cherry luxuriating over the fence from the cultivated picturesque. Above red campion, unfurling ferns, hart's tongue and giant nettles, a wren's whole body shudders with the violence of its song; wood-doves calm the air with their voices; chiff-chaffs and, it seems, every other bird in the book saturate the morning with their music. A pheasant's jagged cry echoes in the amphitheatre above. Up there, the greensand farmhouse, the rubble outbuildings, the lawns and beds of Quarr's old grange, and its cattle grazing by the pond are an idyll posed for the painter's brush. Down here, a thatched cottage sunk in rank growth is unaffectedly picturesque.

Farmer Jolliffe insisted that the Excisemen search Luccombe Farm, even the bedroom where his wife lay with their newborn child. The officer was diffident, but satisfied. The baby was a doll, and the tubs in the bed. The old smugglers' path drops through dark woods, hung with lianas of honeysuckle, towards the sound of an invisible stream and the brightness of sunlight on fragments of sea. As at Shanklin, the stream that cut the Chine was a headwater of the eastern Yar before the cliffs were eaten back; here it runs out of the Gault, over the Carstone, and falls through a wild chasm in the Sandrock; then pours over a ledge of green clay and grit and cascades on to the rocky beach. Above the ledge, there is a cave in the pale rock. I jumped the stream, clambered up with roots for handholds, and crawled inside under a roof concentrically patterned with the Sandrock's eroded laminations. Light flooded its angle, and I emerged at a further cave-mouth, perched high above the rugged bay. I retreated, and climbed down the wooden steps that descend from a ledge crammed with horse-tail, bog pimpernel and marsh helleborine. The spring gushes, and water seeps from the ledge along its length. Worn, weed-covered piles of wrecked groynes resemble giant asparagus. Abraded bricks and hunks of masonry are mementoes of the fishermen's cottages that perched on the ledge, and of houses that fell in 1951. Bleached trunks lie at the cliff's foot; living trees lean oddly, as the shifting ground slowly fells them; the face of the ledge is festooned with the roots of those that still stand upright.

Pebbles, rocks and stones strew the beach; white, grey or yellow, egg-like or gnarled; brown, red or purple ironstone, smooth as sandpaper, rounded and regular as sculpture, or eroded like pine bark. A big rock stands, bare head and shoulders above a crowd of weed-shrouded boulders; it is hollow, with a miniature grotto whose floor is water holding the pale pink, skeletal tree-shape of corallina, and the vivid swaying arms of an anemone monster. But the real giant, growing up out of the shore—high above the rock pools, wet clay and sand and luminous stones—is a Sandrock monolith, a raw brooding presence that seems to embody and emanate the *genius loci*. As you step past it on the stones towards Dunnose, it undergoes a slow metamorphosis. Always it breaks the skyline above the tree-tops far above, and behind. The head's aspect shifts, then becomes two, those of a mother and child: a gaunt madonna presiding over the terraced cliffs, the clefts at their base, the rocks and the glistening sands towards Yellow Ledge where the latest tide has abandoned a black sash of wrack. Then the image becomes one again, a leaning figure scouring the horizon with blank eyes. Sandown and Shanklin are blotted out behind rock faces and rife ledges stepping down to the sea, but the Culvers shine white and alien across intervening shades of blue. The light changes, and the mood. Luccombe Bay is a fugitive place, and a place of escape. It is a scene of flux and of peace. It is a hard haven, a temporary paradise.

15

THE BOWL OF THE ISLAND

A rich and fruitful valley lay immediately beneath; it was adorned
with cornfields and pastures, through which a small river winded in
a variety of directions, and many herds grazed upon its banks . . .
The noble mansions of the rich, and the lowly cottages of the poor,
added their respective features to the landscape. The air was mild
and the declining sun occasioned a beautiful interchange of light and
shade upon the sides of the hills.

Legh Richmond   *The Dairyman's Daughter*

A BADGER SETT'S pungent nostril dilates between the roots of an
oak. The bole's reptilian bark rears itself to three times a man's
height. Then, limbs flail outwards as if impelled by an acorn-
memory of hurricane, angular, layer upon layer scratching a mad
pattern against the mild May-Day sky, a Medusa-head of gnarled
serpents whose writhing has been slowed to near stillness. The thick
rope of a beech trunk hangs upwards, and frays into branches.
Nothing seems to move, but at the trees' far nerve-ends frail yellow
and luminous green leaves break out of blunt and sharp buds, like
winged insects unfurling from chrysalises. Hungry for light, they
will spread a canopy over Borthwood Copse. For now, the sun
lights upon a floor of bluebells, wood anemones and celandines.
Flowers like dream-raspberries illuminate the dusky green of larch
needles. The almost painful green of grass islands is set in dun seas of
dead leaves. Here are the dark points of holly, trunks shimmering
with ivy-scales, hazel and elder saplings like spars, and the old
rigging of honeysuckle. Here is the blushing haze of new birch
shoots en masse, the ruddy glow of pine bark under shadowy
boughs, and coppiced chestnut unsheathing saw-toothed leaves.
Paths lead from dense wood to glade, from high trees to coppice, up
and down the levels of 50-odd acres bought in 1924 by Frank Morey,

timber merchant and founder of the Isle of Wight Natural History and Archaeological Society, and given to the National Trust. Borthwood Copse furnishes their properties with gates and fencing, and is being nurtured back to something of its old glory. Broad-wood, or Bordwood Forest contributed 30-foot lengths of oak, weighing three or four tons apiece, to the construction of the first Sandown Fort. Cultivation of surrounding commons and continual felling of its fringes have eroded its breadth. The medieval forest was stocked with goodly red and fallow deer, heath-cocks and hens; it was a royal chase for kings, lords of the Island, and ladies, like Isabella de Fortibus and Phillipa, Duchess of York, to whom it was granted by Henry V. It was a preserve protected by strict prohib-itions; Sir Edward Horsey came down hard on one, Forder of Newchurch, for shooting game-birds within, and therefore out of, bounds. A knoll in the Ferruginous Sands, capped with plateau gravel and a heathy crown of fern and gorse, rejoices in the title of Queen's Bower, site of a hunting-lodge from which to preside over the chase. Wind-blown trees embower the summit; shelter for cattle who graze the meadow, spangled with buttercup and star-of-Bethlehem, that falls away towards Borthwood Farm.

All around are the fertile undulations of the Lower Greensand, rutted by deep lanes, steep banks vivid with bedrock or, at Skinner's Hill and Newchurch, the gravels of the plateaux. Northwards is Alverstone Garden Village, laid out between the wars and since extended like a leafy suburb, where Richard Webster, Lord Alver-stone, had his game reserve in Youngwoods Copse. The old village and the mill lie across the disused railway and the River Yar. Ducks, heron, moorhen and kingfishers, water forget-me-not, bur mari-gold, iris and kingcups adorn waterway and marsh, but the village is dry because Lord Alverstone's deeds preclude the building of a public house. Downriver, though, the Yar meanders through wetlands to Yarbridge, with Adgestone's vineyards on the hillside above. Uphill from Alverstone, the Ferruginous Sands peter out and are overlaid by the poorer Sandrock. The ancient farm of Kern, once property of the Knights Templar, lies snugly under the downs there, underpinned by rumours of its subterranean passage and the underground activities of the past. To the west, past oak-woods and ploughed land thick with pheasant and partridge, an opencast pit yawns like a planet-scape of banded ochres, of yellow and grey and white, eaten at by orange, yellow and red machines. Higher still, a belt of pines marks the Carstone ridge; then the Gault Clay traps water from the Upper Greensand and Chalk above, and feeds the reservoir at Knighton beside the vanished house of Knighton Gorges.

It is said that a Saxon chapel stood at Alverstone, Alfred's tun, but that when FitzOsbern endowed Lyre he had a new church built on a grander site. Newchurch's All Saints tops the sandstone bluff above the Yar at Langbridge; its parish embraced Ryde and Ventnor. Lancet windows, that were shuttered not glazed, survive in the chancel; but by the time Henry V gave Newchurch to Beaulieu Abbey, the Norman building had acquired side-aisles, transepts and a porch. Upon the latter, the monks built a tower, though the present white lapped weather-boarding and spire date from George II. They glorified the interior with gaudy murals, plastered over and limewashed during the Protectorate. They built a rood loft and excavated stairs to it through the massive masonry. A ceiling was knocked down, in 1883, to reveal the roof timbers and the sanctus bell's splayed aperture above the chancel arch. A gilded Pelican-in-her-piety, from Frome in Somerset, stands as lectern opposite a soberly-panelled pulpit whose tester, inlaid with a dark star, has been relegated to the vestry. This transept was a chantry, built by Eudo de Morville in 1204, where a mass-priest might intercede on behalf of his father, one of four knights who had murdered the turbulent Thomas à Becket. It became a mortuary chapel for the Dillingtons, the next masters of Knighton, and is lined with memorials including one to Jane, "delivered of her eleventh Child the second day of February 1674, and died the ninth of February, in the 30th year of her age. Shee lieth here interred with five of her Children Thomas, Frances, Willia^m, Elizabeth and the youngest a son abortive." Of her husband, the parish registers record, "Received of Sir Robt Dillington, Bartt., the sume of fifty shillings, being one moiety of five pounds for Sir Robert his father not buryed in woollen,—the other 50s. p^d to Mr David Urry, informer." Urry's interest in sheep may have made him keen to enforce the 1667 and 1678 Acts which forbad that any, other than plague victims, "be buried in any shirt, shift, sheet or shroud or anything whatever . . . other than what is made of sheep's wool only." The registers record "a very smart shock of an earthquake" in November 1811, and the desolate meditation of a parson uncertain of the hope that was in him:

> When these my records I reflecting read,
> I find what numerous ills these births succeed,
> What powerful griefs the nuptial ties attend,
> With what regrets these painful journeys end;
> When from the cradle to the grave I look,
> *This* I conceive to be a melancholy book.

There was exuberance too: "Pd. William Callaway for Ringing Beer, when King George came to England, and when he was crowned, Sept. and Oct. 1714, £0.15s.0d.", and the gallery of 1780 thrummed with viols, flutes and bassoons for 77 years before the barrel-organ and pipe-organ usurped it and its musicians.

A tablet high in the nave celebrates a boisterous character, Squire William Thatcher of Wackland, breeder of champion fighting-cocks. Not far from Fighting Cocks Cross and the Fighting Cocks public house on the Arreton Road, Wackland is a substantial farmhouse of 1736, set between lakes, with a viewing-tower above an arena in which spurred birds were urged to spill each other's blood. The Pointer Inn at Newchurch shows that a nose for game was valued here, and a fox weather-vane, now in Brading Museum, was presented to a later Squire Thatcher in recognition of his rearing a litter of Portsmouth fox-cubs, the first to be seen in the Island, in Wacklands withy-bed about 1830. The Harriers found new sport, at the first meet of the season, when they turned their dogs on to one of the foxes and were taken for a ride beyond the moor, beyond Bleak Down and the Wilderness, down to the cliffs of Atherfield. The graveyard at Newchurch is a grand balcony from which to watch autumn hunting summer, and spring hounding winter through the Arreton valley.

On Plough Sundays, a hundred farmers and their families still meet to bless the Ransome plough bought by Michael Reed's great-grandfather in 1869. The foot of the shute was washed by the waters of the Yar. Now, grey and chestnut horses crop pasture beside Parsonage Farm. From the site of a newly discovered Roman villa, the swell of rich red arable ground laps along the length of the downs and has eroded marl-pits there, like little coves glowing white in the green cliffs. Ruddy ploughland greens up with shoots of barley and wheat, grows golden and white, and is shorn by combines in due season. Camden comments on its export potential, for it "consisteth of soile very fruitfull, and is thankefull to the husbandman, in so much as it doth affoord corne to be carried forth." He was writing, however, of a time deplored for depopulation, by reason of lords of manors and farmers getting together as many farms as they could. By the time the Revd Warner compiled his *General View of the Agriculture of the Isle of Wight*, 150 years later in 1794, the aim was self-sufficiency in the face of the Napoleonic blockade. In 1770, Matthew Peters had published his *The Rational Farmer* at Newport; it is dedicated "To all lovers of Husbandry, particularly, to those of the Isle of Wight", whom he then berates for their ignorance, idleness and insularity: "It is well known what opposition was made to turnips but a few years since by the farmers: what now would they part with them for?" He threatens French agricultural advances, "a circumstance more to be dreaded than their mighty armies, or their encreasing fleets." He is advocate for the spike-roller, the scarificator, and for Ducket's two coulter and share plough. He propagates the doctrine of vegetable manures, of sea-weeds, of manures found at the bottom of marl-hills, ditches and mill-ponds, and of cheap clay ashes from the kiln, "very fructifying in cold strong land". He exhorts the farmer "to have done with the expensive horse, and cherish the profitable ox", and proposes a ten-year rotation which will yield a profit, on 100 acres, of £11,076.15s. Such increase was readily to be gained, if only they would learn from experience, as William Sivier of Dungewood and Emmanuel White of Compton Grange had done, from their experiments with pigs, for "we must not mistake the meaning of Solomon where he says, 'there is nothing new under the sun', that being metaphysically spoke relative to the knowledge of God: short-sighted man is always seeing, but can never see; always learning but never learned."

The middle of our century saw Island farms joined into empires, with overners taking advantage of cheap land. Exports now include sweet-corn, asparagus and garlic. From our Newchurch promontory we can see land shining like water, covered with acres of polythene; and, westwards, at Hale Common, the sun glints off the panes of great tree-screened crystal palaces dedicated to the production of carnations, chrysanthemums, cucumbers and tomatoes, though the price of oil, and oil subsidies to European growers, are making the glass-house business a fragile one indeed. The Bowl of the Island is so hospitable to horticulture because of the free-draining Ferruginous Sands, whose colour and fertility was put down not just to underlying geology, but to a celestial phenomenon: John Speed quotes reports "that in the yeere of man's salvation, 1176 . . . in this Iland it rained a showre of bloud, which continued for the space of two howers together, to the great wonder and amazement of the people that beheld it with feare." Sunlight, reflected and refracted between the surrounding sea and the stratosphere, seems to attain a peculiar intensity in the lap of land between Wight's spine and its southern bulwark. The clarity of the air keeps glass-houses clean and "is commmended both for health and delight, whereof the first is witnessed by the long continuance of the Inhabitants in the state of their bodies before they be decayed, and the other for quantitie gives place to no neighbouring Country."

The alchemy of soil, light and air combined to draw Quarr's monks to Haseley at the behest of the Norman baron, Engelger de Bohun. For four centuries it was an Abbey grange, set on a Greensand island in the marshes by the Yar. A tributary fed fish stews, and a track known as Straight Mile or Shepherd's Lane still runs north to a marl-pit in Arreton Down, first way-mark on the monks' trek back to Quarr. Haseley's barns, its wool room, and its fulling-mill, whose wooden hammers had pummelled cloth with fuller's earth and pioneered the Wight's rise to prominence in the cloth trade, passed to John Mill and his brother George at the Dissolution. They transformed working buildings into a Tudor mansion, the best house on the Island in its day, by re-using its stone, and perhaps that of other Quarr properties. Here, Douzabelle Mill opened her house and her heart to Sir Edward Horsey, estranged from his wife in France; days of hare-coursing, bull-baiting or hawking ended with voluptuous feasting; a week's fare included two beeves and eight sheep, and was supplemented with "gifts" of spices, sweetmeats and Canary-wine from privateers based at St Helen's and Cowes; to follow, Douzabelle danced the Straight Mile with a piper at her heels. The plague took Horsey from her, but Oglander tells us that she held sway in the Island, and finished its young ladies' education, for another twenty years, before dying in the same year as the mainland Queen, Elizabeth.

Sir Thomas Fleming, Lord Chief Justice and judge of Gunpowder Plotters, soon bought Haseley, along with Quarr, Binstead,

Newnham, Combley and the tithes and advowson of Arreton. Though roof-timbers in the south wing are fourteenth-century or earlier, and the main building is a Tudor long-house, Colonel Fleming did his best, in the late eighteenth century, to insinuate Georgian features and proportions into the old structure. The dining-room still has its Tudor fireplace, but the drawing-room has been given height and a cubical shape by removing the first floor; it is graced by an Adam fireplace, the old stone one having been re-cut to frame the south-facing Palladian window. The present owners believe that a quarter of the arms of Henry VII, now a building-stone in the south wing, came from this fireplace. Stonework around the window is covered by geometric tiles, but much masonry was replaced by real red brick when Tudor windows were succeeded by larger Georgian ones. Redundant stone mullions edge beds in the gardens. The date 1567 is carved on one of the timbers of the drawing-room wall; Tudor wattle and daub was rendered with Georgian plaster, and a nearby batten is inscribed 1787. A view from the west side shows how the house has grown by accretion and patching: great chimney stacks, gables, a variety of windows, and a pantry, kitchen, scullery and dairy tacked on to the old hall. A mummified cat and two attendant rats were found interred in the walls; clay marbles, shoes, darned socks, clay pipes, an old comb and a hairbrush base lay, long lost, under first-floor boards. Truckle-beds scored marks in the six bays of the maids' small dormitory. There is a convenient slop-hole next to the housekeeper's bedroom, but when Raymond and Krystyna Young took the house over in 1976, water was cascading down the servants' staircase, three-quarters of the roofing had to be renewed, and the whole house rescued from dereliction.

Now, they have embarked on a programme of accretion in reverse, stripping it back to the earliest features they can find. Victorian brickwork in the hall was pulled out to reveal the 22-foot fireplace where carcases once turned on spits; sadly, the north wing's Georgian three-storey bay, whose sagging timbers were held together by the windows' weight-boxes, has also come down. The cart-house is now a craft shop and pottery. The fish-stews are part car-park and part pond, endowed with a toy Noah's Ark and Castle. The courtyard has been embellished with a startling white rococo fountain, which perhaps accounts for the dummy Douzabelle's surprised expression and the effigy Sir Edward's death-bed pallor in the vaulted upstairs room. The appeals to visitors and to historicity are uneasy bedfellows, but there is no doubt that Haseley, split into farm workers' accommodation and abandoned to the elements, has been revived and restored to stand for the future as one of the most interesting houses on the Island. Whether it is the oldest is another question. The Wax Museum at Brading and Haseley have set themselves up as contenders for the title; the Tourist Board, the Advertising Standards Authority, the County Archivist, the Curator of Carisbrooke Museum and Dom S.F. Hockey of Quarr have been enlisted as unwilling referees. In the cause of truth and tourism, cautious academics have tried to arbitrate between enthusiastic owners and, in a debate stuffed with ifs and buts, have had the temerity to suggest that neither property may have as strong a claim to be the oldest domestic building as the hall at Swainston or the manor house at Chale. Who knows?

The farm buildings at Haseley are still owned by the Browns, who bought the manor from the Flemings in 1952. They can claim the longest stone barn in the Wight; its four sets of double doors lead into an interior stacked with bales and sacks of feed; a corbel-course, wall-posts, tie beams, queen posts, purlins and rafters support, not thatch, but a corrugated roof. At Arreton, the "tithebarn" is roofless, a sad and magnificent stone ruin, whose timber predecessor groaned with the weight of Quarr's corn. Later barns at Arreton have been restored and converted to Country Craft Workshops in which a shifting population of craftsmen and women make and sell pottery, leatherwork, furniture, printing, ironwork and hand-knitting. Arreton Manor, with its cottage, dairy and dove-cote, had a chequered history too, but now it is picture-book Jacobean, all mellow Binstead stone and Greensand without, and wood-panelling within, complete with a secret door to the gun-room, a tale of child murder and haunting, and royal connections dating back to Alfred the Great, if indeed this is that Adrintone he willed to his youngest son Etherward. Count and Countess Slade de Pomeroy are old hands at the tourist business, and woo the public with displays of dolls, dolls-houses, costumes, Alum Bay sand pictures, agricultural implements and "The National Wireless Museum", a junk-shop of the air-waves with, curiously, no celebration of Marconi's pioneering work on the Island. Mr Slade showed me into the grand clutter of the private

room to which he and his wife retreat in the open season. He
affirmed proudly that he had been Prior of the Knights Templar in
Britain, but I felt that I should have been a bailiff, a steward or a
tenant facing the Squire with facts about forage or fodder, the state of
the harvest, the disposition of flocks and the marketing of cattle;
discussing the upkeep of property or the collection of rents. His
concern was to maintain the flow of satisfied customers, who
respond to his invitation to "go back in time", when rivals were
combating the economic climate by opening up ever new attractions.

I could imagine the present Squires of Tourism waking from sleep
in a lather of sweat, as though hag-ridden by a wicked witch who, in
the nightmare, had opened all the glorious Elizabethan and Jacobean
houses to the public at once; hereabouts, not just Haseley, but Hale
Manor and Horringford, Apse Manor, Merston Manor and Great
Budbridge; the whole Garden Isle, a jig-saw of Country Parks, Craft
Centres, Zoos and Museums, glamorous Chines and picturesque
Ruins, thrown wide on a day when the Wight, shuddering with
culture-shock, casts loose from its moorings; it drifts down the
Channel into the Atlantic wastes, and goes down, turnstiles clicking,
lights flashing, and every instrument in the wireless room stuttering
messages of fury and farewell; it founders like *Titanic*; it is lost, like
Atlantis, beneath the spume and froth of its mythology.

That day, as I left Arreton Manor, the rain threw itself down as if
to drown us all; but visit it in sunlight and, under the swell of the
downs in a prospect of fertile fields, it effortlessly seduces. A yaffle
guffaws in the graveyard and small birds seem to bray from the trees
there; as you follow the rough music of such sirens, a rat escapes
from under your feet into the grain-store's sanctuary. The battlemented tower of St George's Church was tipped by a spire until
lightning toppled it; marvellous masonry is held up by the rugged
hulk of buttresses which convey a sense of massiveness out of all
proportion to the rest of the building. Saxon stonework beside the
tower and in the north wall of the chancel show the age of the
foundation, given by FitzOsbern to Lyre and transferred, after much
wrangling, to Quarr. The high-pitched, plunging curve of the nave
roof and twin gables at the east end cover a multitude of medieval
and post-medieval modifications, both elegant and crude. Not far
from the Priest's door, sunlight warms the headstone of Elizabeth
Wallbridge, who was brought up in a cottage on Hale Common, put

into service at Knighton Gorges, and wasted by consumption. Legh Richmond charted the progress of her body to this resting place, and chronicled the triumph of her spirit, in his affecting and best-selling tract *The Dairyman's Daughter*. Through him the humble dead are best remembered, but high in the wall a tablet commemorates William Colnet, "gent of Comblie", who claimed to be the great-nephew of the last Emperor of Constantinople. Hannah Urry's rhyme, on her husband James' tomb, strives to make sense of his demise, gored by a bull. William Rayner who died shortly after-wards, in 1823, is celebrated for the way he made the tower and air of Arreton reverberate:

> Skilled in the mystery of the pleasing Peal,
> Which few can know, and fewer still reveal;
> Whether with little Bells or Bell sublime,
> To split a moment to the truth of Time;
> Time so oft truly beat, at length o'ercame,
> Yet shall this Tribute long preserve his Name.

Near the Elizabethan porch is the red-brick tomb of Oliver Cromwell's grandson, William, and his wife, of Horringford. Inside the church are white marble monuments, two by Richard West-macott and one by a local mason called J. Haskoll, to the last of the Worsley Holmeses. The Serles of Stone, near Blackwater, left brasses; one of 1595, set in Sussex marble, describes in doggerel how William Serle left "an hundred powndes of redie coyne" to the needy of Arreton; the money was put to the purchase of Garretts Farm on St George's Down, whose profits furnished the poor with bread in winter. In the south chancel is a headless brass effigy of 1430, and an early English epitaph to a veteran of Agincourt:

> Here is y'buried under this grave
> Harry Hawles, his soule God save,
> Long tyme steward of the Yle of Wyght,
> Have mercy on hym, God ful of myght.

The chancels are separated by a graceful arcade of Purbeck marble columns; in the north aisle, set in a quatrefoil of Purbeck marble, there is a rare though mutilated Christ in Majesty, and, as befits a church of St George, a repulsive dragon's head above the remnants of the old font. The present restored font stands foursquare on its old

Purbeck marble plinth, before the long and short work of the Saxon or early Norman west door into the tower. Twin lancets, half blocked by the tower, and clerestory windows that now admit no light are among many marks of the metamorphoses that this magnificent church has undergone. Worked and re-worked throughout, weathered and repaired outside, colourfully painted and sternly white-washed inside, it stands, a heavily buttressed monument to all the buildings it has been; embodiment of the continual struggle to put down the dragon whose sinuous, sinister length lies along the valley bottom, and to bruise its head by raising up stones upon it to the glory of God.

The chalk-pit on Gallows Hill glistens like a snow-peak. The high plateau of St George's Down, decapitated like an egg, drips with the ochrous yolk of gravels spooned out of it by Vectis Stone's machinery. Crushed white rock from the one is spread, in autumn, on the deep-red furrows that lap around the base of the other; dark soil crests seem to break foaming upon an inland shore. Below, Merstone is engulfed in acres of cabbages like overblown blue-green roses, flanked by chamomile. A rich expanse of mud slumps between the rusting corrugated iron hulks of farm buildings, and the gracious Jacobean red brick of Merston Manor comes as a surprise. With its stone quoins and mullions, it was built by Edward Cheke for his wife, Elizabeth Oglander, and set behind a brick and stone wall amongst tamarisks and chestnuts. A line of poplars screens the house from the weather that scours the Island's bowl. Here a windmill ground corn and pumped water, but it was blown down 30 years ago. Merston's water runs into the Medina, but a little to the south are wetlands, streams and ditches that feed the eastern Yar, the luscious depths of the valley around Great Budbridge Manor. Here are cedars, willows and poplars, a pond populated with moorhen and Aylesbury duck, and more Jacobean stone shrouded by Virginia creeper. It was home for Urrys and Dillingtons, and from its seclusion Captain Richard Cook of Sandown Castle rode out in his wrought velvet gown, escorted by a dozen soldiers with halberds, to worship at Arreton Church. Great Budbridge's glass-houses are dedicated to tomatoes, though figs ripen against the manor house wall. Rooks croon raggedly in the crowns of the conifer and chestnut wood, but from here to Godshill the going is wet. Everywhere, water sucks and seeps, sedges and rushes flourish, with sundews and heath-spotted orchids, bog asphodels and pimpernels. Across the reaches of the abundant waste is Munsley and Moor Farm, and somewhere, swallowed in the peat beds of the Yar's upper reaches and in the slough of history, are the lost settlements that bore the Saxon names of Tidelingham and Tidearding Mor. You can cross the redundant railway embankment, and climb slowly from the bogs of Little Kennerley to Bohemia. From there you can survey the bed of the Yar, the ripples, knolls and plateaux of the Ferruginous Sands running away towards Sandown, the whole fertile mix of soil and water in the bowl between the northern and southern downs; then turn your back on it and make for the less productive greensands and gravels, the "golden nuts" of Rookley.

Over the hill among trees is Pidford Manor, but Rookley itself was an unpretentious, proletarian place, long since shorn of most of its timber, and therefore of its rooks too. Many of its inhabitants were reluctant to call anyone master; it was a place of gravel, brick-clay and an independent spirit; it metalled roads, built houses and kept an open mind. It is at the confluence of routes from Chale, Niton and the Undercliff, and from Godshill, Ventnor and Shanklin, gathering their traffic before flowing north to Newport. Gossip of ships and shoals and wrecks, intelligence about the movement of Preventive men and their prey, the contraband, was collected here and passed on at the discretion of Rookley men. Highwood Lodge was the staging-post for the Ventnor-Cowes coach, and many a less public place was stopover for travellers in under-the-counter commodities. It is a bald, bare-faced, straightforwardly crooked cluster of houses, whose walls harboured non-conformist, dissenting talk.

The established church's reign at Rookley was a brief one; the hall it occupied was sold to the Women's Institute in 1960; but Rookley is notable for the formation of the Wight's first Bible Christian Society, in the cottage next door to the present post office, on 3 October 1823. This radical inauguration was presided over by James Thorne, of Shebbear in Devon, less than three months after Mary Toms of Tintagel had first preached the Bryanite gospel in the Island. If Rookley souls were to be reformed, it was not to be with conventional decorum; ecstatic love-feasts, celebrating new-found fellowship in the Body of Christ, made Rookley ring with song which needed no illicit liquor to abet it. Mrs O'Bryan came, and

William Strongman, who wrote that as far as he knew there was nowhere in the kingdom so destitute of the power of godliness as the Wight. Firebrands went out and preached in the open air, in cottages, in makeshift chapels. Revivalist fervour filled Grandfather Bartlett's cottage at St Helen's, resounded from the preaching-post at Queen's Bower, and rang out on St George's Down. There, the Revd Richard Uglow's prayers were interrupted by the Vicar and Clerk of the parish of Arreton, who declared the meeting illegal and as magistrate commanded the assembly to disperse. Uglow continued in prayer, for the Vicar. He was taken into custody, and later acquitted, to the parson's fury. Clergymen and landowners incited violence, rough music and all manner of disruption. The Revd Bailey had his head cut open on Chale Green, but continued to intercede for his assailant while a Niton woman staunched the blood. William Henley of Brading risked the loss of his place, and penury, if he continued in the faith; so threatened the clergyman and his employer's wife. But his master refused to discharge a faithful servant, and increased his wages. So it was, through standing up to the establishment, that Rookley's landmarks are chapel and school-house, both born of radical dissent.

In 1933, another landmark rose up, the chimney of Pritchett's brick-works. They had expanded southwards, from brickyards at Gunville and Northwood, to Rookley in 1924. Fifteen years later they were making 5,500,000 articles per annum here; they were famous for Henry Edmund Pritchett's terracotta grotesques, but bricks were their staple. The weathered Gault Clay was shifted by light railway, moulded by power press, baked in continuous kilns, passed through a battery of drying tunnels, and carried away to Newport or Portsmouth or further afield. When Rookley's chimney was felled, it marked the end of brickmaking on the Island, and of six generations of Pritchett clay-getters. Now, the workings are lakes stocked with fish, the ravaged landscape has been planted with 1,200 trees and with all the impedimenta of a Country Park. Rookley's rough edges have been rubbed off; it is respectable now, with a merely respectable share of non-conformity.

After the rich delights of Newchurch and Arreton, I like Rookley's practical stoicism. The landscape, plundered for gravels, is of a barer beauty. Just north of Bleak Down, poised between Munsley Bog and the Wilderness, stands the solitary Chequers Inn, an old house with slate-hung walls unusual in the Wight. There must have been a wild service, or chequer, tree here once to give it its name. It was certainly manned by checkers for, before it was a pub, it was the last Excise House before Newport. Hard by the road to Rookley, it kept a wary eye on the traffic and an ear open for information. Now, it has a very private snug, a basic stone-flagged public bar, and a lounge furnished with the comforts of a cottage. The talk is of horseflesh and booze and love. You can come in your suit, your slippers, your overalls or your leathers; they are all here, farm-worker or builder, businessman or stable-owner, holiday-maker or biker; and, standing on the right flags in the right pub in the right place in the Island, clad in denim and studded leather, the most beautiful girl I have seen. It is that sort of place. Outside is air and light and land falling away to the barbarically beautiful Wilderness, where peewits cry over the snake fern, *Osmunda regalis*, over sallow and alder and furze. It adds up to that inexplicable oneness that dreams are made of; a clarity that is itself a mystery.

16

THE BACK OF THE WIGHT

... How the cellars of North Court, the Kitchen, the rooms
Were all waiting for me, with the housemaids and grooms;
How the books and the cooks with a Rhyme or a Jelly
Were to stock *uti decet* my wisdom and belly ...
                    Count Waldstein   Letter to Richard Bull

I have lived nearly all my life on a storm-swept, rocky coast ...
where, in the fifty years that I can clearly remember, many ships,
great and small, have struck on our outlying rocks and been broken
to pieces by the violence of the sea. Very many stout-hearted
seamen have been drowned, but ... over one thousand lives have
been saved by our Island life-boats.
                    Lord Mottistone   *Launch*

FROM ITS INLAND roots, a tongue of Lower Greensand runs,
eloquent with bucolic delights, between Shorwell and Brighstone
with hills to the north and the Wealden Clays to the south, until it
meets the coast at Compton Bay. The stone, thatch and colourful
cottage gardens of Shorwell are settled in a crook of the downs, and
behind it, set below the road to Bowcombe and surrounded by hills,
is secreted the glorious mansion of North Court. The manor of
Northschorewell had been devised to Lacock Abbey by Amicia,
widow of Baldwin de Redvers and, not long after the Dissolution, it
came into the possession of the Leighs. Sir John Leigh built North
Court's principal wing in 1615. Elizabeth Sewell, who stayed here in
1835, based her Emmerton Hall in *Amy Herbert* on an inflated version
of the house. The main porch was moved to the north wing in 1837,
and a gun-room and music room after Lutyens completed the picture
in 1905. What confronts you now, as you sweep down the drive, are
red-brick chimneys and many gables punctuated by pinnacles like
little obelisks rising against a backdrop of billowing trees. It looks all

Jacobean, but feels Georgian, especially when you step inside the old east-facing front door into the spacious hall with its Venetian window and its grand staircase after Grinling Gibbons. Richard Bull first walked in here with his "heifers", his wife and daughters, on an Island visit in 1783. Bull was heir to Watchingwell, and bought North Court from the Leighs' heir in 1795. Elizabeth, his daughter, must have loved the story of the North Court Thimble Cairn on Brighstone Down: it marked the resort of a sailor's lover, who sewed for her wedding up there, and watched for the return of his ship from a three-year voyage; it never came, and she plied her needle till she died, leaving a vast trousseau. The spinster Elizabeth had a round tower called Miss Bull's Folly erected on the down. She inspired the mausoleum, inscribed with florid verses, to her sister Catherine. She was behind the construction of terraces, a dairy with stained glass windows, an Alpine Bridge across the road to a Temple of the Sun on Mount Ararat, and a rustic summerhouse cobbled with the knuckle-bones of sheep. She abetted her father in his passion for "head hunting", the collecting of portrait prints, in collaboration and competition with Horace Walpole and Joseph Gulston. Ten years ago, 95 prints from the North Court collection were sold for £109,000, so one can only guess at the value of Richard Bull's library of three thousand volumes.

Sunlight flooded in from the canted bay windows, and the table sported a net and two table-tennis bats, when I was shown in to the Library. In the dark season of 1863–4, "when the hounds of spring are on winter's traces", Algernon Charles Swinburne covered the table with large sheets of drafts for *Atalanta in Calydon*, the poem that was to establish his reputation. North Court had passed from Bull, via the female line, to Sir James Willoughby Grant, one of Wellington's least trusted commanders, and on to Swinburne's aunt, Lady Mary Gordon. Her daughter was Mary Charlotte Julia Gordon, Swinburne's cousin and love who, it is said, drove the poet deeper into the world of de Sade and alcoholism when she married General Sir Robert Disney Leith. For the time being, Mary's presence as she worked, played or rode with him, or delighted him with her rendering of Handel on the organ, illumined and warmed the brief months. The Island was Arden or Eden to him, but she involuntarily drove him out and, a decade later, he could write of returning to the Wight "at the risk of realizing the sensations of a damned ghost revisiting earth".

Mrs Gladys Harrison, widow of one of three brothers who had bought this the largest Jacobean house on the Island for £9,000 in 1963, showed me downstairs to the Withdrawing-room and served me tea, kept hot in a cosy like a padded handbag. The walls were full of photographs of meets and old prints of the house; drawers debouched carefully preserved mementoes of its past, including Mrs Disney Leith's sketchbooks, worthy of a lady whose mother had been coached by J.M.W. Turner. Twenty years ago the kitchen, where cooks had concocted delicacies for the likes of Count Waldstein, was a near-cubical underground chamber seventeen feet high; it had satisfied soldiers' appetites in 1940, when North Court was the headquarters of the 2nd Battalion, The Royal Fusiliers, which manned posts between St Catherine's Point and the Needles. Now, in spacious seclusion, a swimming-pool heats in the sun and a spring still issues softly from its source in a flint-built shelter; it is hard even to imagine the thunder of air-raids, though a 500lb bomb fell opposite the Crown Inn, just missing St Peter's Church, and a German air-crew suffered North Court's hospitality. Once, the chimes of the Brighstone bell-buoy, carried by the wind into this retreat, were mistaken for those of St Peter's bell signalling imminent invasion.

In the days when French and Spanish forces were feared, St Peter's vestry was a gun-chamber with an arch for a gun-port, now blocked up. At first the church was one small chapel, dependent upon Carisbrooke; then the nave and chancel of the church of "Suthshorwell" were added; and, about 1440, the church was remodelled with a third nave and chancel, and a tower. This symmetry, together with the eccentric pulpit inserted in a pillar of the north arcade, required the pews to be orientated in collegiate style. The stone spire, with its weathercock dated 1617, was probably given by Sir John Leigh who undoubtedly garnished the interior with many of the richer details, which enhance its singularity and set off the fascinating memorials to Leighs, Bulls, Bennets and Gordons which it contains. In 1899, Mrs Disney Leith purchased a painted altarpiece from the turf and stone church of Thingvellir, for one kroner; she brought it back from Iceland and installed it in the south chancel, in memory of her son killed in action in India, above the portable altar used by General Sir Willoughby Gordon during the Peninsular War. Through the intervention of Magnus Magnusson, it was returned to Iceland in 1974, in exchange for a replica and an Icelandic bible, which joins St Peter's collection of early bibles and other books. Under the tower is a charming exhibit of local finds: mesolithic flints, neolithic arrow-heads and pottery fragments spanning two millenia, which add to the pleasant sense of disorientation and shifting perspectives which the church induces. Above the north door, so that as many eyes as possible may glimpse it and gain its blessing, is a fifteenth-century mural painting of St Christopher. At the left, he rides with the devil and, having renounced him, gains a blossoming staff; at the right, a hermit stands by his hermitage, while the saint is shot through with arrows below; in the centre, he crosses a river, full of frolicsome fish and ships, bearing upon his shoulder the infant Christ who pro-nounces, on a scroll like a cartoon balloon, "Ego sum alpha et omega". A statement and a blessing to redraw all perspectives, disrupt time itself and re-orientate the vision of creation.

The springs that rise at North Court or in the dells, pungent with wild garlic, above it, join to form Swinburne's "one loose thin pulseless tremulous vein" that used to power a mill at the end of Fine Lane; it flows past Wolverton Manor, whose ancestor, built a little to the north and surrounded by a deep moat, was the principal seat before North Court; now it is a beautiful E-plan Elizabethan house haunted by a ghostly musician and linked to the rugged Tudor charm of West Court by a footbridge across the stream and, some say, by a lost underground passage. Downstream, Yafford Mill's wooden overshot wheel turns as a tourist attraction, and grey seals gambol in the pool below the mill-race. Next is the site of the grist mill at Grove, near the old farmhouse of Waytes Court, Brighstone. There, the stream is joined by the Buddle brook that runs down from Rock, site of a livid quarry and of a Roman corridor villa, now under the plough. The flow sustains rife wilderness and productive plots in Moortown's combe, an ideal place for concealing contraband tubs. "Bung" Russell, of Buddlebrooke Cottage, let it be known that Moortown Lane was haunted by a flying hare, especially when the moon was new and the tides were right. From 1865–79 he lived at Lilygrove which, as Uggleton Manor, is reputed to have been a possession of the Knights Templar. On the chalk blocks of Casses

Cottage, opposite, are carved the silhouettes of ships, supposed to have been smugglers' signals. The thatched Five Bells Inn, now a shop, once profited from the trade in cheap liquor. The new inn was called the New Inn until, in 1973, it was re-christened the Three Bishops.

St Mary the Virgin is the church of the five bells and the three bishops. The bells, now six, have been re-cast and re-hung at various times, notably in 1740 when the brass gun, housed in a gun-house at the north side of the tower, contributed to the melt. The church is bulky and businesslike; four massive pillars of the original Norman north arcade remain; the south aisle was divided into two chapels, one at the east for Waytes Court, and one at the west for Limerstone. The latter, a seventeenth-century stone farm, set around a great courtyard, was farmed for 43 years by the late Frederick Fortesque Hollis, MBE, chairman of the parish council for half a century and Methodist lay preacher for longer still; but in the fourteenth century, Limerstone was the site of an Augustinian chapel of the Holy Ghost. The fabric of St Mary's bears the marks of waxing and waning fortunes, and its list of incumbents is evidence of the turbulence of history. Hopton Sydenham, chaplain to Charles I, was ejected in 1653 in favour of the Puritan Thomas Dingley. Bishop Ken, when rector here in the 1660s, wrote hymns—"Glory to Thee, my God this night" and "Awake my Soul, and with the sun"—in the shadow of the yew hedge in the Rectory garden, before taking the throne of Bath and Wells, and a cell in the Tower of London for repudiating the Declaration of Indulgence. Ken's Rectory still contains a carved oak door depicting biblical episodes, and what is said to be a smugglers' hideout. The slavery abolitionist, William Wilberforce, stayed here in his last months, when his son, later Bishop of Oxford, was rector. Before taking on Huxley and the Darwinians, "Soapy Sam" campaigned against the Island Bible Christians; notices were posted about the parish, "Beware of the doctrine of Martha Toogood", and he urged that all labourers who attended their meeting-house should be discharged. When all houses were closed to them, the Bible Christians met in an old marl-pit on Brighstone Down and, on one winter's day, rejoiced to find it miraculously clear of snow; they successfully sought legal protection from Wilberforce's persecution. The third rector to attain a See was Bishop Moberly of Salisbury, who served Brighstone from 1866–9.

Up at Combe Farm, Harold Lack's care is the cure of soils. He recently won a Conservation Award for the restoration of a sand-pit to grazing land, for the creation of a carp pond under the quarry cliff, for planting trees and allowing hedgewillow and bulrushes to regenerate themselves, and for re-thatching his buildings. His 150 acres was split into 23 fields a century ago, with names like Rock, Mead Butt, Pond Butt, Mare Ground, Sandy Ground, Barren Field and Green Piece. Now there are five, divided between cereals and beef grazing, with pigs besides, but they are mainly fertilized with farmyard manure; the remaining hedges, devastated by the loss of elms, are being replanted with seedlings and saplings. South of Brighstone, Shate Farm boasts one of the two oldest Jersey herds in Britain, served originally by the bull Windsor from Queen Victoria's Osborne herd. The nearby mill has worked since the sixteenth century. Here, a young officer from the garrison at the Chine was killed after leaving Brighstone Fair, a scene of gaiety and rioting, drunkenness and whoring in the last century, when the villages of the Back of the Wight were denominated "Drunken Shorwell, Fighting Brighstone and Runaway Brooke". Brighstone men have always worked the land, but farmers and labourers, as well as tradesmen, like the Bucketts who have long been builders and gravediggers, traditionally reaped a rich harvest from the sea; fishing, smuggling, beachcombing, wrecking and life-saving are all skills rooted in this salt-swept soil. The stream we have followed cuts down through the gravels and underlying Wealden Beds, carving a chine; a defile whose shelter and humidity conspire to cherish a dense vegetation full of the charm of birds. It runs beneath a great viaduct—built of bricks dug, moulded and baked on the spot—which carries the Military Road, and is joined by Marsh Chine's stream before opening its sombre mouth of blue-grey and ochrous clays to the sea.

Charles Seely was born in 1803, of a family of Lincolnshire farmers and millers. In his 'teens, he was sent to Chale to recuperate from a chest complaint. As he walked along the downs from Shorwell to the Needles, the Back of the Wight seemed a dream incarnate; he swore that, if he made his fortune, he would own all the land he could see. When the family mill burnt down, he moved the business to Nottinghamshire and found himself sitting on the wealth he needed;

coal made him mine-owner and iron-master. A long-term contract with the Admiralty, to ballast wooden ships, lasted long after they were obsolete, left Seely rich and mountains of "Seely's Pigs" to rust on Portsmouth Docks for a century. At the time he became MP for Lincoln, he was described as "a cross between a brigand and an Italian organ-grinder", a strangely appropriate landlord for Brook. He bought this, the manor of Bowermans and Howes, in about 1854, with land stretching eastwards towards Brighstone and westwards to Freshwater Gate. His son, Sir Charles, the first baronet, extended the property patchily to Atherfield and was required to build the Military Road in the 1860s, to service the coastal garrisons and permit swift deployment of troops in the event of French invasion. Until the 1930s it was a track punctuated by many gates; then it was sold to the County Council and re-surfaced by the labour of unemployed men turned stonebreakers. Now it is a fast road riding the cliffs and the gentle swell of pasture and arable land, with spectacular panoramas of pacific or bellicose seas, of Compton, Brook and Brighstone Bays, and of Chale, the "Grave-yard" or "Bay of Death".

A westerly gale drove the schooner *Sentinel* on to the rocks at Brook and sank a 900-ton Maltese barque off Grange Chine on the night of 4 December 1859; a bronze medallion, in Carisbrooke Castle Museum, was presented "for gallantry in saving life" to farmer Thomas Baker, one of the Brook coastguard's scratch crew that night, when nine out of 23 lives were saved. The calls for a lifeboat reached a crescendo and, in the summer of 1860, Mary Seely launched the Wight's first, the *Dauntless*, at Brook; it and its successors were to save 263 lives. Brighstone's the *Rescue* was launched soon afterwards, and Brighstone crews would save 433 souls. Atherfields boats rescued 157 folk between 1891 and 1915, when the Brighstone and Atherfield crews were disbanded. Jack Seely, the first Lord Mottistone, who had succeeded John Hayter, Ben Jacobs, Thomas Hookey and Roland Hayter as coxswain of the Brook boat persuaded the R.N.L.I. that the *Susan Ashley* should not be retired. She was launched by a team of six horses until about 1927, and for ten years after that by a waterproof tractor; after the last war she was converted to a yacht and recently starred in the film, *The Riddle of the Sands*.

Brook House was the scenario for a strange episode in 1864: spring sunlight warmed its eighteenth-century façade, and lit on the scarlet of Garibaldi's shirt and poncho. In the Library, where she was later exercised by Lloyd George's charms, Mary Seely snipped off a lock of the Liberator's hair, still preserved on a piece of Brook House notepaper and identified in Mrs Seely's reverent script. Off-screen, the Queen tutted at the revolutionary's proximity and wrote tetchily to Charles Seely, but did not send for him until 1887 when she said, "How nice to see you, Mr Seely, after all these years," and he is reported to have replied, "Yes ma'am, as we get older we get wiser." Back in 1864, Garibaldi, looking like "one of the great men of our Elizabethan age" according to Emily Tennyson, bent to plant an oak tree. The oak is a grand creature today, of great stature and generous girth; but its broad, uncoiling boughs preside over divided grounds. Brook House lost its third storey, and was divided into sumptuous flats, after its occupation by the Army in the last war. The property has been cut up and stitched back together, a patchwork of former glories.

After Charles Seely died, folk could no longer set their watches by his daily carriage to Newport, or wonder at his disproportionately long stride, like that of a man on snow-shoes. Parliament could no longer look forward to the eloquent gestures that accompanied his annual speech, described as inaudible but impressive. His son, Sir Charles, had given reading-rooms to the Island and the Seely Library at Newport; he had re-built Brook Church, now a sanctuary for memorials of the lifeboat service, and the lifeboat house, now a garage. He bought Gatcombe in 1890 and, just as his three sisters had married Island men, the next year made Hilda Grant of Cowes his bride. He piped water to tenants' houses. He had a mound erected on top of Brighstone Down, so that he could claim the highest point on the Island. He employed Sir Aston Webb to design Brook Hill House, a version of Dartmouth Naval College, furnished with an interior of red wood, but died, in 1915, before he could move in. In the Great War it was marked as a fortress on German maps, but survived to house J.B. Priestley; then, neglected, it suffered the combined onslaught of language students and weather, before being sold and converted into flats. Gutted or no, its shell stands, set above old Seely land like the bridge of a ship above the deck.

Chekes lived at Mottistone Manor for three hundred years. Sir Thomas Cheke—whose cousin was that Sir John who, Milton wrote, "taught'st Cambridge and King Edward Greek"—transformed the early Tudor house into an Elizabethan "L" by adding the wing called Magna, whose porch is sealed with his initials and the date 1567. Oglander talks of Sir Thomas, "whose son sold all" in 1621 to Sir Robert Dillington "who will buy all", but, 80 years on, the Dillingtons sold Mottistone to the Leighs of North Court as a farmhouse, after 1,400 tons of sandy hillside had slipped and buried the back of the house almost to the eaves. Charles Seely bought it from the Simeons of Swainstone in 1861; a row over inheritance left Charles, the second baronet, with Brook and "spendthrift" Jack with Mottistone. Jack, the first Lord Mottistone, employed the architectural partnership of his son John, and Paul Paget, who both later worked on Eltham Palace, the Charterhouse and Portsmouth Cathedral, to excavate and revive the manor house in 1927. A Tudor arch leads you through the great barn that shelters the house, and gives on to lawns before and behind façades of Elizabethan greensand work and earlier shelly limestone; and on to the mullions and transoms of Magna's windows, and the mullions of the Dower House and the Rectory, whose rear was so recently unearthed like an archaeological find, untampered with since the day of its burial. The lower slopes of the roofs are clad with limestone slates, some still held in place by the original oak pegs, and tiled higher up so as not to overtax the trusses with the weight of stone. The architect, the second Baron Mottistone, left the estate to the National Trust.

Little is left of the twelfth-century church of the de Insulas, standing on its modest mound opposite the manor house, for SS Peter and Paul's has been drastically restored by Chekes and Dillingtons and Seelys; but we must be grateful that the church, decrepit in the last century, is now beautifully light, airy and broad, with painted capitals to the octagonal piers of its arcades, and a chancel roof of cedar from the wreckage of the barque *Cedarine*, whose convict cargo was salvaged by the Brighstone lifeboat in 1862. A parclose screen in the Cheke chapel extols the memory of the first Baron Mottistone, soldier, politician, horseman, mariner and author who, the Latin inscription concludes, "in epitome guarded and passed on the immemorial English tradition which by the grace of God will never die." On Christmas Eve 1977, the Revd Robert Bowyer found the weathervane lying in the snowy graveyard, having spun off from the spire; it was re-gilded and set to ride the winds once more in memory of Evelyn, Lady Mottistone. Molehills prise up clumps of snowdrops and crocuses between graves.

In one large table tomb, the coffins of drowned mariners were stacked to leave room for caches of smuggled tubs, when the loft at the manor was full, or under the Preventive men's eye. Tradition ascribes another, marked by a clumsy cross constructed from a sixteenth-century pier, to eleven French sailors washed ashore at Brook; but it holds the remains of six men of the *Scourge* who put out in the ship's boat to rescue the crew of the man-o'-war *Sphynx*, grounded on the rocks, on 18 January 1847, in the days before the lifeboat. A seventh, Gunner Harris, is buried on the mainland. The *Hampshire Independent* reported that the shore was "strewn with gun carriages, masts, spars and broken boats, in every direction, while the farmers' teams in the neighbourhood were busily employed in conveying her stores to Brooke Farm." Gunner Harris had been ordered to lie outside the line of breakers, but valour overcame discretion and he braved the seas that broke the *Sphynx*. Thomas Sewell, coastguard, said, "No boat could live through it."

From the churchyard you can either follow in the wake of a Friesian herd down the lane to Sud Moor and the treacherous coast, or pass north through double lych-gates, across the road, and up a hollow-way beside the manor. You climb through a clearing whose felled beeches have been replaced by tender saplings, and stumble up a ravine overarched by venerable branches. You emerge, breathless, at the edge of an idyllic valley that the Gault Clay makes between the Carstone ridge on which you stand and the still higher obstacle of Mottistone Down to the north. Standing proud, immediately before you, is the Long Stone, the moot stone or *moteres stan* which gives Mottistone its name. The site was *Calluna* heathland when Neolithic men planted this monolith and its recumbent companion to mark, or focus the light of the rising sun into the chambered long barrow which they raised in veneration of the ancestors who had cleared the downs of timber. Some say that Saxon elders later called men to solemn moot here, on a bald mound by a bare stone. Now, forest clothes the downs once more and the valley is hemmed in by trees which cast deep shadow over the pocked and weather-riven sandstone face of the Long Stone. The sun falls full on a red-brick house and a thatched stone barn, and draws from the earth the aroma of fruitfulness, a scent you can follow eastwards towards wooded Black

Barrow and Grammar's Common. You can plunge back into the
wood's smell of sap and decay along Strawberry Lane, past the Iron
Age Castle Hill whose overgrown banks and ditches are riddled with
burrows and scrapes among roots of beech, alder, holly and pine; or
westwards towards Brook Hill, where light from the sea vibrates
through colonnades and sears the eye, even as frost sharpens each
grass blade and horse-shoes of ice are cast in hoof-prints on the track.

Hulverstone is a few cottages, a cruciform single-storey toll-house,
and the 500-year-old Sun Inn, whose white shell and thick thatch is
floored with stone paves and supported by ship's timbers. When I
last went in there, shrammed with cold, icicles glittered like shards of
glass on the chimney, but a fire blazed in the huge grate and a seven-
week-old puppy played hoopie among the legs of bar-stools. The
night before, the landlord's son had thrown his old slippers on the
fire and their blaze had fired the chimney; he had climbed the thatch
and dowsed it, cracking the pot and decking the stack with icy
hangings, or tinklybobs. The bar used to be full of the Irish brogue
of coastguards, brought in to keep a disinterested watch on the
Wight's back door. Now, they still come all the way from the
Needles, with tales of the foolhardiness of yachtsmen, the heroism of
the Yarmouth lifeboat crew, and the smuggling of heroin. When
there were two bars and the shoot came in, the landlord can
remember beaters crowding the large one, guzzling their gratuities,
and five millionaires in the small one, arguing over the bill.

The Military Road runs from the head of Brook Chine, over a low
plinth of land called Hanover Point and through the territory of
Compton Grange, the smallest of Quarr's granaries; it climbs from
the Wealden bed of the Island, up through a ruddy and rugged ravine
in the Ferruginous Sands, before dropping towards the valley and
chine dominated by Compton Farm, and then up again between
walls of Upper Greensand and Chalk to the slopes of Compton and
Afton Downs. The cliffs shiver and fall; soon the road itself may
founder and its tarmac be pounded to bituminous gravel by the
breakers below. Then, only walkers will enjoy the spicy scent and
rich purple of the rare Hoary Stock whose fleshy stems brave the
weather up here. Shift the focus, and take a long lazy backward look
along the Back of the Wight. Speed up the film, and the fields
between here and St Catherine's would seem like the faces of a

thousand prisms shifting under the passage of a year of suns, reflecting and refracting their energies in a succession of subtle tints—all the warm ochres, the whole spectrum of greens, soft silvers, brassy gilts—the rotation of crops underscored by the furrows' grain—grasses, hay, barley, wheat, brassicas, roots, potatoes—the diurnal clumping and scattering of cattle on pastures and the leisurely migration of sheep between the dip and the shears. Amid the seasonal flux, farmhouses like Dunsbury, Chilton, Marsh-green, Sutton, and the mud and wattle and old stone of Walpan, squat solid like little rocky islands, sometimes screened by reefs of trees, from which tractors daily cast off to trawl the soils' deeps. Water runs down to the real sea, a double octave of streams for ever cutting back from a coast which is itself for ever hacked away by the lunatic assaults and retreats of tides; a litany of chines chanted almost instinctively by mariners and fishermen for whom this shore is an inviting or intimidating threshold to be crossed or shunned: Compton, Shippards, Brook, Chilton, Grange, the twins Marsh and Barnes, Cowleaze, Shepherd's, Whale's deep canyon, Ladder's little desert, Walpen, and lastly Blackgang, decked out but stranded, high above the grim rubble of a tumbled cliff.

Not long ago, there were lookouts above Atherfield, Ladder and Blackgang come the second week of May, watching for the influx of silver, a glittering slick of new-minted mackerel. A signal posted the boats out into the shots, clear of rocks; nets were paid out, a web of thread hemming in the shoal, and heaved ashore, a writhing trove of perhaps a thousand fish to repay the helpers, the oarsman and the boat. Seventy tons of fish came ashore at Walpen in 1910, in the hold of the wrecked *Nemrod*; the same men, Wheelers and Mews, Whites and Cottons, harvested whatever crop the sea gave up, fish or wrecks or tubs. Sir Richard Worsley relates how Chale folk panned the sand for gold dust, the grounds of dollars from a Spanish ship. Every pummelled inch of this coast is thick with stories of wrecks, smuggling and heroic seamanship, tales set down in James Wheeler's log of 1746–1808, in Fred Mew's *Back of the Wight*, in Lord Mottistone's *Launch* and in the memorials of the lifeboat service; and told and re-told wherever old men meet. Robert of Harslade's Calendar notes the death of a youth killed, perhaps in a raid, on 21 March 1211, as the Martyrdom of St Simon. Archaeologists dig and sift the cliffs for even more fragmentary, unspoken stories; enduring

fragments of tools and hearths litter the coast and give us a frail grasp
on the ghostly dynasties of Stone Age man; sherds, and barbed and
tanged arrowheads, a bronze axe from Brook, a Welsh stone axe
from Chale Common, and cremated ashes in an urnfield at Barnes
hint at thriving Bronze Age culture; Iron Age hut sites at Sud Moor
and Shippards, first-century coins at Yafford, and Roman pottery
and roof-tiles at Grange give us glimpses of the life-style that
culminated in the sophistication of rich overners and natives who
lorded it from villas in the downs' shadow. Recent history is often
more fragile: tales of garrisons pickled on smuggled brandy are all
that remain of Napoleonic barracks at Grange and Compton; vivid
memories of flak and fury are mementoes of the anti-aircraft gun-
crews that raised the Island's hackles against the Luftwaffe. Holiday
camps garrison tourists at Grange, and at Stocks Cross, from which
two German prisoners-of-war once escaped over the cliff; but these,
and history's relics, are equally threatened by the invading sea.

Cows parade through a tunnel beneath the Military Road at
Compton to graze above the chine's gash. Climb down the steep
ladder on to the shore at night, like one barbecue party in 1959, and
you might see the lights of a three-masted cutter approaching across
a starlit sea; instead of grounding, it sinks into nothingness, the ghost
of a Revenue ship. More palpable, in daylight, is the rock of the
cliffs. High chalk gives way to the yellows, greys and rusts of the
Greensands, dramatic diagonal brushstrokes taking the eye up and
eastwards again and again until the sombre rainbow of the Wealden
raises its purples, blues, greens and reds into sight, and dips down
again towards Atherfield Point, where the Atherfield clays and then
the Greensands take over once more. Between Brook and Chilton
Chine, the cliffs are capped with alluvium from a vanished tributary
of the western Yar, with valley gravel containing remains of the
mammoth near Grange, and with blown sand between Atherfield
and Chale. On the shore you can pick up brilliant pebbles and
fossilized hazel nuts, known as "Noah's nuts". Below the platform
of Hanover Point, a cormorant launches itself from the sea-mark set
like a thimble on submarine fingers of rock reaching out for prey; at
low tide you can see the bones of a primeval forest of cycads, horse-
tails and giant conifers, the preserved wreckage of trees from a now-
foreign latitude, a Pine Raft washed to the mouth of the delta,
weathering after millenia into lumps of lignite, coal and fool's gold.

The great reptiles left their footprints and bones along this stretch of coast, and the small seven-foot-high dinosaur, Hypsilophodon. Near Shepherd's Chine the base of the cliff is supported by crude arches and pillars of red sandstone; your feet crunch on a coarse orange grit, strangely spongey on its bed of dark clay; rocks rain from the cliff, a thatched ruin stares desolately out to sea beside the holiday camp, and the stream, diverted from its old course, hurries down to salty limbo.

Between the viciously beckoning ledges off Atherfield Point and the bulk of Rocken End, Chale Bay's graveyard yawns, its strata dipping all the way to St Catherine's which looms like a great monument in the sea-mist. Smugglers' craft came and went here like phantoms and, at Christmas-tide 1826, Lieutenant Arnold surprised 50 or more men landing tubs; he summoned mythical reinforcements, but was beaten up before the free-traders fled. If there are ghosts here, they are those of the ships and men that foundered at the rate of more than one a year in the eighteenth and nineteenth centuries; a sad catalogue of brave names that "came ashore" bearing gifts of wine, gold, cheese, lead, figs, almonds, oil, rum, allspice, leather, indigo, tobacco, sugar, hewn stone, china clay, salt, coals, rice, coffee, wool, silk, velvet, brimstone, cork and corpses.

The church registers of St Andrew's, Chale, are laced with grim entries. Its bleak and melancholy graveyard holds more than its share of named and unnamed spoils of the sea. Eighteen of the *Clarendon*'s crew and passengers are buried there, washed up after the 345-ton, full-rigged vessel drove ashore on the morning of 11 October 1836. Miss Gourlay's body was, with others, swept away, but came to rest before her father's house at Southsea. James Wheeler was nearly drowned, rescuing the only three survivors. The ship's timbers contributed to many a house around Chale, and made possible the enlargement of the pub, the White Mouse, into the Clarendon Hotel. But houses hereabouts ride a treacherous geological swell; south of the church is Cliff Terrace, from which Wheelers watched wind and tide and looked for shoals and wrecks and surreptitious signals; the seaward houses have been carried away, like many others above St Catherine's Point. They have joined the flotsam and jetsam cast up and sucked down by the waves, to be punished by the tides, ground slow and small in ocean's mill, with all the other timbers, bones and stones that lie unquiet in the greater graveyard to which the Wight itself gradually succumbs.

PART SEVEN

TROPICS

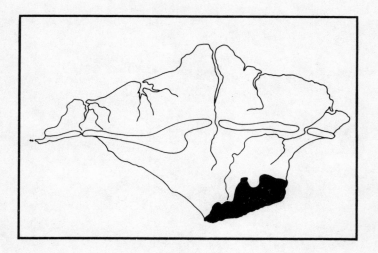

On the saint's down a golden oriole flies
and Boniface's spring flits down, far south
to land-slipped latitudes luxuriant
enough to summon sonnets up; love-songs
whose rhythms, rhymes and stresses must embrace
rock's crack of doom, clay gouts on Undercliff,
diverted roads and streams, the deviant
genius loci of chalybeate springs.

Liquor floods in on the astringent tide,
stocks the long shelf where the infirm adore
their latest god. I breathe an elegy
to Ventnor, last resort on Styx's shore;
where genius thrived, graveyard geology
insists that all things ordinary died.

17

THE SOUTHERN BULWARK

From the top of the highest down there are views which are only to
be equalled on the Genoese shore of the Mediterranean.
                    Charles Dickens   Letter to John Forster

One can stroll here for hours, enjoying both sea- and mountain-air
at the same time.
                          Karl Marx   Letter to Engels

THE *Ship of Blessed Mary*, from Bayonne, broke up in Chale Bay on
the Sunday after Easter in 1313. It disgorged survivors and 174 tuns
of Aquitaine white wine which were speedily salvaged by the locals.
Walter de Goditon—now Gotten Manor Farm—claimed that he had
bargained with the mariners for 53 barrels and one pipe of wine, but
he and other Island men were dragged through the courts of
Winchester, Southampton and Westminster. Chroniclers have maintained that it was church wine, and that as a penance Walter was
constrained to build a chantry and lighthouse on St Catherine's Hill;
but we know that one Walter de Langstrell was admitted to an
existing hermitage there in 1312. There is a medieval lime-kiln built,
of hewn greensand, into the side of a Bronze Age round barrow on
Niton Down, but we do not know whether it furnished mortar for
the oratory's original foundation, or for additions that Walter de
Goditon may have carried out, or both.

Gore Cliff stands, like sheer and rugged battlements, above
rumpled green slopes, frothy with thrift, and hulks of rock upon
which perilously rooted trees raise billowing canopies: a series of
shelves and scarps, of solid and leafy surfaces, stepping and
stumbling down to the chaos of clays and the shifty, dependable sea.
The presiding genius of the Upper Greensand fortress is gravity;

235

abetted by the rock's dip, by its faulting and its bedding of Blue Slipper lubricated by springs: twinkling rivulets and turbid seepage which undermine and dismantle Gore Cliff's bastion, fragment by massive fragment.

Above are the rounded contours of St Catherine's Hill, whose herbage was cropped back to milky chalk by rival flocks in the sixteenth century, engendering a bitter dispute between tenants of Oglander, Worsley and St Mary's College, Winchester. The Salt Cellar, or Mustard Pot, squats at the summit, the roots of a 1785 lighthouse never finished by the Trinity Board because of the mists that engulf "St Cattern's"; it quartered those who manned the Signal Station, successor to the beacons that flared up on the high places in times of alarm, but was then quarried for good building stone. John Harrys of Chale, and others, had long since pillaged the oratory's masonry; what is left is a shadow in the turf and the Pepper Pot, or St Catherine's Tower, dedicated to that saint of Alexandria whose beheaded body spouted milk and was transported by the angels to Mount Sinai. So *Montem de Cheal*, Chale Mountain, became Seynt Kateryn's, and the sturdy octagonal tower, with a roof like a nose-cone and buttresses like the fins of a medieval rocket, became a launching-pad for prayer; intercession for the souls of those in peril from the sea that caresses the wrecking arc of coast between Rocken End and the Needles, the sea that stretches westwards to Purbeck and St Aldhelm's Race and Head and chantry chapel, and to the far bulk of Portland rearing up on the hazy horizon. Prayer and light: once, on clear dark nights, mariners looked up to shafts of light shot from the tower's eight lantern windows like the spokes of a fiery Catherine Wheel.

St Catherine's Down extends northwards like an inland promontory. From it you can trace the subtly shifting lineaments of the southern bulwark: gravel caps, domes and ridges of Chalk, flanks of Upper Greensand and laps of Gault Clay, a marvellous gallery of profiles silhouetted down against down against sky; care-worn and cultivated brows furrowed by sheepwalks and strip-lynchets, pocked with marl-pits, riven by dry valleys and, below, by wet ones; the weathered peaks and silted troughs of a great, slow swell. If tradition is to be believed, swell is not a fanciful word. According to Sir Richard Worsley, Chale men maintained that, in their youth, Shanklin Down was barely visible above Week Down from St

Catherine's Down, and that older men had told them of a time when it could only be glimpsed from the top of the beacon; that therefore Shanklin Down was rising, or Week Down subsiding; tales which geologists find hard to swallow. But then, they don't much like the ups and downs of Brading Haven, or the idea of a causeway across the Solent. In the face of a geological theory that is as rock-solid as the earth's faulted, shifting, crumbling crust, you may prefer to listen to the persistent yoppul, or gabble, of the oral tradition. However, everyone agrees about the land-slips along the coast, though many forget that the inland cliffs, around St Catherine's Down, Gat Cliff and St Martin's Down, are their mirror image: craggy features fallen away into the island's bowl.

The tall Corinthian column topped by a ball, on St Catherine's Down, was erected by Michael Hoy, a Russian merchant who built the Hermitage, to commemorate the English visit of Czar Alexander in 1814. Lieutenant Dawes, of the infamous Sophie's family, appended in 1857 an ironic tablet, carved by Andrew Morris of Afton, in memory of our dead in the Crimea. Trees climb towards the monument, and the walk to the Hermitage plunges you into a different world, of bluebells, hawthorn and sycamore, of sweet chestnut, beech and privet, and the gracious shrubby shelter of a garden; there is a terrace and a fountain, a roofed-in spring and a swimming-pool; faded grandeur embowered among blowsy rhododendrons, a stable-block with a clock-tower and bell-cote, fractured stone urns and gargoyles grimacing head-in-hands on the gateposts. Below Hermitage Wood, a new house has the view: the valley of the upper Yar, gaunt Gat Cliff, Godshill and on to Sandown Bay and the gleaming Culvers. One moment, you may drop down a lush field putting up flustered partridge; the next, the sun heats a dry landscape out of Turkey, where black-faced sheep shelter under pines on livid, sandy outcrops; then, the scene falls open before you like a sheet of flower-spangled pasture where single trees grow out of ponds of shadow.

Soon you come upon the manor of Wydcombe, set amongst old timber and gathering streams to itself in the angle between Head Down and St Catherine's Down. Here, there is a drinking fountain in a niche by the pig-styes, a blind-eyed and corrugated-iron roofed stone farmhouse and derelict yard, with barns in which Tudor work abuts on to breeze-blocks and galvanized iron. The walled manor house exhibits stone-work spanning three centuries, a derelict Frenchified, Victorianized confection now being renovated. One wing has gone, another is roofless, but the main house is oddly enchanting: gables with lacy bargeboards consort with lucarne-style windows, a spired oriel and a pagoda-like penthouse. The garden runs up a steep-sided valley to where a dammed stream makes a pond and waterfall. Two sisters and a brother lived reclusive lives in this nook of Arcadia, but after the ladies died their brother hanged himself, and the house and garden were possessed by rot and weed that are only now beginning to be exorcized. The stream, with sumps of sycamores beached on its bank, purls through parkland and, before it reaches Monky Lands and Southford Lane, the long tall bulk of Moorhills Farm brings it back to Jacobean Wight. Stone it is, but it has a heart of wood, for timber is Clifford Matthews' business as it was his forefathers'. Moorhills' staircase with treads made from a quartered trunk, many of its fittings and much of its furniture were made in the workshop outside. Where another man might park his car, his son's oyster-dredger is in for a re-fit. An elm-trunk is a magical tree-house for his grandchildren. He sat, the epitome of an enterprising Islander, his hands engulfing a glass, and his legs stretched before a blazing fireplace whose ancient-looking Tudor arch and panelling he inserted, and talked of his work on the replicas of the *Golden Hind* and the *Nonsuch*, in photography and television. His success is bred of woodsman's lore; of horse-chestnut for milk pails, of ash zores for hurdles woven with hazel, of the whippances and bodkins that comprise a discriminating carter's set of clutters, of quant poles for Medina barges. When Cliff's great-grandfather and his father called at Princeletts for cocoa on a cold winter's night, the farmer stuffed the boy into a hay-filled sack for the cart-ride home; and Cliff himself remembers oak poles, stripped of their bark for tanning, being sawn for nitches of firelighting and carted to Ventnor, where every hotel bedroom had its fire to warm the hordes of winter visitors. His are the timber spans that bridge the chasm at Whitecliff Bay; his collection of wood-working tools and an innovative mind work hand in glove to solve any problem in wood, he says, however knotty.

Across the valley, at Nettlecombe, a brick smithy contains the forge where malleable pink iron has been smitten into the shapes that succeeding generations have needed. The old bakehouse at Berryl

Farm, Whitwell, has hatched fertile images of germination, growth and decay in plaster, wood, stone and bronze, for in his cottage there the sculptor Colin Riches realizes tough visions of birth, crucifixion and healing.

Whitwell's church of St Mary & St Rhadegunde has been much restored and adorned with crucifixes and images of saints, but contains an old decayed roof-boss displaying the instruments of the Passion and the pierced palms of Christ. A reproduction of the mural that decorated the south wall shows the body of a saint beheaded by wicked powers-that-be, beneath a medieval city, a mountain, and his assumption and coronation in the kingdom-that-is-to-come, the heavenly city. St Rhadegunde's was a chapel of the Esturs of Gatcombe, and a Norman respond to the otherwise Perpendicular chancel arch survives behind the pulpit of 1623. About 1200, the lord of Stenbury added the chapel of St Mary for his St Lawrence tenants; the arcade that links and divides the twin chapels is supported by an octagonal pier of Purbeck marble, from elsewhere and slightly short, with a swollen abacus to make up the height. Outside, beneath the tower's great battlements, are some beautiful eighteenth-century headstones of Purbeck workmanship, whose foliage, scrolls and cherubic heads have weathered better than the etched and eroded stones of the church porch. Behind the church there is a prospect, over Whitwell's roofs, of Hoy's monument growing out of trees on the distant down, and a black and a white horse grazing in tandem over the churchyard wall. The White Horse Inn, once an alehouse known as Chiddles Cottage, draws lunchtime pilgrims in under its thatch; they used to process to the White Well or, more prosaically, to draw water from the pumps erected by Mr Spindler of Old Park, St Lawrence. Now, stout lubricates the progress of spent matches around the cribbage board and the inaudible dialect commentary that issues from the gap-toothed mouths of antique opponents. A greying black dog sleeps and twitches arthritically under the table. A third old man looks on, scratching at his mobile wig, like a taciturn umpire: "Goo on, you gurt chucklehead . . . Iss, iss . . . Wull, Oi'll be daarned . . . There's a pretty zet out!" The louder, younger men in the bar are Island republicans, discussing the royal family: "All this Chas an' Di, wha's blue blud anyhow? Jus' means their grandads wuz bigger thieves'n anyone . . . Fly the flag over the Falklands, but does this Oiland want a Guv'nor. No thanks!"

The Yarborough Arms would have been royalist, rooting for Prince Charles or the Duke of Kent, had it been open; it was the small station hotel for the 1897 line that ran south past Dean Farm, disappeared into the portals of the down, emerged some six hundred yards later, and served St Lawrence and Ventnor West until 1952. Now, this end of St Lawrence Tunnel is a moist, dark spawning ground for mushrooms. Northwards, the railway's truncated embankment runs out of the downs' embrace, leaving the Council housing estate called Paradise to the left and, to the right, Stenbury Farm, a Jacobean manor house on the moated site of its thirteenth-century antecedent. Of the moat, two dry arms remain; of Stenbury mill, two banked rectangles flank the stream; of the de Heyno's chapel, or of the Bronze Age urn cemetery disinterred in 1727, there is nothing at all.

I would have enjoyed descending from my Isle of Wight Central Railway carriage and being conveyed in a trap from the station, between the stone and thatch of Godshill, to the fulsome hospitality of the Griffin Hotel. In the morning I should have dawdled about the village, smelling the products of the bakery's dying fires and listening to the bellows breathing new life into the forge and to the chiming of the smith's anvil. I should have delayed the pleasure of ascending the hill itself, until the sun was high and lit full on its graveyard summit and the glorious All Saints Church. Church, Herb Cottage, Natural History Museum, Bird Garden, Tea Gardens and all are echoed in miniature in the Model Village in the Old Vicarage Gardens. The village is still full of charm; it is no sea-side strumpet; its attractions are those of a demure, country-bred whore who has learned to please city folks. So I climb the hill as quickly as possible, away from knick-knackery, clap-trappery and all her trippery temptations, up into narrow lush lanes sunk into the Ferruginous Sands. For Godshill is not part of the true southern bulwark, but its inland vanguard, a high place to which stones for a church on the water-meadows of Sheepwash were repeatedly and supernaturally raised in Edward the Confessor's time, we are told. The builders gave in, and claimed the pagan hill for God.

The present church is the fourth on the site, and dates from the fourteenth century. With its twin naves, twin transepts, and embattled and pinnacled tower set above picture-postcard cottages, it is the largest and most colourful pre-Reformation church in the Wight. Gleaming white walls and arcades enhance an interior full of air and light, but set off enough details, picked out in Mr Joyce's modern paintwork, to make a Puritan apoplectic: a modern rood-beam, images of saints, memorial effigies and cartouches, as well as rich carpets and embroidery, fat candles and continuously quivering sanctuary flames. Services here are thick with incense from swung censers, with sprinkling and with the tinkling of bells. At the elevation of the Host, a chime is struck within, and the sanctus bell of 1703, hung between corbel heads in the south transept's bell-cote, rings out its proclamation of death and resurrection high across the valley of the Yar. Inside, the sacrament is reserved under the transept's barrel roof. A carved angel on a corbel and painted angels bearing scrolls look down upon the fifteenth-century mural of a three-branched lily which, for all its delicacy of leaf and stem, bears all the agonized, exquisite weight of the crucified Christ. The Lily Cross of Godshill is unique in Britain; its faded brushwork, together with the vivid re-painting elsewhere in the building, give some idea of the gaudy splendour of our medieval churches.

There is a rich gallery of Worsley memorials: effigies of Sir James, the Master of the Robes who stage-managed the Field of the Cloth of Gold, and his lady, Anne, kneel beneath a delicate frieze and a pediment surmounted by a tilting-helmet; Sir Richard Worsley is monstrously commemorated by a 30-ton sarcophagus with lion's feet, now sensibly obscured by the pipes of the elegant organ brought from Freshwater in 1814. Lady Anne's mother and father, Sir John and Lady Agnes Leigh, carved from Derbyshire alabaster, recline in state under a Caen stone canopy between the chancels; Sir John's feet rest on a pig and their soles are carved with the fat, cowled figures of Bedesmen or Weepers who whimsically tell their rosaries out of sight of all but the nosiest sightseers. Godshill was the fattest living on the Island in 1296; it was required to provide three armed horses in time of war, as against Brading and Newchurch's two each. In 1308, the installation of a new rector by the bishop of Winchester, to replace the man nominated by Lyre, was opposed by armed monks who were excommunicated for their pains. In 1570, the vicar was suspected of papistry and tolerance of recusants; he had put away his wife in Mary's reign, had not read the confession of uniformity for nine years, and had not uttered the monthly prayers against the

241

Pope. He would feel at home here now. All Saints is rich and strange and peaceful.

You walk out of the porch over the bones of Richard Gard; despite his epitaph's eulogy, he was for ever stigmatized by Oglander as an estate-grabber and horse-thief; he had his lead coffin interred under the thinnest covering of earth so that he might make a quick exit at the resurrection, as if the last trump was the starting-gun for the sprint to the celestial city. The timekeeper's clock is an eighteenth-century sundial mounted on the tiered plinth of a fifteenth-century cross. Moles throw up obstacles of red earth among the graves which, like the church, are speckled with the ochres and greens, blacks and whites of lichens. Anne Garde, died 1592, lies at the east end of the church; hour-glasses, skulls and cherubs' heads adorn eighteenth-century headstones, while, on Ann Loader's, a hand emerging from heavy clouds plucks off the coffin-lid and a trumpeting angel points at her skeleton and those of her twin children. Who knows who will arise from beneath the oldest slab, which lies beside the path to Churchgate Cottage? It is marked with a sword in weathered relief, dating perhaps from Plantagenet days. Here, at rogation-tide, white surpliced figures process, dropping holy water like dew and wafting clouds of incense, between the black yew trees and the dense scrub which conceals ruins and many birds at the hill's brow. Rooks croak ragged responses from their twig rafts below. When thunder rolls, folk recall apocalyptic lightning strikes: that of 1904, which caused £1,000 worth of damage to the tower, of 1897, and that of 1778, which tore at the tower, melted parts of the clock, rolled up leading, ran the length of the arcade, forked, shook the east end and ploughed a furrow in the boneyard.

Southwards, in the liquid light, you can see the greater obstacle of Gat Cliff's firestone face. High on the summit of Appuldurcombe Down is the Worsley obelisk, like a winning-post; 70 feet of Cornish granite, lopped by lightning in 1831, which the parish council and Sir Richard Worsley are planning to restore. The southern bulwark sprawls to left and right. The sea could be a million miles away. Hilda Piper told me of an old man, Godshill born and bred, whom she nursed in Ryde Hospital. Until that trip, he had been to Newport now and then but had never seen the sea. She took him on to the hospital roof for a glimpse of it. "That what all the fuss be about?" he said, "My duck-pond at hwome's better'n that."

Worsleys were great travellers. After the jury had awarded Sir Richard one shilling damages in the divorce action he brought against Captain Bisset of Knighton, the 27th admitted lover of his wife, Lady Seymour, he set off for the Mediterranean, the Near East, the Levant and Russia. He brought his plunder back to the house below Stenbury Down, begun by Sir Robert in 1701 in the grand manner, and completed by him in a grander manner still. The obelisk and Cook's Castle, of which a few stones remain on St Martin's Down, were eye-catchers on each side of a valley landscape orchestrated by Capability Brown. Freemantle Gate is an Ionic triumphal arch, between Godshill and Appuldurcombe Parks, designed by Wyatt, who also supplemented the English Baroque style of John James' house design. Tuscan columns, giant Corinthian pilasters framing greensand ashlar from the Undercliff, and swags, roundels, garlands and mouldings of Portland stone made an elaborate setting for Sir Richard's collection of Greek marbles, gems, paintings—including the *Daniel in the Lions' Den* after Rubens, now in Godshill Church—and Chippendale furniture. The exhibits, so enjoyed by the young John Ruskin, were catalogued, annotated and copiously illustrated in the rare and sumptuous two-volume *Museum Worsleianum*.

Appuldurcombe had been a Priory of the Abbey of Montebourg in Normandy and, following the suppression of alien houses, was granted to the nun minoresses without Aldgate, who leased it to the Frys. By marriage it came to Sir John Leigh, whose daughter Anne married Sir James Worsley. The house which Sir Robert boasted of having razed to the ground was a many-gabled Elizabethan mansion. The Worsley motto was *Ut Sursum Desuper*—I swoop to rise again— but the new house passed to Sir Richard's niece, wife of the Earl of Yarborough, and was sold in 1855. The Revd Mr Pound ran an academy for young gentlemen here. The Benedictines of Solesmes found it a refuge before moving to Quarr. The house decayed, unsold, and in 1943 a landmine shattered windows and damaged the roof; an echo of the gunpowder explosion in the gate-house that killed two sons of an earlier Richard Worsley, that Captain of the Wight who entertained Henry VIII and Thomas Cromwell at Appuldurcombe. Now it is a roofless ruin, dramatically shot through with shafts of light and shadow, a shell in the care of the Department of the Environment.

Only the arched and vaulted cellars are sheltered from the elements now; but, in the middle of a field of sweetcorn behind the house, there is a hump of scrub hiding an ice-house of fine stonework. Steps descend to an arch where the first of two sets of doors, arranged like an air-lock, used to hang. Deep inside the thick masonry is a brick-built dome where ice, frozen in the nearby shallow pan, was stored like gold in a vault: a cave of ice to be mined in the hot season. From its profound silence, I emerged to the sound of mowing-machines touring between the noble trees that punctuate the lawns beyond the ha-ha, and the chinking of masons' tools on stone. George Newberry was at work restoring the coping around the fountain. He explained that French stone had to be used, because it was difficult to get large enough greensand blocks now from the quarries at Gatcombe, Luccombe, Steephill, or between Whitecroft and Nettlecombe. Blocks tumbled by the shore are more often than not spoiled by shatterwicks: hard, grey, splintery bodies which resist a chisel and are shattered by a punch. Blue-hearted rag, that was used for Appuldurcombe Lodge, can still be found. When the north section of the main house, foundering on its pine raft, was taken down and rebuilt, the blocks measured five feet by four by twenty inches deep. Mr Newberry is a craftsman in the old tradition, proud of his work and that of his forebears; a non-conformist character propping up the bones of a stately home, a radical republican restoring the bastions of privilege for the enjoyment of the public.

The pillars in the Great Hall or Colonnade Room are of ruddy scagliola, in imitation of porphyry. They have sufferd most from the weather and are sheltered under corrugated iron. But stand between them, looking out over the shining star motif in the marble floor, and you still get a notion of the grandeur to which Sir Robert Worsley, friend of Bishop Ken and Dean Swift whose "reigning folly" was planting, and *Appuldrecwm*, valley of the apple-trees, aspired. A gravel path runs between trim lawns to the bowl of the fountain, whose liquid arcs once spread themselves and appeared to tangle with the boughs of a stately tree beyond. Through a filigree of water and foliage, Worsley eyes glimpsed the fertile rise and fall of the downs behind Wroxall. Over there, the buzzard, or *wroc* that gave its name to the village, patrols field-banks for what it can get, quartering the territory towards twin cottages called *Providence* and *Temperance*. Though the old thatches in the village's centre once shrouded smuggled tubs, it is a sober-looking, workmanlike place, where Teknacron's printed circuit works has replaced the bacon factory. St John's Church is weathering badly because its Victorian stonework was not laid with the grain. From the steep porch tower of 1911, lucarne windows ogle the main street and the cottages built there for workers imported to drive the railway tunnel through Wroxall and Littleton Downs to Ventnor.

The Isle of Wight Railway's burrow begins between Wroxall Cross and Wroxall Farm and disappears, but for ventilation shafts like mole-hills upon the downs, for 1,312 yards. The company had intended to link Shanklin and Ventnor via Luccombe and the Landslip, but Lord Yarborough led the opposition to this route and forced them to undertake the largest engineering feat on the Island. At the Wroxall end, a hoard of fourth-century coins was discovered during the digging in 1863, and when the Wroxall moles finally broke through and met the Ventnor moles, deep underground on 10 September 1866, they are said to have celebrated with a free-for-all fist fight. The glinting brass and fiery breath of locomotives daily penetrated the southern bulwark and emerged, from a red-brick portal in the firestone face of an old quarry, directly into the station built there. Old adits were engine sheds and store-houses hacked out of raw rock below the valley that runs up to the elbow of Littleton Down far above. Now clothes, fibre-glass, and venetian blinds are made in the industrial estate that replaced the terminus. The tunnel is blocked, and passengers no longer make a dramatic entry, from darkness into the rocky glare and sea-light above Ventnor.

You can still refresh yourself in the Terminus Hotel, at the old quarry mouth, before tackling the steep path that climbs behind it and up a staircase of rugged steps cut into the hillside. Soon the track becomes chalky as you rise above the Upper Greensand and Chert which the quarry face displays. On an April day I made the ascent to the highest point on the Wight, the 783-foot summit of St Boniface Down. Rabbit-droppings speckled the turf and scores of rabbits scattered like shadows before the rising sun. Every tussock seemed to shelter a treasure of modest violets and proud, trumpeting cowslips. Across the valley, Littleton Down's hide is brindled with patches of gorse, hawthorn and dead bracken; oases of bluebells glittered between concrete outcrops, the surviving footings of military installations. Up here, the top of the Wight's world is gravel-capped, with an acid flora including, in a few months, tormentil and bilberry. Masts rise and spread their wiry webs; green radar dishes swivel incessantly, whining a monotonous lament. Radar made Ventnor a prime target during the last war, and bomb craters pock the brow of the down, recolonized now by heather, brambles and more bluebells. Next time, if the worst happens, the bombs will not be so forgiving. Vain will be the scuttling to makeshift shelters amongst the clutter of roofs below, that seem to adhere to Ventnor cliff. The sirens will sound more like the last trump, and the race be more like that of Richard Gard starting from his shallow Godshill bed; or like the Wroxall and Ventnor moles hurrying to the centre of the earth. Below 30 feet of St Boniface's chalk and twelve feet of concrete, there is a hundred yards of corridor serving chambers that comprise a nuclear war nerve-centre dating from the last war but equipped for its new task since 1974. Communications rooms, operations rooms, dormitories, a canteen, toilets, air conditioning and generating plant are reserved for the use of those civil and military personnel, under Colonel Ian Appleton, who have tickets for the bunker. A think-tank from which to co-ordinate corpses, casualties and those bands of desperadoes which seem to be the first concern of post-holocaust planners. The élite may have a passport for their passage beyond the mushroom cloud, but they are asked to bring their own picnics, knife, fork and spoon.

Today, the view from the top is glorious; St Catherine's Tower makes a clear mark on the distant down, but the story goes that a bishop once picked his way here on horseback in a dense mist. Finding himself riding over the precipice, he let go of the reins and trusted himself to the beast's sure-footedness and the care of St Boniface, vowing that he would donate an acre of land to the saint's church if he got to the bottom alive. Bishop's Acre survives to tell the tale. Folk used to climb up to St Bonny's Well which sprang, remarkably, from near the summit; if they reached it without once looking back, any wish they made while drinking of its water would be granted. On the saint's day, it used to be dressed with flowers. Bishop Wilfrid, to whom Caedwalla granted a third of the Island, was the hero of the young monk of Crediton named Wynfryth who came to Nursling, near Southampton. There is no evidence for it in the voluminous correspondence he left behind, but it may be that he trod these hills in the days before he became that St Boniface, Apostle of Germany, who laid the foundations of the Holy Roman Empire, before being martyred at Dokkum in 754.

Once past the radar and the high fences—with the rich, rife Undercliff and the sea far below, the valley of the apple trees embraced by downs to the north, and the spine of hills beyond like the rim of the Island's bowl—it is possible to think so. It is a miraculous place. Up here on that April day, I followed the flirting flight of a bird in yellow and black livery; it took off as I approached and alighted ahead, again and again. A rare presence and a privileged sighting, for it was a golden oriole that lured me on along the roof of the world, before vanishing at last in the scrub of Bonchurch Down. Suddenly, the south-east coast from Luccombe to Binbridge Isle unrolled before me like an illuminated scroll. Chestnut and white horses grazed on the slopes of Nansen Hill, named after the Polar explorer by John Whitehouse of Bembridge School; and below, to the right, was the Landslip, the beginning of that most magical fillet of land that lies between the southern bulwark and the sea.

18

HEALTH, WEALTH & UNDERWORLD

The Undercliff bids fair to exceed all other winter residences in this country, and the island will have added to its title of the Garden of England, that of the BRITISH MADEIRA.

Dr James Clark   *The Influence of Climate in the Prevention and Cure of Chronic Diseases*

So eulogistic a statement from so eminent an authority set the whole world of invalids in motion.

W.H.D. Adams   *Nelson's Hand Book to the Isle of Wight*

FROM THE HIGH places you drop through the Devil's Chimney to a fallen world, a slipped latitude. From tea-rooms set in trim gardens you clamber down a dank rift and emerge into a contorted place where twisted oaks and hazel brakes, brambles and moss and hart's tongue fern, tangled clematis and ivy grow upon the tumbled, terraced terrain of the Landslip. Paths that ran across the East End, from Luccombe towards the dark snout of Dunnose, were carried away when twenty or thirty acres foundered in 1810. In 1818, even greater portions of chalk-capped greensand were sundered from the base of Nansen Hill, above Bordwood Ledge and Steel Bay. With full-grown trees shuddering and plunging, rafts of ground slid on the blue slipper. They shifted seawards, tilting landwards all the while, and reared new scarps and cliffs with chasms and valleys behind, where blocked streams pooled into little lakes. Heads of water lubricated further slips, while at cliff edge and shore the clays were weathered out of the fallen masses, so that the hard rock was slowly consolidated into a firm bastion. Things stabilized. Raw surfaces, that so awed visitors in the 1820s, soon were cloaked with growth, and the Wight witnessed a terrifying and consoling demonstration of the way in which the Undercliffs, that slump for seven miles between Luccombe and Blackgang Chines, were made. Turf turned the rough diamond's rugged new facets to emerald. Cattle grazed it, and made tracks in a fresh territory.

Dunnose's coarse and pebbly Carstone strata drop to sea level at Monks' Bay. Hulks of Upper Greensand Chert rest on the beach, and a curvaceous array of laid-back timbers protects the coast from erosion. In the 1840s, the last remnants of a "Roman" encampment were washed away, though urns and calcined bones continued to be exhumed for some years.

Tradition wildly asserts that the monks of Lyre first landed at Monks' Bay in the eighth century, and that they founded the first church of St Boniface at Bonecerce, or Boncurch. A coin of Aethelwulf, Alfred the Great's father, was found here, but the tiny Old Church has nothing older in it than Norman masonry re-used in the late twelfth century. The churchyard, though, feels like anciently hallowed ground. Among trees and climbers, shrubs and daffodils, lie moss-quilted table tombs and the simple headstones of quarry-men, fishermen and farmers, in sight of a sea much nearer than that on the old maps, for the glebe has been eaten away. Here, Charles I had brief, mournful respite from Carisbrooke at the burial of Sir Ralph Chamberlayne, where Thomas Mackett already lay in the oldest grave of 1616. Here lies John Hadfield, with John Sterling, whom Carlyle called "the most perfectly transparent soul I have ever known". Here, the Revd William Adams, author of *The Shadow of the Cross* who died at Winterbourne overlooking the boneyard, lies near Paul Moyle Robins Beswetherick, a Bible Christian minister from Cornwall, who died in Ventnor in 1861 aged twenty-four. Between them, they could tell a tale of the metamorphosis of Bonchurch. Inside—before a rococo Flemish cross of black oak given by Mr Surman in 1830, and beneath a wall-painting that might be St Christopher or the Last Judgement—the five-year-old boy Swinburne was christened Algernon Charles.

Captain (later Admiral) Charles Swinburne subjected his son to another baptism when he threw him, giggling and struggling, into the sea at Monks' Bay. For the father, water and flogging were naval prerequisites; for the son, pain and the solving sea were sensuous escape-routes into chaos. The Captain rented and then, in 1841, bought East Dene, the house at the bottom of Bonchurch Shute, built by Mr Surman in 1826 on the site of Bonchurch Farm. With

Macketts Farm, near the Old Church, and Marepool Farm, by the
osier bed which fishermen cropped for weaving lobster-pots, it
divided the parish's territory into a tight mosaic of Closes, Meads
and Wards, opening out uphill into larger Fields, Furlongs and
Downs. Field-names like Mount, Lamb Ledge, Cliff and Lind Ledge
reflected the terrain, while Little Pitts, Great Pitts and Pitts indicate
where stonecutters worked the freestone and rag. A pyramid of
sample stone, dating from 1773, is built into the wall near the pond.
In the cliffs, a cave called Old Jack could hold up to 500 gallons of
illicit liquor. Spirits in the form of a horseman and a phantom coach
kept folk indoors as the hard stuff was carried, on muffled hoofs, to
the combe behind Mr Hadfield's St Boniface House. The house,
demolished after a rates dispute, harboured a more disquieting
presence that ripped bedclothes off sleeping guests, but was booked
by William Wilberforce as having "the best climate in Britain for a
pulmonary case" for his daughter Lizzy in 1832. She died before she
could be moved there, but it is clear that Bonchurch's attractions
were being noised abroad. Already, Joseph Hadfield had cleared the
osier-bed and made a pond; Keats had written of its cottages
"covered with creepers and honeysuckles, with roses and eglantines
peeping in at the windows. Fit abodes for the people I guess live in
them, romantic old maids fond of novels, or soldiers' widows with a
pretty jointure. . . . If I could play upon the Guitar I might make my
fortune with an old song—and get two blessings at once—a Lady's
heart and the Rheumatism." Uppermount, now the sumptuous
Peacock Vane, was built in 1836, the year the Revd James White had
a private Act of Parliament passed to revoke the restrictive conditions under which his wife, Rosa Hill, had inherited much of
Bonchurch. Marepool Farm was superseded by Wood Lynch;
Macketts became Undermount, and its barn, Winterbourne. The
outcrop known as Shakespeare Rock was re-named Pulpit Rock and
given a wooden cross to commemorate St Boniface's supposed
preaching-post. Hadfield's Look-out in Undermount's grounds
became Flagstaff Rock. So the wild crust of the place was tamed,
farms transformed into mansions, and closes into luxuriant gardens
behind stone walls. Hewn greensand was reared against backdrops of
rugged rock. Romantic wildness and bucolic charm were civilized
and enhanced with money and the aid of a sub-tropical micro-
climate.

Where owlers had cheated customs men along haunted runs from the Channel to hideaways and safe houses, now gentlefolk smuggled their sick to cheat the Ferryman. George Brannon feared for the village: "From the bad taste which too generally prevails,—we mean the *vanity of glare*—the *affectation of elegance*,—so frequently carried out at the expense of all propriety, we are not without some apprehension that many of the gentry at Bonchurch will also neglect the essential rule, that *the peculiar character of every scene demands an* APPROPRIATE STYLE *in building and decoration*: for it avails little to have ivy-mantled rocks and mossy cliffs, the sunny knoll and the shady glen, with their groves and streams,—if the Genius of the spot be not consulted, and HARMONY made the rule of every innovation and improvement." A sentiment which the Wight could ill afford to ignore, and did, and still does. Damn the Genius of the spot, when the Genius of the heart is pride or mammon.

The Revd James Hill and Charles Swinburne did a good job, however, when they provided for the new church of St Boniface. The foundation was laid by the Revd William Adams in June 1847; Jonathan Joliffe, builder, and Daniel Day, mason, worked to designs by Benjamin Ferrey of London. They raised an imposing edifice for 360 sittings against the shored-up rockface of Pitts. Lancets cast coloured lights across an airy interior bedecked with tapestry work. The pagan Oak of Thor, looking more like a Christmas tree, is borne on a banner by St Boniface, who miraculously felled it in far-off Hesse. On choir-stall cushions, whimsical animals parade into the Ark and out under the rainbow, whose colours are picked up in ranks of kneelers. Outside, raw and worked stone amplify the light to Mediterranean intensity, and graves squat among mossy rocks and trees burdened with blossom. Dr Leeson, the church's patron who gave his name to Leeson Road, lies with his family in a mausoleum capped by a great pyramid. A marble tomb commemorates the "king" of the Cocos-Keeling Islands, George Clunies-Ross, who rested here for five years before being re-interred in his kingdom in 1915. Swinburne came into his Wight kingdom in 1909, when his body was lowered into one of the half-dozen family graves here. The procession that followed his cortège from Ventnor was an odd one, and the rector who led it a confused man. The family wanted a Christian burial, but the poet's companion and executor, Watts-Dunton, insisted, at William Rossetti's suggestion, on his friend's desire for a godless interment. In the face of the Disney-Leiths, Tennyson's son Hallam, and the daughters of William Rossetti and William Morris, among many other distinguished mourners, the rector gave a harmless address. He avoided any mention of the resurrection, but when his compromise service included the homily, "Man that is born of woman hath but a short time to live . . .", some of the chief mourners greeted it with cries of "Shame!" and "Scandalous!" The next year, Thomas Hardy and Florence stood among primroses here; to the accompaniment of noisy rooks, Hardy laid a sprig of mournful, magical ivy on the grave, and wrote:

> In this fair niche above the unslumbering sea,
> That sentrys up and down all night, all day,
> From cove to promontory, from ness to bay,
> The Fates have fitly bidden that he should be
>   Pillowed eternally . . .

East Dene is now a field-study and conference centre, claiming seventeenth-century fabric and oak panelling looted from the Armada. It has a Victorian château for a lodge, with the stem of a vine, labelled 1870, snaking thickly into it. Brannon's fears have not been wholly realized; exotics have not entirely exorcized ash, hawthorn and whortleberry, and I confess to coveting Monks' Bay Cottage with its octagonal annexe ideal for a study. From there, I could creep out into the heat and light above the insatiable sea, and follow in the footsteps of those who have lived or stayed in Bonchurch: H. de Vere Stacpoole who gave the pond to the village, the young Alice Meynell, Elizabeth Sewell who started her school here, Tennyson who had his wideawake hat sliced up for souvenirs by lady admirers, Edmund Peel and Edmund Venables. At Winterbourne, Thackeray and Carlyle were entertained by Dickens, who interspersed work on *David Copperfield* with climbs up St Boniface Down, gin-punch parties, rounders on the beach, and showers under the waterfall, shielded from the villagers' gaze by a special shelter. But his enthusiasm for Bonchurch waned. He was sceptical of doctors' claims, and wrote, "I am quite convinced that I should die here, in a year. It's not hot, it's not close, I don't know what it is, but the prostration of it is awful."

But Macaulay, who spent the summer of 1850 working on his

History of England at Madeira Hall towards Ventnor, summed up the consensus view: "Here I am, lodged most delightfully. I look out on one side to the crags and myrtles of the Undercliff, against which my house is built. On the other side I have a view of the sea, which is at this moment as blue as the sky, and as calm as the Serpentine. My little garden is charming."

Ventnor had been charming too, twenty years before, and less of a place than Bonchurch. It was then furnished with fine firm sand. A grist-mill, perched on a crag, spewed its race down into Mill Bay, where Turner had drawn fishing-boats, lobster-pots and capstans. The occupants of half a dozen cottages refreshed themselves, in the company of the few visitors who penetrated this underworld, at the Crab & Lobster Inn. In 1828, the mason who worked on Steephill Castle built Cove Cottage, around which the new village was to coalesce, catalysed by Dr (later Sir) James Clark's advocacy of the climate and its efficacy for consumptives. The price of land increased ten-fold in fifteen years. John Hambrough ushered in the Victorian Age with his bleak Early English St Catherine's Church and the parsonage in Albert Street, built of stone quarried at Elm Grove and St Boniface Down. The road to Bonchurch was laid in the 1840s, an Act for "paving, lighting, watching, cleansing and otherwise improvement" was procured and, in 1848, the year Ventnor Mill burnt down, the sea-wall and esplanade were built, though Mill Street didn't become Pier Street for a while. The promontory at the east of the cove was blasted away and replaced by a jetty: it broke up. Seas undermined the new sea-front. The promontory was urgently rebuilt. Some natural laws had to be respected even by the developers of Ventnor, though they seemed to be able to disregard gravity, cramming dwellings into the bowl-shaped Cove, once known as Chicken Pits, and piling the town upon every available shelf and plinth: a game of snakes and ladders played upon a maze of zig-zag roads and steps, with the footings of one house at the chimney height of the next, "in every conceivable style and every outrageous shape," as Venables says, "Strawberry Hill Gothic, Seaside Swiss, and Carpenter's palazzo." In 1862, Holy Trinity's spire rose 160 feet above an interior rife with carved foliage and lit by a kaleidoscope of stained glass. A population that approached 400 in the late 'thirties, climbed to 5,000 by 1866. Ventnor was no longer charming.

But it is still attractive. The stone and thatch of Hadfield's Manor House, once a farm, squats below a precipice of later building styles. Sir Francis Pittis & Son occupy a fine town house. Hurst's, the ironmongers, have marvellously preserved their Victorian façade. Knight's Library drew the cultured to it, as did the Literary & Scientific Institute, and there are now plans for a Local Heritage Centre, which would please old patrons like Andrew Carnegie, and Lydia Becker, who distributed her first Women's Suffrage pamphlets here. There's a Classical Town Hall, a Gothic Albert Hall, and a valiant between-the-wars attempt at a Winter Gardens. St Boniface Court, where Elizabeth Sewell moved her Bonchurch school, is now a show-piece conversion into flats for retired members of the grocery trade. There are ranks of small terraced houses, and bulky detached and semi-detached villas, in permutations of greensand ashlar, rag rubble, yellow and red brick, and flint. In 1880, the six-year-old Winston Churchill and his brother Jack were despatched to Ventnor for August, to stay with their nanny's sister and her husband, a prison warder who regaled the boys with tales of prison mutinies. A troopship in full sail, a mile or so offshore, impressed them, but not as much as the subsequent storm and the knowledge that she had capsized with the loss of 300 souls. "It made a sear on my mind," Winston wrote, "that some of the divers had fainted with terror at seeing the fish, eating the bodies of the poor soldiers." In the winters of 1881 and 1882, Karl Marx stayed at number one Boniface Gardens to recuperate from his lung ailments, to think and write and walk. On his second visit, a relapse required him to call upon the help of Dr J.M. Williamson. From here, he penned his last letter to Engels: "I still believe that with the help of patience and pedantic self-control I shall soon be once again in shape. The Moor." To the young doctor he wrote what was perhaps one of the last letters of his life, enclosing a signed photograph of himself for Mrs Williamson and saying that he had just heard of his daughter, Jenny's death, a blow which could not but damage his own health. He left for London at once, and died two months later.

The 'eighties saw Ventnor put out a solid pier at last, after ill-fated earlier attempts. In July 1863, the paddle steamer *Chancellor* tore free of her berth alongside the half-built pier, and broke her back upon a shore littered with timbers; and in 1866 the harbour was ravaged by a storm. As I write, the Royal Victoria Pier's back is broken, a useless folly. In Marx's day, new hotels flew their flags along the front; fashionable ladies descended into the waves from lines of fourpenny bathing machines tethered along a beach strewn with shards of quartz, called "Ventnor Diamonds", and pebbles of Choanite, Chalcedony, Agate and Jasper. The fishmonger offered sound geological intelligence, and the hairdresser hawked pinned-down specimens of the Undercliff's butterflies. Neat tea-rooms, where Victorian matrons and misses fluttered and sipped, have metamorphosed into greasy fish-and-chip shops and garish take-away beach-tray parlours. The Pavilion on the Esplanade, with its octagonal crown, cupola and weathercock, is an amusement arcade, where the concert-party's song-and-dance and sly innuendoes have been superseded by the nudge-and-wink of machines. Sir Thomas Brisbane's circular tablet of 1881, announcing Ventnor's latitude and longitude, is propped outside: an incongruous relic of a time when people apparently cared where they were, and commented on how much further south they would need to travel to come upon the same climate.

Ventnor clambered uphill into this century, and seems to have gone downhill ever since. Desperately it applies face-packs and plans face-lifts. The Pageant of 1982 brought the smugglers back under sail, longshoremen competing to bring the booty home and up the East Cliff before the Excise men could catch them. No need to smuggle beer to Ventnor, though, for Burt's 1840 brewery, resurrected after being bombed out in 1943, provides a copious flow of staggeringly cheap and deceptively cheering Ventnor Ales, fed by an endless and almost free supply of St Boniface's spring water. Of their handful of tied houses in and around Ventnor, it is in the low warm gloom of the Hole in the Wall where you can catch a whiff of the town's old charm. Once the coal-house and coachmen's quarters for the Central Hotel, it is said to be visited by two ghosts, one civilian and one military, and by the haunting smell of violets. It is thick with the yarning and ribbing of sailors; the vicissitudes of shoals and sandbanks and outboard motors; the virtues and vices of visitors. Now, the talk is a requiem for houses foundered in Upper Ventnor, of a yawning hole that might swallow a bus, and of fears that, if subsidence continues, Lowtherville could be cut off.

And now, fortified by Burt's transmogrified spring-water, comments turn on the new soft-tinted floodlighting in Pier Street, and on plans to put the town back on the map with a vengeance, with the Ventnor Cascade. Where spa waters have lost their sparkle, a pleasure dome has been decreed. They are plotting, not just to tart up the Eastern Esplanade, give the Winter Gardens some plastic surgery and put a splint on the pier, but to back a £3,000,000 fantasy whose centre-piece will be a giant tent-shaped greenhouse sheltering the boating-lake, a sub-tropical forest, hanging gardens and escalators. There will be a scenic railway too. What, like the funicular railway the Victorians kept promising? 'Course, it'll never happen. Wait and see. Cascadia, here we come.

On a good day, the sea could be a clean version of the Mediterranean. A temperamental geology, whose momentary lapses transport you from Eden to primeval chaos, is offset by the seductive power of its climate. Dr Martin wrote that he had "counted nearly fifty species of garden flowers blooming in the borders in December; and sweet-peas blossom on Christmas Day!" All the Victorian guide-books eulogized the winter-flowering heliotrope, verbena, fuchsia, myrtle and petunia. A fine climate for ailing, or elderly lungs. Perhaps the Iron Age folk, who left hut-sites, pots and middens at Gills Cliff, together with a first-century brooch and a third-century coin-hoard, thought the same. Perhaps the Early Bronze Age man, whose ashes were interred under an inverted urn, came to Steephill for his health. Thirty socketed bronze axes were found there during the making of the railway. The same work disturbed a skeleton in a stone cist at St Lawrence, where Iron Age currency bars and crouched burials, including one with fragments of sword and shield, have been more gently disinterred. Cliff quarries have given up first brasses of Julius Caesar and Domitian, and third- and fourth-century coins have trickled on to the shore from a hoard in the cliff. At Furzebrake, an Iron Age woman, with a child, baby and pot, seems to have been buried unceremoniously by a landslip; while at Belgrave Road, Ventnor, a Romano-British lady wearing a bronze bracelet was overwhelmed by the same treachery. Men and plants have always loved and colonized this frail, desirable land-in-flux between the cliffs: the cliff below the downs and the cliffs above the sea.

Keats, living in Wordsworth's shadow, considered that the hill at Steephill was "almost of as much consequence as Mount Rydal on Lake Winander". Then, it overlooked a charming hamlet dominated by Hans Stanley's, and later Lord Dysart's, thatched cottage built on a deep rock terrace. Hambrough demolished both the grand cottage and the humble hamlet, "much to the advantage of the tenants" in Braddon's opinion, and built a mock-Gothic, romantic castle on the plinth, surrounded by gardens of exotics, by fountains, lawns and bowers, by giant fig-trees and an orangery with trees that owed their provenance to the Prince de Condé. Sir Joseph Paxton, doyen of parks and gardens, said, "I have visited nearly every place of note from Stockholm to Constantinople, but never have I seen anything more beautiful than this." In the 1870s, the Empress of Austria and Empress Eugénie stayed here, and it was to be the home of John Morgan Richards, Mrs Craigie's father, for many years. The young Alice Meynell danced at Steephill in its hey-day, "Glorious fun. Captain Sewell many times watched me going round and round . . . I had no regular flirtation, and no particular compliments, save that truest of all, that the men quarrelled to dance with me. . . . To this dance there were *no* drawbacks." Three-quarters of a century later, after the bombing of Ventnor on 12 August 1940, schoolchildren were thrilled to be moved from the school in the shadow of St Boniface Down to Steephill. For five years they were educated under battlements, in the keep, and in round and octagonal towers. Play-time for the "castle kids" took off into the gardens and woods. The Castle was pulled down in 1964 and replaced by a posh hamlet, suburbia on a shelf.

In the heat-haze of the Cricket Ground, white figures shimmer ghost-like through their summer rituals. Beside a new bungalow, built of and in a good Greensand quarry, the path drops down past grazing goats and donkeys to Steephill Cove. On the cottages, that thrust little stone-walled gardens daringly at the sea, only one thatch is left. Instead of upturned boats and lobster pots, there is a discreet café, sea-walls and breakwaters; but sand and rocks and fragile cliffs upholstered with greenery are the main attractions for those seeking respite from Ventnor's Esplanade. The cove heats and fills with bodies snug on towels or bobbing on lilos in its intimate embrace. However full of flesh and brilliant fabrics it gets, one feels the pressure of older presences, of work-a-day bowler hats and sea-boots, of blue serge and jersey, fishermen and smugglers pressing out of darkness into light, their lives ruled more urgently day and night by the rhythm of the tides, than those of the flimsy bikini-clad phantoms who loaf here at their leisure.

A little westwards, a tunnel through the cliff would lead, if it were not blocked off, up into the land of pomegranates, bananas, olives, loquats, locusts and all the other marvels of the Botanic Garden, a landscaped dream laid out above the sea. Garden fanciers nose between fruits and blooms and flowering trees as carp drift amongst weed in the rose-garden pond. Here, too, is the Smuggling Museum in a setting so picturesque that the grim staple of the old Island economy is, despite itself, rendered romantic. The car-park covers the long footings of Dr Arthur Hassall's Royal National Hospital for Diseases of the Chest. For almost a century, until its closure in 1964, patients lay in wards or in isolation in pavilions linked by a quarter of a mile of corridor, or reclined on wrought-iron balconies under the Tudor gables of Thomas Hellyer's design. They walked and played, or worked at stonecutting, landscaping, husbandry or gardening, according to their condition, in the shadow of the Frenchified tower and the Gothic chapel. Then the place was deserted. After so many slow cures and many more slow deaths, antibiotics exorcized its habitués. But demolition men are said to have been confronted by an ethereal white-coated figure in the operating theatre, by childish moans in the X-ray room, and by the persistent smell of ether.

Admiral Jellicoe used to stand before St Lawrence Hall, since burnt down, on the terrace he called "the bridge", looking out across the dark surge of trees to the white wake the moon made on the sea. Below the road rise the famous twisted red-brick chimneys and stone gables of Lisle Combe. There, the poet Alfred Noyes nurtured what he called "the remembering garden", with its Greek temple and five ponds, including the horseshoe-shaped "hoofprint on Helicon", and cliff pasture running seawards "like the bows of a great liner". Here, John Wilkes came to see work in progress on Worsley's marine villa or "Cottage". Here, the Breton, Jean Julian, tended vineyards and seven stepped and trellised terraces, laid out by Sir Richard Worsley in 1792–3, and planted with more than 700 White Muscadine and Plante Verde vines. Salt breezes and the winds of Napoleonic Wars taxed both vines and workers in sabots; by 1808, lawns replaced them and were embellished with cannon from a captured French privateer. St Lawrence's Well was enshrined in the Gothic manner and drew sightseers to it. Its crystal waters still tumble to the idyll of Orchard's Bay, but a Costa-del-Sol-style house squats beneath the cliff. Noyes habitually plunged into the dazzling arc of water, as into darkness in the days of his blindness, struck out into deep water and, aiming for his wife's guiding voice, swam back into the embrace of his Eden.

Guernsey cows tread the cliff path from their pastures to the milking parlour of Bank End Farm, skirting a lake in the lap of the Undercliff. Against the road stands the bulky parish church of St Lawrence, built by Sir George Gilbert Scott in 1878, notable for its scissor beam roof, for the carillon which first chimed for George V's Silver Jubilee, and for its stained glass. Sunlight enriches Burne-Jones' St Peter and St John, flanking Ford Madox Brown's St Luke, the doctor holding a copy of Hippocrates in one hand and corn-flowers in the other. A light-box illuminates William Morris's depictions of the raising of Lazarus and Jairus' daughter, on either side of Ford Madox Brown's woman with the issue of blood touching the hem of Jesus' garment. Jewel-like, clotted Pre-Raphael-ite colours contrast with the lighter, more flamboyant Art Nouveau glass of the west window; there, in Sir William Reynolds-Stevens' marvellous design, Dr George James Shaw takes a patient's pulse, opposite a paradigm of saintly care and a gaggle of glorious 'nineties angels and children, "Angels of Jesus, Angels of Light, Singing to Welcome the Pilgrims of the Night". These healing windows were saved from the chapel of the Royal National Hospital and installed here in 1972.

Uphill is the twelfth-century church of St Lawrence-under-Wath, the smallest in England until Lord Yarborough gave it a chancel in 1842. The old grave-slabs on which the chancel is founded include that of Corbet Shelbury, an eighteenth-century rector who died after hitting his head on the lintel of the now-blocked north door. The bell-cote houses the dinner-bell of 1777 from Appuldurcombe. The font was salvaged from the churchyard, and stands over against a mysterious font-like object behind the harmonium. Lift the lid, and you find a massive, pestle-less mortar. This old chapel of the de Aulas, dependent for centuries upon St Rhadegund at Whitwell, might be a hermit's cell set in a deep glade, were it not for the pews crammed under its contorted beams and candelabra, and the light reflected off the sea below and refracted through the special atmosphere of the Undercliff. Higher up the Shute, Redgun's, or Rhadegund's path, led worshippers to the mother church above the firestone cliff, or enthusiasts to the tunnel from which the fire-breathing train emerged on its way to St Lawrence Station, Steephill station on the site of the Castle's stables, and Ventnor West. Now the track is a road at the foot of High Hat, a sun-trap for twentieth-century ranch-houses and haciendas. How banal and time-slipped their bricks and tiles and porticoes look, glimpsed between the stone and slate and mullioned windows of the cottages below.

Maple Cottage keeps its counsel behind the low Tudor arch of its front door; Vestry Cottage was an early school-house; Spring Cottage was once called Smuggler's Retreat, and then The Duck, after a bedraggled bird—said to have fallen into Week Farm's well, more than a mile away above the Wath—issued with the spring there; at Rose Cottage, the smugglers' underground found a collaborator in Johanni Lovegad, a gardener imported by Lord Yarborough to introduce Mediterranean manners to his grounds. One Sunday morning, the church lacked a congregation because the cottagers were busy relieving a Dutch dogger of her cargo. In October 1811, the celebrated thespian, Mrs Radcliffe, flexed her vocal cords and her vocabulary against the Undercliff beyond, where "we entered upon a scene of the wildest grandeur and solemnity. Many of the ruinous precipices of the upper cliffs project in horizontal strata, yet have perpendicular rents. Some of the shattered masses give the clearest echoes: we stood before one which responded every syllable with an exactness which was truly astonishing.— There is sometimes what may be called an amphitheatre of rock, where all the area is filled with ruins, which are, however, covered with verdure and underwood, that stretch up the sides with the wildest pomp ..."

The Sugar Loaf is a tump, or tout, overlooking Woody Bay, from which wreckers and smugglers touted for the Channel's custom, and the coastguard kept a benign look-out. Eastwards runs a ragged coast of other bays and headlands, a wild front for the exotic shelf of ground that backs up to the tree-shrouded footings and exposed battlements of the Cliff. The eye takes in the high masts of St Boniface, the plush Gardens, Ventnor's perilous huddle and its optimistic pier making a bid for the horizon. The cliff path hugs the hedged plots of the old Coastguard Cottages, and is supposed to be frequented by an elderly black-cloaked lady with an umbrella and a basket of nammit for her husband, a ghost treading to and from a cottage long toppled into the sea. She is only seen by children, and was recalled by Mrs Georgiana Twining of Woolverton House, whose clock-tower rises behind Woody Bay, presumably to tell passing sailors when it is tea-time. Businesses less exotic than the tea-trade funded other villas and mansions that protrude from the Undercliff's arboretum as if to rival the raw face of the cliff that overshadows them.

In 1907, the truly venerable Woolverton Manor caught fire and its thatch was lost. Its seventeenth-century stone looks as stolid as ever, basking in the sun, but photographs preserved by the owners show a mob-capped and white-frilled garrison of maids guarding furniture and effects on the lawn, while fire-fighters strove with the flames. In the grounds gape the lanceted gables of a fourteenth-century ruin, often called a chapel; but its finely-tooled and time-worn fabric is pierced by joist-holes, showing that it was that two storey house named Woolverton-under-Cliff to which Oglander ascribed a sinister character: horses refused to be tethered by it, they sweated and would not be baited.

Men sweat beside furnaces in seventeenth-century farm-buildings at Old Park, which Michael Harris has transformed into the Isle of Wight Glass Works. Gobs of molten glass are gathered on to a blowing iron, blocked in a wooden cup, blown and rolled in a garnish of vivid glass granules before being coated with more clear glass. All the while, the alchemy is enhanced by re-heating in a glory-hole, and silver and gold leaf may complete the transmutation. Vessels grow like shapely crystal fruit; they blossom on the punty like sea-anemones or like the sea itself, like flowers or tropic gourds, blushing deeply or with delicate Japanese brushwork annealed upon a satin sheen. Sown in a fertile imagination and brought to fruition in intense heat, they are a glittering harvest worthy of the Undercliff.

Hunting thrived at Old Park in 1340, but no longer; horses and hounds are endangered by the cliffs, and foxes and badgers flourish. In 1305, a charter was granted for hawking here, but now the lake and walled gardens are home for toucans and peacocks, giant hornbills and cockatiels, macaws and touracos of the Tropical Bird Park, while Old Park House is a Gothic Hotel. Walt Disney's uncle, Sir John Cheape, lived here before it was bought by Herr Spindler, who wished to mastermind a model village, a new Wolverton to civilize the Undercliff between here and Ventnor. He laid out roads and made improvements, including embellishing St Lawrence Lodge for Mrs Craigie, alias the novelist John Oliver Hobbes. He began to transform the wild, rock-and-shingle-strewn coast at Binnel Bay into a harbour. Had he succeeded, one could have disembarked at a pier within sight of Puckaster Cove, that ancient landing-place of smugglers and traders where Charles II found a haven in a terrible storm of 1 July 1675; in sight, too, of the lighthouse whose beam first shone from St Catherine's Point on 23 March 1840, to warn vessels off the race whose fatal attraction draws vessels towards Rocken End as iron filings are drawn to a magnet. No doubt he would have tamed the rumpled land, quilted with scrub and shrub, mayweed and willow-herb, horse-tails and giant lords-and-ladies, that sprawls down to the bay. As it is, the wildest tract of Undercliff lies between Binnel and St Catherine's Points. But where tides play and storms mean business, the territory's natural wreckage of boulders is augmented by ungainly masses of masonry standing in the sea, the battered relics of sea-wall and esplanade, a German millionaire's dream, Spindler's Folly.

Almost-lost paths twist and switchback up through deep woods whose canopy is thick with birds and sunlight. In a sudden glade set on a step of land, the scarlet streak of a green woodpecker's flight seduces the eye upwards towards confections once called, by some quirk of snobbery, cottages. There is Mirables, and there, The Orchard whose prospect, sketched by Lady Willoughby Gordon and sent to her old tutor, gave Turner raw material for his light-hearted *View from the Terrace of a Villa at Niton*, exhibited at the Royal Academy in 1826, and stimulated him to visit the Wight the next year, after a 30-year absence. Swinburne's return to its neglected grounds, and to memories of childhood bliss, provoked one of at least four Undercliff poems, *A Forsaken Garden*:

> In a coign of the cliff between lowland and highland,
> At the sea-down's edge between windward and lee,
> Walled round with rocks as an inland island,
> The ghost of a garden fronts the sea . . .

The Repository of Arts had described how "the gushing fountain, rocky fragments, verdant slopes, with shrubs of every hue embellishing the winding lawns . . . are backed by a gigantic wall of cliff;

for this varied tract, though far below the beetling cliff, stands high above the broad blue ocean that eternally moves beneath." If you want to beetle up the cliff, you can cross the road and tackle the ascent called, tongue-in-cheek, the Cripple's Path. You edge along a shelf in the firestone face, head down to avoid the lowering overhang of gnarled chert that gives it the feeling of a secret passage open only to tree-tops and the secret place below. Then you emerge from the underworld and stand once again on the outer edge of normality, the threshold of the path to Niton.

But our road is below, and leads to Undercliff Niton. Little Kerenhappuch Newnham was blown over the cliff and re-christened "Happie Ninham" because she landed unhurt; but it is wiser to climb down gracefully and make for the Sandrock Hotel in the footsteps of last century's health-fiends. The eighteenth-century cottage under West Cliff became a hotel after Mr Waterworth, the appositely-named surgeon of Newport, discovered the Sandrock spring towards Blackgang in 1807. He leased ground, made a reservoir and erected a thatched dispensary for this valuable addition to the *materia medica*, a chalybeate water of great strength. The hotel was extended in about 1830, and ennobled by the visit of the Duchess of Kent and Queen Victoria, thenceforth claiming the prefix *Royal*. Victorian guidebooks complained of its distance from the shore, and welcomed the opening, in 1851, of the Victoria Hotel above Reeth Bay. How the proprietors of the Royal Sandrock must have laughed behind their potted palms to see the upstart Victoria drop out of sight in 1875. Their house had already seen and survived the largest landslip of all: in February 1799, a farm called Pitlands and a hundred acres were carried away when Gore Cliff let a chunk of itself loose on the blue slipper: one labourer's cottage stayed the course intact, but the one where Mr Arnold served teas was buried, all but for a memorial chimney. By 1838, a proper road had been laid across the new landscape to serve the chalybeate spring and Blackgang; in 1853, blasting of overhanging rock to render the route safer actually destroyed it completely; it was re-laid once more, but in 1910 the grand property of Southlands fell away, and 23 July 1928 saw falcons and jackdaws lift off from Windy Corner as 120,000 tons of rock cracked and moaned and left their perch. The new Undercliff moved for months, a surreal, anarchic sea of mud and rock, of shifting streams and uprooted trees that slowly settled, settled, settled down.

Not for long. After two premonitory falls, when the dreaming terrain seemed to shift in its fitful sleep, March 1978 saw the road and 25 acres on the move. Briars snapped and cracked like whip-lashes, roots screamed in the soil, broken electricity cables flailed like useless antennae and lit up the cliff at night with eerie blue flashes. Folk carried furniture and effects to safety along a tortuous footpath as the shrubs and trees of their gardens fell out of sight. Cliff Cottage and Sandrock Cottage were destroyed, crumbling as their foundations split beneath them, or bull-dozed away by sliding soil. On the Blackgang side, an ivy and hart's tongue covered knoll beneath towering Gore Cliff still bears the rotunda erected by Thomas Letts, of diary fame, in honour of the tercentenary of Shakespeare's birth. Nearby is a battered scallop surrounded by a fragmentary inscription from *Two Gentlemen of Verona* which once read, "The water nectar, and the rocks pure gold". No spa water issues from the scallop now, and the rocks, embedded in a wilderness of mire, are like beads fallen from the broken string of the road that hangs uselessly around the neck of Gore Cliff.

Thomas Letts' house, Southview, is recalled by its stone gateposts, one felled and one standing, with a gate hanging askew and a notice proclaiming DANGER. Below are the wrecks of houses, of huts and of the chalets of the South View Naturist Holiday Estate. The dedicated can pay their money, to a naked lady in a surviving house, for the privilege of struggling down over slumped ground, on a barely defined track and planks across quagmires, towards Rocken End and the expanse of beach where nudity is the rule. To strip off anywhere is exhilarating, but to strip off in the shadow of a cliff below a cliff, both of which threaten to tumble, is doubly, triply so. Dark clay, Ferruginous Beds, Sandrock and Carstone step upwards to the villainous Gault Clay, and are a forbidding backdrop to shingle and flesh heating in the sun. A deceptively pacific sea rides on a reef whose race reaches out greedily for one-and-a-half miles. Men and women lie, stroll and brave the sucking breakers, far from the fig-leaves of the Botanic Garden, in an attempt at Eden-innocence before the Fall, on a narrow fillet of gold between the devilish cliffs and the deep blue sea.

There is no danger that the tourist hordes that pour from buses and cars above Blackgang Chine will stumble, all unsuspecting, upon naked bodies. The coastline has receded half a mile—300 yards in the last half century alone—and the Chine stops way up the cliff; indeed, it hardly starts any more. As the sea has undercut the natural advantages of their site, so the Dabells' attractions have proliferated on the western extremity of the Undercliff. The first Dabell was a Nottingham lacemaker who came to work in Newport. His son established the Newport store, and Alexander Dabell saw that a rugged chasm's romantic wildness would appeal to the 1840s' sensibility. By 1843 the old black gang, or gangway for fishermen, beachcombers, wreckers and smugglers, was open to the public. An 80-ton whale, languishing off the Needles and washed up dead at Totland, was towed to Gurnard and auctioned. The skeleton was reconstructed at Blackgang: the bones of a pavilion through which the awed tripper entered the grim wonderland. In Boys' Adventure style, the name Black Gang was taken to refer to a sinister smuggling mafia and, after the last war, a Smugglers' Cave, Hall of Mirrors and Model Village began to make a fairground of the place.

For twenty years, the entrance and exit was through an Eastern Bazaar, recently superseded by a man-o'-war gun-deck. The present, fifth generation of the Dabell family see their inheritance as a theme-park; consequently, the balance has shifted from kitsch and fantasy to historic reconstruction. Now, after the Fairy Castle, Crooked House, Mouth of Hell and the Water Garden, you can stroll up and down crooked paths among glass-fibre dinosaurs, through Buffalo Creek, the Gold Mine, the Sawmill, and a maritime show whose centrepiece is a 1906 steam-engine from a River Dart pleasure steamer, that was lifted into the Chine's new museum by crane. Where guttering lanterns were processed up and down a dark stream-riven gully on stormy nights to and from a wrecking shore, the Chine now leaves you in mid-air. Coloured lights illuminate a make-believe world. Plastic smugglers stand guard. The loot rolls in. As natural glories are eroded, hard-headed fantasies take over. The lesson for the Wight is clear, the choice stark.

19

BACKWARDS ON THE TIN-TRAIL

The fact is that these early discoverers ate the gingerbread and left us the gilt.

Edward Thomas   *The Isle of Wight*

One marvels, again and again, at the peaceful beauty and delights of this wonderful island. It seems that about one million other people think the same ...

Isle of Wight Official Holiday Guide 1982

THE ISLAND'S SOUTHERN superstructure—St Catherine's Hill, Niton Down, Gore Cliff and the Undercliff—steps down to the deck of St Catherine's Point, the Wight's prow set on a course for Pointe de Barfleur. The tides' regular rhythm and the unpredictable power of weather build seas and knock them down around the Point's foundations. Like some unimaginably concentrated *aqua fortis*, brine digests the rough diamond. Parts of the cliff-top, as at Cranmore on the north-west facet, have receded at the rate of ten feet a year in the last 40 years; along the south-west coast, farmers continue to draw in their field-boundaries and, to prevent stock plunging with the landslips, hack the overhanging pasture back, as they have done time out of mind, at least since the days when Grange Chine ran out another half mile and disgorged its fresh water at the Roman shore. The Island, which geological tides folded into troughs and extremes of climate abraded, is a temporary quirk of the earth's crust.

Knowles Farm's horned bullocks nuzzle and nurture rough turf in a web of dry-stone walls on the pocked Point. They crop and cud against a backdrop of sky, water or the white walls of the lighthouse complex which, in 1943, was crippled by an air-raid that killed three lighthouse keepers. Now, with its beaming beacon, it stands on *terra infirma*, against the sea's *terra incognita*, like a miniature glistening

266

celestial city. Just above the savage salt-rinsed rocks, behind a lime-washed wall that bears the brunt of the gales, wallflowers and bluebells flourish in the southernmost garden of the Garden Isle. When fog obliterates the model city, and extinguishes its light and its gardens' blaze, the thick atmosphere and earth's thin crust seem to tremble as the sirens open their throats, horns blown up to warn sea-borne prey that the race is on. When he had seen one ship wrecked, and others struggling off the Point, the poet Sidney Dobell wrote wryly, on 27 February 1860, "if that hideous Pagan be right, who says the top of human happiness is to stand safe onshore and see a shipwreck, we ought to be enjoying a frightful Elysium."

One balmy day when I walked the cliffs to Reeth Bay, the sea soothed the shore with its low lullaby and, in a crook of the cliff, I came upon a girl suckling a baby at her breast, presences which with the sun blessed a place of wildness and of terror. Onwards, beyond an accursed heap of scrap, caravans clustered around the water-hole of a refreshment-hut and the notice, "OASIS", nailed to a post. A small spade hung there, and smaller painted letters spelt out "Dog Shovel". Neither the alsatian nor the terrier there would pose for my camera. At Castle Cove, walls of boulders and concrete fortified a cottage and a slipway; ranks of worn piles, like the bones of a wicker basket, bulged with their burden of pebbles and the empty cases of a thousand crabs. Sand made a soft way before the bleeding Carstone face of Reeth Bay, and led me around the headland into Puckaster Cove.

The very name is magical. With Puckpool Point and Puck Hill near Ryde, it seems to claim Wight's territory for the playful sprite. Even when the seas at the Race are steep, Uffa Fox maintained that you can land or launch at Puckaster. I have spreadeagled myself to sunbathe here in October, while a cormorant, on a post above blindingly bright water, offered up his broad span of feathers to the warmth. Fishermen's nets, capstans and huts of stone are gone; boulders and masonry are draped with wrack like black crêpe; a line of posts stilt-walks out to sea like a forgotten boundary; tiny triangular caves in the cliff offer scanty shelter for contraband, and the Undercliff's treachery has blocked the direct climb to Niton. It is not so long since a great haul for the revenue men put an end to the scenario Sidney Dobell describes: "Here are fishermen who never fish, but always have pockets full of money; and farmers whose farming consists in 'ploughing the deep' by night, and whose daily time is spent in standing, like herons, on look-out posts."

Here was older trade still. Here, a gold coin of Maximus was found in the cliff. Here is Old Castle, the Roman *Porta Castrensis* of romantic historians, corrupted to Puckaster. Writing in 1855, the Revd E.W. Kell held "that Niton, as early as 300 BC, was the southern depot of the ancient tin traffic, and continued to be so till the entire conquest of Britain, by the Romans, supplied other and more convenient marts." Pytheas, Marseilles' Greek astronomer, described the land-route for tin and lead from north-west Gaul to his city; and the Sicilian, Diodorus Siculus, told of ancient Britons taking tin at low tide to the island of Icta for transport to France. It has been suggested that the Greeks, wishing to avoid piracy on the high seas between Cornwall and Ushant, preferred the tin brought overland to Stansore Point, across the Solent; that Ictis, or Wight, was a defensible "bank" and market-place for the ore that could then be ferried shortly across the Channel. *Stannum* is Latin for tin, Stansore may mean what it says, and it is interesting to note that Southampton was the market for the tin staple until the fifteenth century, a hangover, it is said, from this ancient trade-route.

Mythical or not, the tin-trail offers a rich trek back through the Wight, through all that we do not know and can no longer discover. A hint, too, at all that wealth I have left untouched; and at the seams I have mined, panned and, in the end, discarded; at the spoil-heap of archives, anecdotes and observations, the mound of memories. The metal has run reasonably clear, I trust, from the mass of rock, but there are many more ingots that might have been cast. The tin-trail is one of ignorance as well as knowledge, a dark passage through the Isle's secret garden.

It is a stiff climb, sometimes on slippery clay, up from the Cove. You wish yourself as sure-footed as the goats tethered near Puckaster Farm. Then you reach the steep track that runs up beside walls and palisades that protect the privacy of the rich. In less paranoid days, Uffa Fox enjoyed the orchards, the cedars, the walnut trees, peaches and grapes of Puckaster House, and savoured the delights of its library and dining-room panelled with carved biblical scenes, and its circular music-room. The local, once Buddle Farm, is the Buddle Inn; so called, they say, after the "buddle" or frame in which

Cornish tin-miners wash the ore. It is a source of excellent food and drink, and, during the water-workers' strike of 1983, the landlord offered copious supplies of Adam's ale from the spring behind the pub. Its source, the melting snows of the Alps, they said: "It comes from Switzerland under the sea-bed and bubbles up in our little spring." Believe that if you like. Uphill from Undercliff Niton is the source of the eastern Yar, in Niton proper—called Niton Regis once, to celebrate a royal pedigree derived from Edward the Confessor, or Crab Niton, to distinguish it from Knighton and to advertise the shore's crustacean harvest. George Eliot called it the prettiest place in all the Island. Tracks, now either paths or roads like Chalton Lane, Munt's Lane and Cow Lane, converge on cottages dating back to the fifteenth century.

Bargains were traditionally struck, contracts sealed and declarations made on the steps of the Playe Cross in the churchyard of St John the Baptist, the sixth of Lyre's Island churches. Though the church was renovated in the thirteenth, fifteenth and nineteenth centuries, Niton young have always been baptized in the Norman cauldron font. One day, when I had been watching the organ being rebuilt, I emerged from the dark Romanesque interior to meet Mr Eldridge, who had pumped the old organ, as a boy, for thirteen years. In boots, gaiters, trousers of coarse cloth, ancient jacket and cap, he was tending the grave of one Charles Boyd who had given money for the organ on condition that, though he was an overner, he would be buried in the boneyard he loved best. Mr Eldridge, whose dialect and accent were of a quality only found in old men of these parts, respected his wishes and pointed out the memorial to another overner who died here in 1886: Edward Edwardes, co-founder of municipal public libraries, who established the reading-room in the village. Mr Eldridge could mind the palaver over the wreck of the *Russie* on Easter Day 1902, which proved that old habits die hard. Its cargo, declared as fishing-gear from Newfoundland, turned out to be wine and spirits for Niton throats, the beach a scene of debauchery. Before this time, Smuggler Mussel and his mates found refuge in the graveyard from the customs officers; W.H. Long quotes how one man reacted when, on his way to work at dawn, he saw the top of one of the tombs move: "He stopped short, and stared wi' all the eyes he'd got, when up goos the stooan higher, and a man's face peeps out at one corner, and zays: 'I zay, mayet, can ye tell me what time 'tes?' . . . hes hear lifted hes hat clane off hes head; a couldn't move, but stood there staren like a stuck pig . . . he run into the vust house a come to, and zays to the people: 'Whatever wull become on us! the dead vokes in the churchyard be gitten out o' their graaves'."

From Niton, with its supposed Roman Port, its Bury, its Old Castle and its camp or tin-mart, the road now takes us back around St Catherine's Hill, from good corn country down to the cabbage country of Chale. Chale Street runs north from the church, the school, the Clarendon and the Wight Mouse, past Chale Abbey Farm whose fourteenth-century hall was built by John de Langford, Warden of the Island and Constable of Carisbrooke Castle. With its buttressed barn of the same date, it is one of the oldest houses on the Island, though "Abbey" is a Victorian title conferred on it by virtue of its arched and ogee-headed windows. Then, with a ghostly carriage-and-four in hot pursuit, we leave Chale Rectory behind us. The Star, at Chale Green, was Sprake's Brewery that made strong ale from local hops and barley, and where still stronger stuff was pumped through a hole in the hearthstone from an illicit cask below. Our track deserts the infant Medina, which runs on into the Wilderness; we run under the lea of the sandstone escarpment that links Pyle Farm to Kingston. From the walled wilderness, on the hill that is St James' graveyard, you can see the backside of the seventeenth-century Kingston Manor, with its massive chimney-breast of masonry topped by five blind brick arches and five stacks. Its small walled garden with a little bridge is a cultivated focus for Arcadian fields and woods that climb away to the horizon.

On the right fork of our road north, the five ashlar-faced bays of Little Billingham are reflected in a duck-pond opposite Edward Worsley's Billingham Manor, whose venerable flat roof supported J.B. Priestley's modern study, with five big windows, like the bridge of a ship. The lower decks are famously haunted: Edward Worsley's bride is said to walk, the clash of his duel with her French lover cuts through the silence, and the head of Charles I appears whenever a prisoner escapes from Parkhurst. Chillerton Street bucks and plunges between hills on which a low sun casts stripes and squares, the shades of medieval lynchets and Celtic fields. ITV's mast stabs 750 feet into the air, while Iron Age earthworks on Chillerton Down transmit a confused, ambiguous picture. Did the then Caulkheads leave their fort unfinished? Were they massacred by Belgic invaders? Did Vespasian take it? Was it, as Richard Frost's purple prose suggests, a sacred shrine of head-hunters, a high place where mis-mated Druidic and Atrebatic religious impulses venerated the severed head? The only evidence, he tells us, was thrown into a river. Until some soberly imaginative archaeology is done up there, speculation remains on a par with King Charles' phosphorescent head, or spring-water from the Swiss Alps.

A chain of wells rises in the valley below, though Chillerton was for many years a "dry" village, between the demise of the beer-house at Verandah Villa and the recent bar in the Village Club. Springs in Hollow Lane fill the sheep-dip on the Green and feed into the Medina. The tin-trail leaves the road, the "streets", fords the brook and starts up the hollow-way behind Sheat Manor. Soon it has to press, in zig-zag fashion, through narrow hedged paths, up on to a dome of ploughed land. Across Sheat's roofs, the southern bulwark looms. Beyond the Medina valley and Champion Farm, St George's Down raises its red, ravaged crown. The Wight's spine undulates eastwards under broken streamers of white cloud like the ghost of the chalk. Then, through a dark wood of sycamore and beech, with ivy and hart's tongue fern glistening on a muddy floor, the track drops into the numinous Gatcombe valley.

Through the trees shines Worsley's house of 1750, where summer visitors come to see a display of Monte Carlo Opera House costumes, old bicycles and horse-drawn transport, and a complete collection of George Brannon's engravings of the Island. The great snowstorm of 1861, when drifts reached a depth of 45 feet in places, detained Gatcombe House's Christmas guests until Easter. Between the Georgian house and the lake, St Olave's churchyard is hedged about and planted with flowering trees and manicured yew; the turf between the stones bursts with bulbs and carpets a secluded garden set about the thirteenth-century chapel of the d'Esturs. But the peace here is tinged with unease: the porch, built with timbers from the 1910 wreck of HMS *Thunderer*, is surmounted by a mason's fantasy, or nightmare, a bestial grotesque crowned with a cross. Inside, an octagonal Purbeck marble font and a sumptuous east window by William Morris are strangely outshone by delicate golden fragments of fifteenth-century glass, contemporary with the tower; wheels out of Ezekiel turn, unturning, one under the feet of a feathered angel hovering above a chequered ground like a celestial chess-piece. Mystery is added to mystery in the chancel where a fourteenth-century oaken effigy of a cross-legged knight lies with an angel at his head and a dog at his feet. Around this figure the Revd James Evans wove a fantasy that has passed into folklore: the legend of Lucy Lightfoot of Bowcombe, in which her obsessional adoration of the figure of Edward Estur culminated in her disappearance as she knelt before it during a violent storm and an eclipse of the sun in 1831: a hoax elaborated in detail and at length. Is it, in fact, a memorial to the crusading Knight Templar, Sir Ralph de Gorges of Knighton, taken to Gatcombe as reparation for damages, which we know of, done to the estate by the knight's grandson and his cronies in 1307? Is the little dog, as the church guide suggests, the totemistic Flacon-Caprice who awakes on midsummer-night to dance and draw the spirits from the downs of Chillerton to revel in the churchyard glade? Paganism stirs its oaken limbs as it always has. We know that the church-wardens were sacked in 1572 for lighting a bonfire on the feast of St John the Baptist, not because it was old midsummer's day, when sacrificial fires flared up in honour of the sun, but because it was a Roman Catholic custom, and recusancy was rife on the Island.

Outside, the charming rectory on the hill was the scene of a tale with a sting in it. Farmer Grayson was fed up with the rector chivvying him for his tithe, so he walked into the study with a skep full of bees, opened it and suggested he take his tenth. Down the road, chisels buzzed and chimed on stone as the mason Colin Wickham and his mates worked on Tucker's Farm. Thousands of pounds were being spent on walling, terracing, and creating a waterfall, pond and swimming-pool: a miniature Elysium painstakingly built of greensand, clunch, Binstead stone, some Quarr stone and red sandstone, with Purbeck slabs and quoins. Colin is an exponent of Isle of Wight coarsing, and proud of it, though he said that he was no Islander: "My great-grandfather came from Wiltshire." He told how, when his grandfather attended Chale School, the teacher asked all those who were related to go outside for the 1910 school photograph. Of 92 children, 91 left the room and Colin's grandfather found himself alone at his desk. Seelys succeeded Worsleys at Gatcombe, and the valley idyll is safe from development because of the limitations of the Seely water-supply. Our route leads on past Seely's cottages of stone, with their characteristic yellow-

BACKWARDS ON THE TIN-TRAIL

brick quoins and gable-end windows, past the stables and kennels of
the Isle of Wight Hunt, and up on the footpath across the tops
towards Carisbrooke.

Up here, on Dark Lanes, if you ignore glimpses, through the
foliage flanking the old green road, of the red-brick fantasy of
Whitecroft Mental Hospital beneath, and the stones of Veyers, Great
Whitcombe and Valleys Farms, you could believe yourself on the
prehistoric track to Wightgarisburgh. Then the curtain wall and keep
appear, with St Dominic's Priory nestling below. Patricia Sibley
recalls how, on cold nights during the war, nuns used to take the old
Love Lane and climb up into the cemetery on Mount Joy, benign
apparitions with soup for the observers posted there. The tin-trail,
however, runs west of the Castle, across Lukely Brook that cleaves
the chalk backbone, and on to St Austin's Gate, the threshold of
another landscape. After Carisbrooke comes Gunville and the
industrial estate; does Gunville echo Gonville and the French
connection? Here was the Bible Christians' "cows'-house" chapel
built of mud, until a new one was erected in 1848 and equipped with
a pulpit presented by White's of Cowes. Here, too, was Carisbrooke
Priory's leper chapel of St Augustine, supported by a pension from
the de Redvers, though Dom Hockey has discovered that there was
only one inmate by 1322. The road or street runs straight, and
straight into the depths of Parkhurst Forest where it has been
obliterated. At the far side a path emerges at Mark's Corner and joins
the road to Hillis Corner and Rew Street. Rue? Street? Here Baskett's
Farm, bisected by the Street, boasts an incongruously gracious
façade and a marvellous cart-shed of four bays. Then the road climbs
down beside Cliff Farm and issues, with the stream called Gurnard
Lucko at Gurnard Bay.

The bay's west end is a shanty-town of chalets, and the beach is
bedecked with grim green huts gazing at the Solent. At the east end,
Prince's Esplanade, the royal way to Cowes was opened in 1926.
During Gurnard's regattas, dogs were launched overboard in a race
for the shore. At the end of the eighteenth century, Bembridge
limestone was quarried here for Portsmouth's fortifications, and
Hassell says that three or four sloops trading in stone were often in
the bay. Charles II made, in 1671, a happier landfall here than at
Puckaster, and in 1583 Gurnard was described as "a common passage
of the isle". Ploughing disinterred a stone block with a mooring-ring

at Harts Farm. A Norman cooking-pot was trawled up in the bay, but, by 1864, recently excavated Roman ruins were lost to the Solent for good. Gurnard was a port, it seems, at least as early as the Roman occupation, and Roman coins have been found at Rew Street and other points along the route we have followed. Was Gurnard, earlier still, the landing-place for tin ferried across the Solent from Lepe, where names like Needs Ore Point, Stansore Point and Stanwood Bay are suggestive. Was the Solent narrower and shallower? Did the rumoured limestone causeway enable the ore to be carried or carted across? Most doubt it. In any case, the honours have long since deserted Gurnard, and gone around Egypt Point to Cowes. But it is still a launching-pad for a madman's trek through the secret heart of the Island: an enigmatic pilgrimage full of hauntings and half-answered questions, a dig southwards through history to Wight's snout and a little deserted cove called Puckaster.

Fame and trade are fickle creatures, as the Wight knows. Pride in the past, the real or the romance, is not enough. The influx of fashionable overners in the last two centuries was finished off with a Victorian veneer and not a little French polish. The décor of those days looks outmoded now, is scratched and battered. Since the war, the engines of industry have either faltered and stalled, or been re-tuned to new conditions; but always the economic fluctuations, the waxing and waning of business, have been more extreme by virtue of the Solent, that "most expensive strip of water in the world". The Island has repeatedly applied for Assisted Area Status on the grounds of "severance by sea", and for the establishment of Enterprise Zones.

Since 1890, when the Wight was divorced from Hampshire and became a separate administrative county, some have wished for a reconciliation and a shared rates burden, given that power and responsibility were substantially delegated. In 1972, in order to maintain its independence under the new Local Government Act, two new district councils—the Boroughs of Medina and South Wight—were formed by merging the old local councils; and Newport renewed its importance as the seat of the County Council. Many are adamant that the Island must be separately governed, but smart under the necessity for overlapping authorities in so small a territory; there are not enough responsible people of talent, they say, to be elected to office, and too many opportunities, too gladly taken, for internecine strife. Some want UDI, though the old Vectis Nationalist Party has been replaced by the Independence (Isle of Wight Residents') Party which aims for Jersey-style self-government, a tax-haven rather than an off-shore republic. In the 1983 General Election the Liberals consolidated their capture of the Island from the Conservatives.

Meanwhile, the unemployment rate rises above 16 per cent, compared to less than 10 per cent across the water. The illegitimacy and suicide rates rise too, symptoms of the fraying fabric of Island life. Young people emigrate to England, and elderly overners are imported, making them 25 per cent of the population, compared to the mainland average of 16 per cent. Hotels by the dozen apply to become old peoples' homes. The rates burden grows. Building land runs out, and a country already overrun with suburbs and ribbon development is put under even greater pressure. Agriculture thrives, but requires fewer and fewer men; farmers continue to rip up ancient boundary hedges and to plough out archaeological sites, opening up big fields to larger machines, and to erosion. But the Island's assets are still largely intact. Businessmen, farmers and the moguls of tourism must learn to understand and appreciate them, and to capitalize upon them creatively, for people seldom exploit what they love. Prince Michael of Kent, tipped by some to be the next Governor, recently expressed his pleasure at the Islanders' attitude and buoyant approach to business, though Caulkheads are more frequently exasperated by immigrants' exhortations to "Get off your behinds". They say they do not want the rat-race their would-be mentors left behind, and they add, with a grimace, "There's four ways on to the Island, and five ways off, and God only knows the fifth."

As the Falklanders saw the Argentinian invasion, so Islanders saw a recent tourist-trade proposal, that Disneyland be builded here on the Island's green and pleasant land; they were jubilant when, as the journalists said, the Goofy idea was bowled out for a Duck. The appointment of an ex-Aston Martin boss, with Japanese high tech connections, to look at the Wight's potential, was also regarded with suspicion. We have got enough experts of our own, they said; it does not take a highly-paid consultant to tell us to upgrade our airports, raise our sights, take the tourist-trade up-market rather than down, and exploit our extraordinary potential. It takes hard cash, investment.

It takes understanding too. An inheritance means nothing if you don't know what's in the will. Heritage is not just what happens to be left over when you have taken care of essentials; it is an essential state of heart and mind, a cherishing spirit. People are learning how practical it is to look again, with the eyes of the poets who celebrated and still celebrate the Wight, at the eccentric place where they live. Just as Caulkheads have always wanted their children to marry Caulkheads, and have been jealous of their rights, so they must be willing to show hackle, to fight for the Island itself; not out of insular nationalism, but out of love and a desire to keep what is good. Attrills, Bucketts, Cottons, Dores, Eldridges, Fluxes, Gubbinses, Hayters, Jolliffes, Mews, Osmans, Pittises, Ratseys, Sibbicks, Urrys, Wrays and Yelfs do not want to find themselves exiled in the place where they were born, imprisoned on Devil's Island, when they could be enjoying the freedom of a little paradise.

Our word *paradise* stems from the Persian word for *garden*. There are signs that the Garden Island will be cultivated once again. It is an idea, and an Island, worth defending; and well worth offering, on its own terms, as a refuge and retreat to those temporary invaders, the tourists. It is an all-year Garden with the best climate in the country, with a thousand places in which to stay, with 60 official "places of interest" and a thousand miles of footpaths amongst a kaleidoscope of land- and sea-scapes. It is a rough diamond of many shifting facets.

In one short chapter, we have travelled from the Undercliff's frightful Elysium through several versions of Eden. We have penetrated secret and forsaken gardens, and traversed the high places. We have trekked across the fields of Arcadia and threaded a trail through the forest of Arden. And we have emerged on the Solent shore of Sieglinde's Island, facing familiar, foreign England across that old river whose marriage with the sea gave birth to Guith or Guict, meaning severance, to Ictis or Icta, to Vectis or Vecta, to Whit or Wight. Now, between Purbeck and Wight, an oil-rig perches above the water and plumbs the depths. For me, it is a short distance and a long way from that high window of my childhood which first gave me a glimpse of white stacks in the sea. They exercised a unique attraction and evoked in me an appetite never entirely satisfied, and a sense of mystery I have not quite shaken off.

SELECT BIBLIOGRAPHY

ADAMS, W.H.D.   *Nelson's Hand Book to the Isle of Wight*   London   1869

ALBIN, J.   *A New, Correct & Much Improved History of the Isle of Wight*   Newport   1795

ALMON, J. (ed.)   *The Correspondence of the late John Wilkes*   London   1805

ARNOLD, C.J.   *The Anglo-Saxon Cemeteries of the Isle of Wight*   British Museum Publications   1982

ASPINALL-OGLANDER, C.F.   *A Nunwell Symphony*   The Hogarth Press   1945

BASFORD, H.V.   *The Vectis Report*   Isle of Wight County Council   1980

BEDE (trans. Sherley-Price)   *A History of the English Church and People*   Penguin   1955

BEVIS, KETTELL & SHEPARD   *Flora of the Isle of Wight*   Isle of Wight Natural History & Archaeological Society   1978

BLAKE, Robert   *Disraeli*   Eyre & Spottiswoode   1966

BLOWS, W.T.   *Reptiles on the Rocks*   Isle of Wight County Council   1978

BOULAY, E. Du   *Bembridge, Past & Present*   1911

BOWEN, Marjorie   *The Scandal of Sophie Dawes*   John Lane   1935

BOYNTON, L.O.J.   *Appuldurcombe House*   H.M.S.O.   1967

BRANNON, George   *Picture of the Isle of Wight*   c.1847

BULLAR, John   *Guide to the Isle of Wight*   Southampton   c.1831

CAMDEN, William   *Britannia*   1586

CANTWELL, Anthony & SPRACK, Peter   *The Needles Batteries*   National Trust   1981

CHARLTON, John   *Osborne House*   H.M.S.O.   1960

CHURCHILL, Winston S.   *A History of the English Speaking Peoples*   Cassell   1956

CLARK, Dr James   *The Influence of Climate in the Prevention and Cure of Chronic Diseases*   Underwood   1829

DARBY, H.C. (ed.)   *Historical Geography of England before 1800*   Cambridge   1963

DAVIS, Terence   *The Architecture of John Nash*   Studio Books   1960

DEARDEN, James S.   *Turner's Isle of Wight Sketchbook*   Hunnyhill Publications   1979

DICKS, Bruce   *The Isle of Wight*   David & Charles   1979

DOWLING, R.F.W.   *Smuggling on Wight Island*   Ventnor   1978

ENGLEFIELD, Sir H.C.   *A Description of the Principal Beauties, Antiquities & Geological Phenomena, of the Isle of Wight*   London   1816

FERNBANK, Eleanor   *Island Memories*   Saunders   1974

FLORANCE, Arnold   *Queen Victoria at Osborne*   Yelf Bros.   1977

FORSTER, John   *The Life of Charles Dickens*   London   1872–4

FROST, Richard   *Isle of Wight Mysteries*   W.J. Nigh & Sons   1980

GARMONSWAY, G.N. (ed.)   *Anglo-Saxon Chronicle*   Dent   1953

GERNSHEIM, Helmut *Julia Margaret Cameron, her Life and Photographic Work* Fountain Press 1948

GREEN, Margaret *Churches of the Isle of Wight* Winton Publications 1969

GUEST, Montague & BOULTON, William *Memorials of the Royal Yacht Squadron* Murray 1903

HAKLUYT, Richard *Voyages & Documents* Oxford 1958

HARDY, F.E. *The Life of Thomas Hardy* London 1928–30

HAY, David & Joan *The Solent from the Sea* Stanford 1972

HOBSBAWM, E.J. & RUDÉ, George *Captain Swing* Lawrence & Wishart 1969

HOCKEY, S.F. *Quarr Abbey & its Lands 1132–1631* Leicester University Press 1970

— *Insula Vecta* Phillimore 1982

HOGG, I. *Coast Defences of England & Wales, 1856–1956* David & Charles 1974

HUDSON, Derek *Lewis Carroll: an illustrated biography* Constable 1976

HUTCHINS, R.J. (compiler) *An Island of Poetry* Saunders 1979

— *Isle of Wight Literary Haunts* Saunders 1979

— *Rambling round Brighstone* Hunnyhill Publications 1981

— *Smugglers of the Isle of Wight* Saunders 1980

— & TURLEY, R.V. *Young Algernon Swinburne* Hunnyhill Publications 1978

INSOLE, Allan & PARKER, Alan (eds.) *Industrial Archaeology in the Isle of Wight* Isle of Wight County Council 1979

JOLLY, W.P. *Marconi* Constable 1972

JONES, Barbara *The Isle of Wight* Penguin 1950

JONES, Jack D. *The Royal Prisoner* Lutterworth 1965

JOWITT, R.L.P. & M. *Isle of Wight* Batsford 1951

LAURENCE, A.E. & INSOLE, A.N. *Prometheus Bound* Isle of Wight County Council n.d.

LEE, James *An Introduction to Botany* 1760

LELAND, John *Itinerary in England & Wales* c.1535–43

LONG, W.H. *Dictionary of the Isle of Wight Dialect* Brannon & Co 1866

MARTIN, Ralph G. *Lady Randolph Churchill* Cassell 1969

MARTIN, Robert Bernard *Tennyson: The Unquiet Heart* Clarendon Press/ Faber & Faber 1980

MEW, Fred *Back of the Wight* The County Press, Newport 1962

MOTTISTONE, The Lord *Launch* Hodder & Stoughton 1932

NOYES, Alfred *Orchard's Bay* Sheed & Ward 1939

NOYES, Hugh (ed.) *Isle of Wight Bedside Anthology* Isle of Wight County Press 1951

OGLANDER, Sir John (ed. W.H. Long) *The Oglander Memoirs* London 1888

ORTON, Ian *The Isle of Wight at War* Isle of Wight County Library n.d.

PARKER, Alan G. *The Story of Victorian Shanklin* Shanklin Rotary Club 1977

PETERS, Matthew *The Rational Farmer* Newport 1770

PEVSNER, Nikolaus & LLOYD, David   *The Buildings of England: Hampshire and the Isle of Wight*   Penguin   1967

PHILLIPS, Kenneth S.   *For Rooks and Ravens*   Isle of Wight County Council   1981

PHILLIPS-BIRT, Douglas   *Waters of Wight*   Cassell   1967

ROSE-TROUP, Frances   *The Western Rebellion of 1549*   Smith, Elder & Co   1913

RULE, Margaret & STURGESS, Keith   *Brading Roman Villa*   1974

SCAMMELL, Hilary & BLACKMORE, Timothy   *Past & Present Sandown & Shanklin*   Isle of Wight County Library   1980

SELINCOURT, Aubrey de   *Isle of Wight*   Elek   1948

SHERIDON, R.K.   *Lords, Captains & Governors of the Isle of Wight*   H.M.S.O.   1974

SIBLEY, Patricia   *Discovering the Isle of Wight*   Robert Hale   1977

STEEDMAN, Gay & ANKER, Ray   *Ghosts of the Isle of Wight*   Isle of Wight County Press   1977

STONE, P.G.   *The Architectural Antiquities of the Isle of Wight*   London   1891

THOMAS, Edward   *The Isle of Wight*   Blackie & Son   1911

TOMALIN, David J.   *Newport Roman Villa*   Isle of Wight County Council   1975

VANCOUVER, C.   *General View of the Agriculture of Hampshire*   London   1794

VENABLES, Edmund   *The Isle of Wight*   Stanford   1860

Victoria History of the Counties of England: Hampshire & the Isle of Wight   vols. ii & v   Constable   1903 & 1912

WARD LOCK'S   *Guide to the Isle of Wight*   c.1926

WARNER, Revd   *General View of the Agriculture of the Isle of Wight*   London   1794

WHITE, H.J. Osborne   *A Short Account of the Geology of the Isle of Wight*   H.M.S.O.   1921

WHITEHEAD, J.L.   *The Undercliff of the Isle of Wight*   Ventnor   1911

WILSON, Laurence   *Portrait of the Isle of Wight*   Robert Hale   1965

W.I.   *Isle of Wight Village Book*   Isle of Wight Federation of Women's Institutes   1974

WOOLCOCK, J.   *A History of the Bible Christian Churches on the Isle of Wight*   F. Lee, Newport   1897

WORSLEY, Sir Richard   *The History of the Isle of Wight*   London   1781

INDEX

INDEX